Coming Out of the Bl

The Cassell Lesbian and Gay Studies list offers a broad-based platform to lesbian, gay and bisexual writers for the discussion of contemporary issues and for the promotion of new ideas and research.

COMMISSIONING:
Steve Cook

CONSULTANTS:
Liz Gibbs
Christina Ruse
Peter Tatchell

Coming Out of the Blue

British Police Officers
talk about their lives
in 'The Job'
as lesbians, gays
and bisexuals

Marc E. Burke

CASSELL

To Jens (Hase Zwei),
and to my loving family

Cassell
Villiers House, 41/47 Strand
London WC2N 5JE

387 Park Avenue South
New York, NY 10016-8810

First published 1993

British Library Cataloguing-in-Publication Data
A catalogue record for this book is available from the British Library.

ISBN 0-304-32716-6 (hardback)
　　　0-304-32714-X (paperback)

Typeset by Fakenham Photosetting Limited, Fakenham, Norfolk
Printed and bound in Great Britain by Mackays of Chatham PLC
Designed by Peter Guy

Contents

'One old copper came up to me after I'd left the Job and said, "You can look after my kids anytime." I took that as a compliment.'

'I've been cottaging myself and so I wouldn't like to have to go on an importuning squad but at the same time I know what the risks are and I know it's against the law. It's a very difficult area for me.'

'I remember when I first thought I might be gay. There was this toilet on our ground that I'd heard was used by gays. So when I got posted on the beat where this place was, I would sometimes hang around in the hope of seeing what homosexuals looked like. Anyway, I didn't really see many but now I know that probably had something to do with the fact that I was standing across the road in full uniform.'

'So common is the random trawling of public lavatories that I never go into public loos – not even for the purpose for which they were designed. It's safer, when caught short, to use an alleyway or a tree.'

'I wouldn't be here if I didn't think this kind of research was important. I hope it lands on every Chief Super's desk in the country and they learn something from it.'

Foreword

ANY mention of homosexuality or gayness in police circles usually produces a standard reaction of derision and contempt for those who are or are suspected of being 'that way inclined'. Being gay or lesbian is not acceptable in the eyes of the majority of our law enforcers and the further up the police sub-culture you go, the more scathing and brutal the condemnation becomes. The cruel jibes, the crude accusations, the sudden transfer to uniform, the destructive whispering campaign are just some of the treatments dished out to those who are labelled 'queer'. Is it really possible for a social agency, charged with respecting all law-abiding members of the community, whatever their colour, creed, gender or sexual orientation, to behave so obscenely towards some within its own ranks? The answer is found most clearly in this carefully researched and painstakingly honest book by Dr Marc Burke.

The portrayal of the misery, fear of discovery and guilt of countless homosexual men and women who dared to join the police makes salutary reading and stands as a sad indictment of those 'straight' officers who hold positions of power and influence and have allowed such negative attitudes to flourish and take root. Marc Burke exposes the hypocrisy of those who sit in judgement on officers who prefer a different sort of relationship from what is regarded as normal. In doing so, he has opened up the entire topic for proper and more informed discussion. This is the first time that serving police officers and those who have left the job in fear and despair have ventilated their own most personal thoughts and desires so frankly and articulately. Marc Burke's timely and sympathetic account of the problems of being gay in the police may now allow the police service to come out into the open and to acknowledge that gay and lesbian officers do exist, fulfil their duties and are represented in large numbers, albeit generally under cover of secrecy, within most ranks.

The time has come to stop this homophobic witch hunt once and for all, whether the resistance to change is found within the ranks of ACPO, the Superintendents Association or even in the higher echelons of the Police Federation. The police service must strive to accept that everyone is an individual who is entitled to be valued and respected whatever his or her sexual preferences. Those forces who have already altered their policy and have tried to eliminate all forms of unfair discrimination will still learn something from this book. Officers who have not yet made that crucial quantum leap from bigotry and prejudice to enlightenment and equality have indeed much to learn from Marc Burke's poignant case studies. He is to be congratulated for giving us all so much food for thought and for the opportunity of examining our own prejudices.

Alison Halford

Preface

THE origins of this book's contents are various. The bulk of the material has been transcribed from interviews with currently serving and retired British police officers; the remainder consists of original essays, letters and other short pieces, all of which attempt to relate and analyse various aspects of homosexual or bisexual experience within the British police service. It is not claimed that the views expressed here are representative of all officers whose sexual orientation is other than exclusively heterosexual; rather, their expression attempts to build a mosaic-like picture of police life from the position of the men and women who live those alternative lives, thus giving an important insight into an interesting and largely unrecognized section of society.

Apart from providing a unique account of a previously undocumented set of lesbian, gay and bisexual experiences in Britain, it is hoped that this book will serve a number of purposes. For those readers who are neither police officers nor homosexual or bisexual, the material combines a characterization of police culture and practice with a fresh perspective on this highly controversial population. An unusual view of 'the homosexual experience' is offered. It is hoped that through listening to what contributors have to say, a deeper understanding of both these communities may be achieved.

For those readers who are heterosexual police officers, the book has two main aims. Firstly, it is hoped these writings will produce a police awareness at grass-roots level that the same spectrum of sexualities found outside the service are also to be found within police ranks. Many of those who speak in this book will be their colleagues and close friends; they are not criminals *per se*. Secondly, it is hoped that the writings will alert both middle and senior management within Britain's fifty-two police services to the real problems faced by a large minority of their workforce, and encourage serious consideration regarding effective policy (and attitude) amendments within those services that have not already taken steps to amend them.

In addition, the collection should provide food for thought to the ever-growing police-bashing contingent within the lesbian and gay communities. Like these communities, Britain's police services contain a wide variety of citizens who carry with them a multiplicity of attitudes and opinions on all issues. They cannot and should not be thought of as a unitary entity.

In short, it is the goal of this book that both the police and the lesbian and gay communities learn something of the problems faced by the other, and give recognition to those lesbian, gay or bisexual officers who, as part of each community, are often comprehended by neither and persecuted by both.

Finally, for those little-understood officers who exist within that no-man's-land, this book establishes their existence for the first time in this country and serves as a record of their experiences.

Acknowledgements

I would like to thank those officers who gave me their time and their considerable trust in the writing of this book by allowing me into the most personal and vulnerable facet of their lives. I hope that this work repays them in the accurate expression of their fears and their pain, as well as their hopes and aspirations for the future. My desire for them is that it may go some way towards the achievement of a more tolerant and open-minded police service. My thanks also go to those who obstructed me. Their hindrance provided a constant source of motivation.

My gratitude goes to Jens for both his practical assistance and his enthusiastic support, particularly when the tide was against us. I am also indebted to Justin Johnson for his word-processing assistance and to 'Oscar' stationery supplies. Finally, my thanks go to Professor Peter Campbell, Dr Nigel South, Michael Kellett, Lisa Power and Tony Murphey for their observations and suggestions in examining the text.

Author's Note

FIRSTLY, because of the serious nature of some of the events which are related in this book, it has been necessary to alter officers' details, as well as some of the case details, in order to protect those concerned from harassment.

Secondly, the terms 'homosexual', 'lesbian', 'gay' and 'same-sex (partner)' are used throughout the text to refer to homogenous sexual relationships or sexualities. The terms 'homosexual', 'gay' and 'same-sex (partner)' are intended to encompass women, unless clearly inappropriate, although the word 'lesbian' is also used with some frequency. This convention reflects the various ways in which female officers in particular have chosen to describe their sexual orientation. The terms are used throughout this book interchangeably and without prejudice. I have also used the term 'non-heterosexual' with some frequency in preference to (a) the term 'homosexual', which excludes the bisexual (and is often perceived as excluding the female), and (b) the rather cumbersome 'lesbian, gay or bisexual'. The term 'non-heterosexual' is also intended to be more specific in referring primarily to *sexual orientation*, thus avoiding connotations with issues of *identity* inherent in the terms 'gay' and 'lesbian'.

For those unfamiliar with police terminology and abbreviations, a glossary is provided on pages 250–3, and a glossary of gay speak appears on pages 253–4.

Introduction

MUCH has been said about the police academically in recent years, and their work is well known to the public by virtue of its extraordinary and relentless media coverage. In fact, no other profession has been so widely represented on television: barely an evening passes without a police documentary or drama. Issues surrounding alternative sexualities are also better understood today than previously, and have become increasingly well documented. Media coverage in the area has expanded dramatically over the past decade, and a number of popular television soaps have tackled sexual orientation, with gay characters appearing in 'EastEnders', 'Brookside', 'Dynasty' and 'Eldorado'. As myth and misunderstanding are gradually eroded, both gay and lesbian lifestyles are becoming increasingly acceptable in Britain, in line with our European counterparts.

Whilst we now know a considerable amount about what it means to be homosexual or bisexual in terms of orientation, we still know virtually nothing, despite many theories, about why sexual orientations differ. And in a society that can still be overtly hostile to same-sex relationships there is much to learn about how discovering that one is attracted to one's own sex, particularly in conjunction with various other co-factors such as occupation, can affect self-esteem, the development of personal identity and general psychological function.

The fact that there is little love lost between the police and the lesbian and gay communities comes as no surprise; indeed, their conflicting values and philosophies would predict such friction, and the theme has been the subject of a sprinkling of (mostly US) studies. However, whilst the subject of homosexuality *and* the police has been probed, albeit rather shallowly, virtually nothing has been articulated on the direct combination of the two: homosexuality *in* the police.

    This book looks at the effects of belonging to two marginal and antagonistic communities at the same time and addresses a number of important issues. Which community, if any, has the loyalty of these officers, and how do they feel about their dual identity in life? Which of their two identities represents their 'true' identity, or is it modified according to company? How does living a double life affect officers and how do they manage their relationships? Do any of them come out at work and if they do, how many suffer prejudice or discrimination as a result? Is the situation any worse for women? And what makes people choose to put themselves under such pressures in the first place by combining what would appear to be the uncombinable? In answer to these and other difficult questions, officers from the various forces, departments and ranks of the British police service, many of them members of the new Lesbian and Gay Police Association (LAGPA), speak out for the first time, offering a pot-pourri of views and opinions on their sexuality and the profession that they have chosen.

Chapter one

Sketches

IN this first chapter, broad sketches of lesbian, gay or bisexual lives in Britain's police services are offered. They cover a wide number of general issues and most touch on, and therefore serve as good introductions for, the more specific topics which will be covered in greater detail in the chapters that follow.

● *Metropolitan PC, age 26, five years' service*

Being gay and a police officer. Can you be both? Not many members of the public ever think of gay police officers. I am gay and was twenty-one when I joined the Metropolitan Police. I've been a police officer for the past five years and have worked in Hackney, East London, since leaving training school. When I joined the police I knew I was gay – I've been gay ever since I can remember and I've never had any relationships with women. I know of officers who have gotten married in order to conceal their sexuality or because they were gay but denied it to themselves. I don't believe in covering my sexuality like that. I am happy with my sexuality, I have never had any problems with it and I feel sorry for people who can't accept that they are gay, be they police officers or anyone else.

I had a couple of relationships with men before I joined the police but since I lived outside London in a place where there were no gay bars or discos, I found it difficult to meet other gay people and that's partly why I came to London. Firstly because of its large gay community and secondly to join the police.

4: Coming Out of the Blue

During my stay at Hendon police training college I didn't meet any other gay police officers or venture into any gay venue until after I left the college. Shortly after I left, I went to a Monday night social group called Gay Young London at King's Cross. At that meeting I thought I saw someone I knew but couldn't quite place him. After the meeting I got talking to him and discovered that he had been a class captain at Hendon whilst I was there. We had a brief relationship which didn't work out but we still remained friends. I now have a boyfriend whom I live with, and whom I have been having a relationship with for over three years.

Sometimes work can be difficult because I am not out; I try to keep my work life and my social life separate. For a period of time, I had a nine-to-five job at my station where I worked mainly on my own, but now that I'm back on relief doing shift-work, I sometimes find that keeping my work and my sexuality separate is difficult. Luckily, I know a number of gay and lesbian officers of all ranks. We meet up socially and are a support to each other. I've considered coming out at work but I don't think it would serve any useful advantage at this stage as I would like to take promotion and (hopefully) rise through the ranks. I think it's a shame because I do my job as good as anyone else. In my service so far I have earned two bravery commendations and I've never had a complaint about the way I do my job. At work there is a gay pub on our division and as I walk by sometimes I see other gay people and I smile to myself and carry on, knowing that I am just the same as them and if they need me as a police officer that I can help them and relate to them.

One of my best memories since I joined the police happened about three and a half years ago. I was at work walking down the street in my uniform on a summer's day when this very good-looking man walked by me in the opposite direction on the same side of the street. I continued to walk on but at the same moment we turned around to look at each other. We both stopped for a moment, about twenty yards apart and looked at each other again, but I suppose he was afraid to approach me because of my uniform. At that moment a car stopped to ask me directions and by the time I had finished and looked again he was gone.

I am happy being a police officer and also being gay. Sometimes rumours go round at work about me but I think it should be up to them to make the move and ask me if they're interested, not the other way about. The trouble is, if you don't tell people, then you get accused of being secretive and seedy about it, and if you do, then you're ramming it down their throats. Luckily my boyfriend is very supportive.

● *Avon and Somerset PC, age 29, six years' service*

I joined the Job¹ at the age of twenty-three, having completed a number of years' service in the British forces. I've always known I am gay, but because it was illegal to be homosexual in the forces and not heard of in the police, that has restricted the way I have expressed my sexuality, both in the choice of my partners and in the way I operate in public. I had a number of sexual encounters with colleagues in the forces, but no long-term relationships.

During my interview to join the police, questions were asked about whether I had a girlfriend. Of course I made out that I was as straight as the next man. I was not out at that stage and I did not have any plans to come out. I'm still not out at work, but I'm quite active on the local gay scene, where I haven't made a secret of my occupation. I suppose now it's only a matter of time before I am seen by one of my colleagues coming out of a gay pub or club.

I don't think any of my other colleagues suspect I'm gay. I've told my parents; my mum was quite upset at first, she doesn't know any other gay people and she had all the classic stereotyped, homophobic ideas. I have assured her I don't fancy little boys or wear women's clothing! I think she now accepts the way I am, but I don't think she will ever truly understand. She thinks and hopes that I'm just going through a phase and that once I've got it out of my system and the right girl comes along, things will sort themselves out. Well, she's going to have a long wait! She won't let me bring any boyfriends home because there are younger members in my family, and I presume she thinks I could influence them. My father is OK about me, but he never mentions the subject or enquires about my friends. He hates Julian Clary, and so long as I don't act or dress like him I think he will be able to tolerate my sexuality. My best straight friend and his wife know about me.

6: Coming Out of the Blue

When I told them I feared I would lose them, but it hasn't made the slightest difference to our friendship.

I've started to look for alternative employment, as I feel I am under such a great deal of pressure. Some days I just want to walk up to my Inspector and tell him I'm gay, but I haven't yet had the courage to do it, not until I know my Chief Constable's views on the subject. But even if he publicly expresses a favourable opinion, he might say one thing when he means the opposite. So unfortunately I believe the only answer is for me to leave the Job. It is a sad reflection on society when someone feels forced to leave a career they enjoy, just because of their sexuality.

I believe that because of the macho image of policemen, most of my colleagues openly condemn and criticize homosexuals. For example, my Sergeant is a Catholic and he hates policewomen, masons and homosexuals. He thinks they're defective. I was talking to him one day and he said, 'When I went for my Inspector's board, I was asked how I would react to, and treat a homosexual officer on my group. Of course I told them what they wanted to hear, and not that I would really make his life hell – until I had persuaded him that it would be best for everyone if he resigned.' He obviously didn't know he was talking to one. On the other hand, in my opinion, lesbians in the police don't seem to bother most policemen. This is probably because they don't pose a direct threat or challenge to their ego or masculinity.

I had my last fling with a woman about twelve months ago, just before I decided to come out, and since then my partners have all been men. I've no intention of having a girlfriend again. At the moment I have a steady boyfriend. He's quite a bit younger than me and I feel a lot for him, but to be honest I don't think our relationship will last because of his age. I live on my own at present, but I would love to have a live-in partner and lead as near 'normal' a life as possible.

● *Metropolitan WPC, age 21,*
three years' service

If I could tell everyone in the world just one thing about being a lesbian it would be that it isn't a choice. I never chose to be *gay and I never wanted to be. Why would I? But there was nothing I could do about it. It chose me. I've known since about thirteen but I refused to accept it until about nineteen or twenty. That's how it is for a lot of people. In that time, I tried everything from religion to psychology to change me, but of course none of it worked, and I'm pissed off now that I was led to believe that it might. That's just the way I am, and I'm quite happy to be that way now that I'm old enough, mature enough, and intelligent enough to realize how little difference it makes. I know now that the reason I wanted to change had little to do with me not liking my sexuality (I clearly did like it) and everything to do with being brought up to despise it by a society that is totally hung-up on sex and sexuality. What aliens would make of the way we fuss over it, God only knows. I nearly killed myself once because I thought I was some kind of Gorgon, and when I think about that now it pisses me off. To think that I nearly gave in to such a cruel and warped society. If anyone ought to be ashamed then it's a society that teaches its children to hate what they are before they even know it, so that they contemplate suicide when they find out what 'monsters' they are – just for loving their own sex. Big deal. I say this to the people who nearly killed me: future generations will laugh at you just as you laugh at those who burned the so-called witches and thought that the world was flat. I don't waste my time trying to justify my existence to people any more. You do when you're younger because society tells you that you're not worth the same space as everyone else and when you're young you believe it. Once you've grown up of course, you realize that you've been totally fucked over by society, and you took the lot. As far as I'm concerned, if the police don't like it, then they can spin because I now know that I'm a better human being than most of them put together.*

● *Cambridgeshire PS, age 35,
resigned with seven years' service*

I am a gay, Christian, ex-policeman. It is tough to be a Christian; it is even tougher to be gay; it took most of my physical, mental and emotional resources to be an effective policeman. To attempt to integrate all three of these aspects of my life was the most demanding challenge of my thirty-five years' existence.

I'm not a policeman any more but I am still a Christian and still gay, although I readily admit to a dislike of the narrow stereotypes often attached to the latter two groups. After all, what is a Christian? What exactly does 'gay' mean?

I'd like to share some of my experiences in the hope of suggesting that there are police officers out there who are more than queer-bashing, thoughtless thugs, though these surely exist; and that gays are more than leather-clad, deviant toilet-loiterers. My hope is that this will help to encourage just a little more understanding, even compassion, towards those people who struggle to live their lives as part of a minority group, police, Christian or gay.

I was a policeman. I am gay. Yet I dare say that I fit into neither of these two stereotypical extremes, though I have learned much about what might lead people to either of them. I am now thirty-five and living and working in France, as a prelude to returning to what grew in me as a passion: to resume working for, and in, the Third World, having lived and worked in Africa earlier in my life. I left the police late in 1990 in order to pursue these plans.

I am now perhaps the most contented I have ever been because after an immense spiritual and emotional struggle, I now know and accept that I am predominantly homosexual. Furthermore, I celebrate and express that fact in the context of an established, committed, mutually respectful, even prayerful relationship with a man I love. Despite the lack of societal, legal and ritual supports which surround a heterosexual couple sharing their lives together, Adam and I are determined to explore and find our futures together as companions – as best friends. The story of my own self-discovery and acceptance is also a chronicle of that growing and ever-deepening relationship.

I joined the police when I was twenty-seven years old, having been a teacher of English for three years in Kenya. I can never satisfactorily answer the question, 'Why did you become a policeman?' But the clichés of feeling the need to do something useful with and for people in an organization as vitally important and potentially constructive and exciting as the police, held much truth for me. It was, at least, something I had always wanted to try.

9: Sketches

I did all the usual early career postings, on foot in the city centre, driving the panda / incident response car, attachments to the CID and so on. Remarkably, my short seven-year career was quite successful. Promoted to Sergeant early in service, before my five years were up, I was also chosen for a couple of fairly specialist, organizational roles. Apparently I was kept on my own force's 'special potential' list and was marked out for fairly rapid promotion.

The police reader will be aware, and other readers need to be aware, of the immense pressures involved in being a police officer but also of the tremendous, fascinating insight the work can give into the variety and mechanics of human nature. I have had my periods of intense tiredness and stress. I have known the fears of cocking it up or of being investigated by the Discipline Branch for something you know you didn't do. I have faced the violent, the armed, the unstable, the drunk, the frightened, the battered, the injured. Having been a part of this environment, I understand why policemen and women need to 'belong' — to identify with, and seek the support of, their own police companions. I understand the need for the canteen culture of cynicism, gossip, jokes and stereotyping. It all helps to let off the pressure of accumulated tension. But I have also seen how this often highly charged atmosphere, created by the enormous expectations laid on the individual police officer, particularly those on the front line, can lead to a peculiar bottling-up of emotions; a creation of the tendency to deny one's true feelings and beliefs on a number of issues in order to maintain the acceptance and affirmation given by the group which is so vital in fighting off the pressures both from the outside, and unfortunately, sometimes from the higher, managerial ranks inside the police.

It was within this framework then, in a job which I both loved and hated, that at thirty-one years of age, the most important crunch of my life came. I remember being asked quite directly in my first police interview — and I always respected the man for it — 'Are you a homosexual?' I said, 'No.' At the time I was being truthful: I did not know at a conscious, acknowledged level that I was. I knew of a sense of attraction to some of my peers throughout school and university, and of a growing 'disturbance', the only word I can use to describe it, within me. But so comprehensive I believe is the job done by the patterning of social conditioning, pressures and 'norms' with regard to the issue of homosexuality, promulgated through the omnipresent media of advertising, education and community, that I had very efficiently repressed those feelings and denied them – even to myself.

Throughout my twenties I had three important relationships with girlfriends, each one ending partly because we were not suited but partly also, I now see, because I was not truly fulfilling myself. Again though, I put it all at a distance. Then I met a girl whom I genuinely felt, as I got to know her, was someone I could increasingly love and eventually marry. We were suited: we had a wonderfully vivacious and satisfying friendship and we were compatible in many ways. Others agreed. I loved her. However, once more, what I then perceived as the 'ogre' of my truer self raised its head. I just could not give myself fully to this beautiful woman. Something else was crying out from deep within me, something I gradually came to realize must be answered and confronted – or buried. If buried, it would not die, but slowly infect through lack of air, and kill off my real nature. I would be caught in a destructive web of pretence and half-truths, living out a form of acceptable conventionality, but forever being eaten away inside. I have seen this before in the lives of many middle-aged gay men I know. Goodness knows I wanted to be 'normal'; to have a wife and kids, to be invited as a couple for dinner, to be a 'respectable' member of society. I did not ask God to make me gay! And at that time, I really did not want to be. Fortunately, something from my internal resource tank gave me, at last, and quite late on, the strength to admit and confront the side of my nature which had called to me for so long.

The hurt of the break-up with the girl I loved was followed by months of confusion and loneliness as I thrashed around in the wilderness of my hitherto unacknowledged nature. But I was now determined to sort it through, until I could be sure that the next serious relationship I had, whether with a man or woman, would be the one to which I could give myself fully.

The rest of the story is one of a growing fabric of self-realization, self-acceptance and self-expression. It was interwoven by thick strands of fear. How do I now find out about this part of myself? Who do I turn to for help? How do I meet like-minded people? (*I was much too afraid to go to the local gay pub in my town.*) What happens if my colleagues or bosses find out that I am even beginning to explore this personal issue? What about my future career? Could I be open? And what will the Church say? My family? My friends?

I will be eternally grateful to my family, a few significant friends in England and America, the local lesbian and gay Christian group, but chiefly, to Adam and to God for the increasing support, love and affirmation that I was to receive over the next few years. The fight goes on of course. There is still much residual homophobia, self-hatred and lack of understanding to deal with inside of me.

And the police? I resigned from the force, partly because I was becoming increasingly frustrated from a professional point of view, quite apart from the gay issue. It is true, however, that coming to terms with myself seems to have released new and creative resources within me, urging me to find and do what I truly want and reassuring me that I do not need authority, status or wealth to afford meaning and value to my life. But partly too I resigned because I felt, rightly or wrongly, that my determination to be increasingly open – not militant but not self-denying – about myself and my partner would not be well received within the organization, perhaps making it difficult to do my job effectively. I can't be sure of this because I didn't stay long enough to find out. Perhaps I should have done. Perhaps I should I have been more of a pioneer. There is something attractive about that, if it were not for my greater desire to return to Third World development work.

The problem is, perhaps, not so much any actual oppression or prejudice there may be within the police against gay people, but the *perceived* expressions of these, the fear that one may be harassed, alienated or mocked. It is therefore to this fear that I would recommend senior police officers address their attentions, if they wish to help the suffering minority both within and without their ranks. To the gay community I would say two things: Be aware that there are gay people within the police who need your support. Be aware also that, of the close police friends with whom I shared my secret, I received unreserved affirmation. Secondly, I believe that it will only be through gentle, tactful and honest communication with *the police organization that progress towards harmony will be made.*

To society at large I say: Please let me be. Let me share the desire to be truly and openly 'in love'; to not only be categorized in limited and insulting terms of 'genital contact' but to be able to take my proper place in the community.

● *Metropolitan YACS PC, age 33, fourteen years' service*

When I hear anti-gay jokes from colleagues, or talk about what the queers are up to on the common, I do my best to educate them – in a low-key fashion – and try to get them to take a broader view of things. It upsets me to hear such hogwash on the subject and I tend to think of it as a limitation of people's intelligence to hold such medieval views. But when all's said and done, a change in police culture is required if attitudes towards this sort of thing are to improve. At present, what we've got is a building-site culture and it's very disappointing. The culture of the junior ranks revolves around reading the Sun, *whistling at schoolgirls in the street and yobby boozing. It's anti-intellectual, anti-compassionate, anti-tolerance, anti-reasonable, anti-change, and it's very, very worrying. If you get one of them on their own, you can often have reasonable conversation and you find that they're OK as individuals. It's the collectivity of it that causes problems.*

I don't see the police as a profession because they don't qualify as professionals in the accepted sense of the word, even though some of them act in a professional way. I think one of the basic problems is to do with recruitment. I just don't think they recruit the right people. They say that they get the pick of the crop but when you look at what they select it's not very impressive: recruits that are not able to think for themselves – of weak character and easily moulded – they follow like sheep and it leaves one wondering about the judgement of the selection boards.

Thankfully, it's not as bad as it used to be and these days you can see a fair sprinkling of newspapers in the canteen. Things have changed a lot over the past ten years; attitudes are changing –

chiefly at more senior levels. It's getting better, but there's a long way to go yet. You still get Chief Superintendents giggling like school kids at meetings regarding this sexual orientation business – I was at one the other day – they find it difficult to deal with the subject matter, I guess it makes them feel insecure. But in the end they settled down and got on with it.

● Kent PC, age 34, twelve years' service

I am a PC with the Kent Constabulary and have been in the Job for twelve years but I have known that I was gay for about twenty, so obviously I knew I was gay when I joined. I was in the army for five years prior to coming into the Job (another occupation which society does not associate gay men as being members of). In point of fact, in the whole of my working life since leaving school in the 1970s, I have only been in one industry between leaving the army and joining the Job in which gays are totally accepted and thought nothing of; indeed, anyone who does have a problem with gays doesn't last long or even do well. That industry was the film production business. So why did I leave an enlightened and liberal industry to join a profession which, to say the least, is conservative in its social outlook? Well, the simple answer is, 'Why not?' I had always wanted to be a copper from an early age and had gone into the army as a second choice, having been told that my eyes weren't strong enough to join the police cadets. This is something about which I am now quite pleased, since it has given me an opportunity to experience life.

I am not open at work about my sexuality, or 'out' as it is frequently described. However, a thirty-four-year-old single police officer who is seldom, if ever, seen by his colleagues in the company of a woman has to have a question mark over him. I have, for my own part, no doubt whatsoever that there are those at my station who suspect, or who are convinced that I am gay, but none to date has had the bottle to come right out and ask me to my face. Whilst I fully realize that there are some gay officers who are so deep in the closet at work that they are almost in Narnia, I do not count myself amongst their number. If I were to be asked by anyone at work if I were gay, then provided that I felt they were asking for a genuine reason and did not have an ulterior motive, then I would have no hesitation in saying, 'Yes, I am'; otherwise, I wouldn't lie, I just wouldn't answer the question. I'd side-step it. I normally deal with it by not talking about my sex life much – unlike the rest of the station – which makes me a suspicious oddity in itself. Personally, although there are those who would strongly disagree, I see no reason to be open at work. It is a personal thing and after all, it's nobody's business but my own.

When I hear PCs pulling homosexuals to bits in the canteen and trotting out the same old stereotypes that all gay men are either limp-wristed Marys like Larry Grayson, or else are seedy little men in raincoats who molest little boys, I feel like going up to them and screaming, 'What the fucking hell's the matter with you? I'm gay, does that make me any different to the person you thought I was five seconds ago?!' They always seem to conveniently forget the fact that most molestations of children are carried out by heterosexuals and not gay men. Police officers should know better. But I don't say anything. I keep my gob shut.

● *Metropolitan PC, age 35,
seventeen years' service*

I wasn't quite seventeen years old when I joined the Job as a cadet, although I knew I was gay before I joined. I always wanted to be a police officer and although I was gay, I thought I could cover up the fact without too much trouble. Ever since a small boy, maybe seven or eight years old, I have been attracted to members of my own sex. Initially, I thought this was 'hero worship', as in the case of film stars but when I got a crush on a boy the same age as me, I must have been about nine at the time, I knew that this was 'not right' but I still thought I would grow out of it. That's what you hear, isn't it? However, by the time I'd reached my early teens, I had had crushes on several boys at school and realizing that girls did not interest me, I concluded I was definitely gay.

I have never been part of the gay scene and have never frequented gay bars or clubs. My first sexual experiences as a teenager were through cruising at a known cruising area near to where I lived. Now I'm older, and knowing the law, I don't cruise any more.

I am now thirty-five years old. It is nineteen years since I joined the Cadet Corps. My mother is now dead and I never came out to her. Nor have I come out to my father, who incidentally is also a retired police officer. I am certain that he knows about me but the subject has never been discussed and I have never found any reason for bringing it up.

Apart from a few boyfriends over the years, the only people who know I'm gay are the members of the Lesbian and Gay Police Association. As far as my colleagues are concerned, I will come out to them when I feel the time is right. That will be when I have no fear of being persecuted or discriminated against and straight officers have been educated on gay issues and lifestyles, thereby eliminating any fears or ignorance they may have on the subject.

● *Metropolitan PC, age 31, six years' service*

My name is Alan, I joined the Job in 1985 and have served at the same station since completing training at Hendon. Being a gay policeman has never been an impediment to carrying out my job from my point of view. From my colleagues' point of view, well, they don't know officially, although occasionally I suspect they suspect.

The only consideration I gave to being gay before I joined was the location of the force in which I wanted to serve. Obviously, being the largest force in the country, the Met was the best choice; less chance of being found out. Much the same reason many gays come to London. I didn't fancy getting stuck in a small town in the counties where everyone knows everyone else's business, although for all that, I chose London mainly for other reasons: I am a Londoner, I have family living there and the money is better.

When I first joined, I knew that there was no statutory discrimination against gays in the police as there is in the armed forces, but I wasn't sure how things worked in practice. It seemed likely that there would be a good deal of anti-gay sentiment; after all, the police are not renowned for their even-handedness towards those members of the public who happen to be gay. Equally, it seemed a virtual certainty that in a force of 27,000 officers there would be a substantial number of gay men and women amongst them – 10 per cent if the Kinsey figures are to be believed. Well, if it is true, that's more than the sum total of officers in many of the smaller forces in this country. The mind boggles!

I had expected to come across a few other gays at Hendon (after all there were so many people there) but I only heard a few whispers about a couple of blokes in the intake following mine. Not that I would have been bold enough to have sought out any kindred spirit. I've always been very reticent when it comes to approaching someone like that. Anyway, that was Hendon. Not very exciting from the point of view of meeting other gay police, but I enjoyed myself just the same.

I'm lucky I suppose, in that I have the support of my parents. I've always found it easy to talk to them and we've always been an extremely close-knit family. When I first told them that I was gay, I was sure they already knew. I was wrong. Neither of them had any idea, and it came as quite a shock. My mother cried all day. She said afterwards that all she could think of was the seedy side of homosexuality. But Mum and Dad both talked it over and agreed that I was still the same person after they heard the news as I was before, and they both still loved me just the same. A few weeks later, I received an envelope containing two letters: one from Mum and one from Dad. Both were very supportive and said everything I would have dared hope for. I remember I cried with relief. I still have both letters.

After leaving Hendon, I bought my own place and started work 'out on division', as it's known. It was all very new and exciting and I soon encountered the much-talked-about 'canteen culture'. I soon realized that no matter how keen or well intentioned a new probationer is, it is difficult to go against the grain of the existing 'old sweats'. So when the talk is of 'spades' and 'queens' and 'lefty bastards', it would take a very brave individual indeed who voiced any sort of protest. Most people just keep their mouth shut and wait until they are 'confirmed' in the rank (after two years' probation) before they're ready to stand up and be counted.

It cannot have escaped everyone's attention that I never

mention girlfriends and they don't ask any more, so I've come to the conclusion that there must have been lots of wagging tongues when I was out of the canteen. They must have guessed by now but no one has said as much and I haven't confirmed anything. That's how I prefer it just now. I know a few other PCs who are out at work and although I don't think they've suffered any hassle from colleagues, who knows what discrimination may have taken place behind the scenes? The time when a gay PC can be confident at work of equal treatment hasn't arrived yet – but we're working on it . . .

Shortly after starting at my first nick I met my other half. Although it wasn't quite love at first sight, we did hit it off remarkably well together and it wasn't very long before we were in a serious relationship. He moved in with me and not long after that we bought a place together. He's not in the police himself, so it took a while for him to cope with my shifts and things. We've now been together for three years and have just moved into a bigger house. No one knows what the future holds but at the moment we're both happy; good jobs, nice house, security and a steady, stable relationship. We've had our ups and downs like everyone, but we're still very much in love and planning for a long-term future together.

● *West Midlands PC, age 26,*
resigned with eight years' service

I've known that I am more attracted to men than women since I was about twelve or thirteen, and I joined the police as a cadet when I was sixteen. I was fed up with school and I didn't know what to do but I wanted to do something exciting. I would probably have joined the army but my mum told me that if I didn't like it, I wouldn't be able to get out. So I joined the police instead.

People (mostly gay activists) often ask me, 'How could you join the police if you knew you were gay?' Well, I didn't really think about whether or not homosexuality was compatible with police work when I joined. It's not the sort of thing you really think about. Looking back now, perhaps I was a bit naive, but as I say, I was quite young, and I think I was still hoping the whole thing would go away anyway. I knew I fancied men more than women

*but I didn't have a gay identity in the way that I do now, which is
entirely different. In any case, I had absolutely no idea at the time
what I was joining, or that police officers could be so thoroughly
nasty. How the hell was I to know, for God's sake? I was just
seventeen. There are lots of cops that aren't of course – nasty, that
is – but there are a lot of assholes too. Funny thing is, contrary to
popular belief, the police don't recruit assholes. Not deliberately
anyway. They try hard, I think. It's just something that you get
turned into once you begin to absorb police culture, that is, it's a
social phenomenon, but all that psychological stuff is too complicated to get into here. But I know I definitely found myself doing a
few things which I promised myself I would never do when I
joined, mostly little things, like using police jargon: words like
'nick' and 'body' and 'landline' – it all sounded so pathetic when I
joined, but after a few years some of it begins to sound OK. I also
started to 'embroider' the odd bit of evidence in court, which is not
as bad as it sounds actually. Everybody does it, not that I use that
as justification, but you soon learn that without it you'd never get a
single conviction, not even on Jack the Ripper. That's the way the
system works here, but you won't understand that unless you've
been in the Job. The point is that the change is an imperceptible
process. It doesn't happen overnight.*

*I left a couple of years ago – not because they found out I
was gay – no one knew about that (except for two of the PCs on my
shift, and I knew that I could trust them 100 per cent). I just didn't
fit the mould, or rather, I refused to fit. And when you don't, life
can get pretty shitty, believe me. And it did. I got totally stitched up
in the end for something I didn't do and was transferred with the
quiet word that I was to be given a hard time. I was. Fuck knows
what would have happened if they'd thought I was a faggot. In the
end, I got an offer I couldn't refuse from elsewhere, and left.*

*It's only since I left that I've really been able to get my act
together about my sexuality – I mean, learned to accept it for what
it is. The police force just isn't the place to try and get to grips with
that kind of thing. If I'd have stayed in for much longer, I'd have
been a basket case by now for sure. I know plenty of others who
went that way. It's just so hard to develop and maintain a positive
self-image of yourself as gay in a repressive organization like that.*

I'm sure a lot of people in the police like to think that they don't have any 'poofs' in the force but that's a load of crap. Every job has gays and bisexuals and they're fools if they think otherwise. Most of them don't come out though for obvious reasons, so it's hard to find others like yourself. Not many of them are camp like they so often are in the pubs and clubs, so they can be hard to spot. I didn't know a single gay copper whilst I was in, though I suspected a few and heard rumours about others – but I thought that was just the normal nastiness.

I did eight years altogether. I can't say I'm sorry I joined, I learned a lot. Can't say I'm sorry I left either. I know a lot more would like to leave, and I'm talking about straight cops now. But it's a question of what else to do. It pays pretty well, it's got security, prestige, and a lot of police officers aren't qualified to do anything else. It's all they know. Besides, it's not easy to get out, psychologically I mean, and like everyone says, it's better than working for a living. It's not a bad job actually. It's the assholes in it. Like a lot of jobs I guess. I know lots of lesbian and gay police officers now that I've left, although I didn't know any whilst I was serving. A couple of the guys are actually out at work and seem to be having no problems. They say that I should join again, they say that it's all changed. But these people are not the norm. They're accepted either because they're better than average at their job or because they've got the personality to carry it off.[2] They have to be whiter than white to get by. And the minute they put a foot wrong, you can be sure they'll get shat on. That much said, things do seem to be improving and although an organization like the police doesn't change overnight, the educational standard has never been higher and that ought to have some bearing on the levels of internal prejudice. So the police force has had a big facelift. That's something that very few people seem to appreciate and for some strange reason I still get protective about the Job on occasions. Mostly when people who don't know diddly squat about it, usually gay activists, start putting their oar in. At the end of the day though, an organization like the police is bound to be a bit of an old dinosaur. When change comes, it comes slowly, and overall values and politics are bound to stay mostly conservative. After all, they're paid to stay that way.

20: Coming Out of the Blue

I think it's about time society grew up on the whole issue of sexuality, if you really want to know how I feel about it. Big fuss about nothing. Who gives a toss anyway? What difference could it possibly make to the universe, if I can get philosophical with you for just a moment? I just don't need that kind of shit any more. I've outgrown the guilt I used to feel. And I certainly don't need it when I'm at work. So no, I don't imagine I'll be joining again. But thanks anyway.

● *Norfolk WPC, age 24, three years' service*

The problem is that everyone thinks they can spot homosexuals. OK, some of them you can — we can all do that — but most of them you can't. The other problem for me are the labels 'homosexual', 'gay', etc. It automatically makes people think all kinds of weird shit. Although that's what I am technically, I hate using the word because it's a label which distorts the person that I am. People suddenly see you differently if they think you're gay, so I don't use the word any more. Sometimes it's quite funny because I end up saying things like 'I'm not gay, I just prefer to sleep with women.' For me, that's all gay (or lesbian) means. I saw my idea summed up in a book once and I copied it out and kept it. I think it says it all. It says what I am, and also that what I am doesn't need a restrictive label:

> *Homosexual. I find the word hard to relate to because it puts me in a category which limits my potential. It also prescribes a whole system of behaviour to which I'm supposed to conform which has nothing to do with my day-to-day living ... I reject the word homosexual. I reject a category that defines my central life thrust in limiting terms. I am a human being.*

Notes

1. The expression 'the Job' enjoys almost universal usage as a synonym for 'the police organization'; hence, throughout this book the word 'job', where it refers to the police service, has a capital 'J'.
2. In his MA dissertation ('Homosexuality in the police', University of Exeter, 1992), Chief Inspector Robert Anthony of the Metropolitan Police refers to this as the 'Good Copper Syndrome'. This refers to the tendency to accept and even respect individuals who may be in some way 'odd', so long as they are perceived to be effective police officers.

Chapter two

Selection and Training

Selection

As far as selection for Britain's police services is concerned, it seems that most gay recruits are sufficiently concerned about their prospects of selection to conceal their sexual orientation throughout the entire selection process.

● *Metropolitan woman Inspector, age 39,*
twenty years' service

I've known I was gay since I was about sixteen, but I'd always wanted to join the police and being gay wasn't going to stop me. If the selection board had known that I was gay when I joined, I'm sure I would never have got in because at the time police women had only just got equal rights and equal pay, and prejudice against everyone who wasn't white, heterosexual and male was rife.

● *Metropolitan PC, age 29, seven years' service*

I'm pretty sure I wouldn't have got in if they'd have known about me because after I'd had the interview and gone on to the next stage, the trainer at Paddington Green said to us when we were all together in a big group: 'There are two things we don't take in the police and that's criminals and poofters.' It hit me like a bolt when he said that, but I didn't say anything of course. No one did. We were all silent. But it's always stuck in my mind.

Although there is little evidence that forces have a common policy to systematically sift out the sexually atypical at the selection stage, electing not to select candidates who are either openly gay or suspected to be so, and 'deselecting' those who are subsequently discovered to have slipped through the net would be one of the simplest ways to frustrate the stability of 'sexually deviant' populations within the service.

● Metropolitan woman Chief Inspector, age 34, twelve years' service

I was at a selection training course at Paddington a couple of years ago, and whilst I was there a civilian came up to us and said that she'd just taken a call from a man who was gay and had been in a stable relationship with his boyfriend for the past fifteen years. He wanted to know if we had any ruling on accepting gay officers. The answer came back that there was no policy, but a senior officer who was standing there at the time said in the next breath that it would be a very brave officer, wouldn't it, who signed such a person's acceptance form if they were gay.

● City of London PC, age 36, nine years' service

By the time I went for my interview I'd thought a lot about what I would say if they asked me about my sexuality or whether or not I had a girlfriend because I'd just come out of the army. I'd had to lie about myself there all the time and I didn't particularly want to spend the rest of my life lying – which was one of the reasons I left. I wasn't about to begin that process of deceit all over again in the police because I knew I didn't have to, so I had to decide in advance how I was going to handle the interview. In the end I couldn't make a decision, and luckily, they never asked, so I didn't bother to bring it up. If they had, I probably would have lied and blushed.

24: Coming Out of the Blue

● *Derbyshire PC, age 46,*
twenty-one years' service

There's no way I would have got in if they'd known I was gay. When I joined, our Chief Constable was ex-army and he ran the force like an army – everybody knew it – and of course homosexuality is still illegal in the army.[1] I wouldn't have stood a cat's chance. It's as simple as that. In fact when I joined, I thought that there probably weren't any gays in the police anyway.

● *Kent DC, age 30, ten years' service*

I have a suspicion that the woman Chief Superintendent who interviewed me might have guessed about me when I went for my interview because one of her questions was, 'You realize that if you were out on the street you could get assaulted?' I said, 'Yes.' 'And marked?' I said, 'Yes.' Then she said, 'Because you are rather pretty ... aren't you?' I'm not quite sure if she knew about me or not. But if she did, she obviously didn't care because here I am.

● *Gwent PC, age 36,*
resigned with fourteen years' service

I would have failed for being gay when I joined because attitudes then were not so good towards that kind of thing, and as a young applicant I might have been seen as a bit of a liability. In any case, they asked the guy before me if he was gay because he had highlighted hair. I don't know what he said but I don't think he got in. They just don't want the risk of embarrassment, and so it's easier just not to have them in. But today I think that senior management are a little more enlightened, and the subject is more open for discussion, although I'm not sure about that in my force. It's pretty small-town mentality here.

A London officer makes a similar point and identifies what he sees as the service's main problem when it comes to young male officers.

25: Selection and Training

● *Metropolitan PC, age 23, five years' service*

I was only eighteen at the time I joined the Job, and if I were to have a sexual boyfriend before I was twenty-one then it would be against the law. I doubt they want to risk that. It's far easier for them to pick someone else who is less risky for them. It's a totally ludicrous situation we're in in this country. I can take on my shoulders one of the most responsible jobs in this country and all the shit that goes with it – and believe me there's a lot of shit – I can make that decision OK – even if it means getting shot by an armed robber – that's OK – I'm old enough to know that that's what I want and what the risks involved are. But can I decide that I simply prefer sleeping with men than women? Can I, hell. I need to be twenty-one to know that. Come on, who are they trying to kid? I knew perfectly well what I wanted at the same age as everyone else.

The observations of this officer are particularly interesting in comparison to the legal situation in many other countries. Britain's unusually high age of consent for (male)[2] homosexual activity, apart from its inherent unfairness, results in a number of bothersome practical consequences with regard to the lives of non-heterosexual policemen. Since the age of consent for same-sex activity between men is twenty-one, and the minimum recruitment age for the police service is eighteen and a half, then the issue arises that it is possible to be at the same time both a police officer and below the age of consent for homosexual activity. Within Europe, this scenario is now only possible in Cyprus, Ireland, and Romania, since all other countries have an age of consent that is either equal to, or lower than, the police recruitment age. (See Appendix D for a full listing of European ages of consent.) In most of the United States, the age of consent for same-sex activity is eighteen whilst the minimum police recruitment age is twenty-one; a full reversal of the situation in Britain and one which (on both counts) seems more sensible. In Canada, the recruitment age is also twenty-one but the age of consent is sixteen; again the scenario does not arise. In the Netherlands, the recruitment age, as in Britain, is only eighteen but the problem is yet again circumvented because the age of consent is considerably lower.[3]

It is, however, worth noting that although it was a significant worry for many of those gay, lesbian and bisexual officers who were eventually successful in their applications to join the police that their sexuality might somehow be exposed during the interview process, for others the issue was never a concern because at the time they applied to join the service, they were not conscious of any homosexual orientation; thus, it is doubtful that homosexuality could ever be successfully purged from either the police or the armed services, whatever the methods of selection.

Training

The uniformed police constable is the principal regulator of policing where it counts most – on the street. As the political scientist James Q. Wilson put it, 'the police department has the special property ... that within it discretion increases as one moves *down* the hierarchy.'[4] The ownership of this property means that the police also have a special duty to ensure that their younger constables and those who are less experienced are appropriately trained to deal with the mass of diversity that they will encounter during the course of their daily duties. That mass of diversity will include people with unusual backgrounds from all classes, a host of ethnic and religious values that they will not share nor even understand, and alternative ways of living and loving. Whilst the first two areas are now comprehensively covered at most urban training schools under titles such as 'Policing Skills' and 'Awareness Training', at most training schools the latter issue is seldom addressed at all.

In his 1830 essay 'On Prejudice',[5] William Hazlitt wrote, 'Prejudice is the child of ignorance.' He continued, 'Mere ignorance is a blank canvass, on which we lay what colours we please.' This notion suggests, as recent studies have shown, that increased education helps to reduce prejudice. Dissimilarly, notes Hazlitt, 'The fewer things we know, the more ready we shall be to pronounce upon and condemn, what is new and strange to us.' In accordance with what we know about the nature of prejudice today, the training schools of Britain have a duty to dispel the ignorance and misunderstanding in the minds of recruits on a wide variety of issues, including same-sex attraction. At present, information on the subject is at best sporadic and idiosyncratic. Although some schools were discussing the topic, most of the officers in this study (and particularly those who had been recently trained) were both surprised and disappointed that they could spend six months at training school without touching upon such an important issue.

● Kent PC, age 21, two years' service

I think that good information at training school would be immensely beneficial. Recruits are so receptive to things during that period, and today's recruits are more open-minded than they've ever been. I think that the subject has to be discussed in open forum and I think that someone gay should go and talk to the recruits like people from other groups do. When I was at training school there were projects we had to do with race relations and stuff, and at the end of it all people were as positive as anybody could possibly want them to be. But of course training school is an ideal world which ceases to exist outside its doors. On the streets it's different. Nevertheless, at least they would know what kind of behaviour is acceptable and expected of them. Training school should at least set a proper standard, or ideal.

● Metropolitan Detective Inspector, age 44, twenty-four years' service

Training will become increasingly important for recruits if sexual orientation is to be introduced into police equal opportunities' policies. Training will become important not just at training school, but at middle and senior management level because it's not just a question of not discriminating against public and officers; if people are going to come to Chief Superintendents with problems connected with their sexuality, then those managers are going to need to know how to deal with it just like they deal with everything else. At the present time the Job is totally ill-equipped to deal with it. There's an awful lot of work to be done yet. Having said that, it would appear that, in the Met at least, the Job is beginning to change in its attitudes towards sexual orientation, which are definitely improving. It seems to be trying to align itself with the softer, more liberal views of the 1990s, rather than the enterprise culture and Thatcherism of the 1980s.

● West Midlands WPS, age 35, twelve years' service

More training is required because the police are policing the whole of society, and they should know what they will be dealing with when they get out there. That includes training on homosexuality and gay lifestyles. Those entering the service should be screened for homophobic attitudes as they are for racist ones, and either put right or dumped. The ways that some recent incidents on the streets have been dealt with demonstrate that such training is desperately required. There was nothing really anti-gay when I was at training school but there was no positive input either. The only input I remember was under the heading of 'Unnatural Offences', which was very negative, so a young impressionable bobby, with no real experience of it, might come to associate homosexuality with breaking the law because the only time it was mentioned was in connection with criminal offences. That has to change.

● South Yorkshire PC, age 29, three years' service

All I got at training school was a two-hour tutorial on homosexuality, bisexuality, heterosexuality, bestiality and necrophilia. It was all lumped together in a light-hearted way and not taken very seriously. The training is definitely inadequate at this time on sexual offences. Whilst the law has to be carried out, officers must be made aware that the law does not equal 'right' when it comes to sexual offences any more than it does on any other matter. Adultery may be immoral but it is not an offence, and there's a perfect example. We should just get on with our job without all this moral superiority crap.

● *Metropolitan WPC, age 27, four years' service*

When I came up from the West Country to join the Met I didn't know what the word 'lesbian' meant, except that it wasn't very nice. I certainly didn't know that it meant me. Recruits must have something to combat that ignorance and any prejudice they learn in the playground. They get a lot on blacks and Asians, but nothing on gays. And where I was in Earls Court, there are tons of gays. People who aren't heterosexual make up one of the biggest minority groups in this country, especially in London.

● *Hampshire PC, age 29, seven years' service*

A whole session should be given to homosexuality and what society defines as 'unnatural'. It's important to teach the police what it means to be gay; to educate those who have this negative attitude towards homosexuality what it's really all about. What PCs need is to have an ordinary person like me come and speak to them at training school and we could all have a whole afternoon thrashing out these issues once and for all. They could see then that I'm a copper the same as them and a person who basically has the same values as them. They could ask me all the usual crazy questions they wanted, like 'What do gays do in bed?' and stuff like that and be as aggressive about it as they liked. I can handle that, and hopefully, by the end of the afternoon I might actually succeed in convincing them that we're basically the same as they are – except we prefer to form relationships with people of the same sex. Then no one could say that they've never met a homosexual and maybe they'd feel more comfortable about the whole thing and be able to deal with it in a more adult way.

It's also important for them to know that being gay doesn't affect your ability as a police officer. That's really important. It's not good enough simply to tell them that they have to accept it, and if they don't they'll be disciplined. They need to understand why their attitudes are wrong. And they need to hear it from someone who is actually gay, who can tell them what it's really like to be gay and to be treated like shit. Otherwise it would be like having a white officer explaining what it's like to be black. How can they? It *always comes better from the horse's mouth. They need to look at the faces of those who they've been taught to hate and see that they look just like they do and that they're actually OK. They need to see for themselves that they've been conned by society – it's no good just telling them they're wrong.*

It has been suggested that in London at least, training is improving and homosexuality is being covered in a more systematic manner. A number of the officers I spoke to were able to confirm such adjustments.

● Metropolitan WPC, age 23, one year's service

We had a rather unorthodox instructor who did a 'domestic' role-play with us. It went like this: The first officer on the scene sees these two guys sitting at a table with a woman, and the woman is talking to one of the guys. To start with it was dealt with as a heterosexual relationship gone wrong where the woman has come between the two men. But it turned out to be a gay relationship with a problem, and the woman was a friend who was simply comforting one of the lads involved. The instructor explained to us that it was a situation that most police officers are outside of, but that it needs to be dealt with objectively just as anything else – the same things apply – the empathy and what have you. I thought it was dealt with very well.

● Metropolitan WPC, age 28, two years' service

We had a couple of discussions where the subject came up. In one we were designing a make-believe community and one of the things we had to decide was whether or not we would allow gay clubs and pubs to exist. Most of the people in the class said no and the instructors challenged that and said why that attitude was wrong – they were more positive than the class. I'd like to see a little more though. One whole lesson would be nice and perhaps some handouts. After all, we had several lessons on the Sikh community and stuff like that, and notes to go with it and most of the officers will end up working in areas where there are no Sikhs at all, whereas all officers will come into contact with homosexuals whether they know it or not.

● *Metropolitan WPS, age 26, four years' service*

We had a discussion on sexuality once when it came to dealing with Aids. Most of the people in the room said the usual kiddy stuff like 'Err!' and 'Yuk!' about how disgusting it all was. The instructors tried to encourage people to be understanding towards homosexuals which was good, but it was pretty obvious that they didn't think for one minute that anyone in the room was actually gay. I found it all a bit condescending really. There's a tremendous pressure to go along with the jokes and stuff in circumstances like that so that no one guesses you're gay. I know I did. You'd think that the instructors would realize that, but they take you all at face value.

It is not necessary that officers understand the socio-psychological dynamics of sexual orientation and physical attraction, but it would be a useful learning exercise for officers to try and understand and come to terms with what it is that makes them respond so strongly when confronted with homosexuality. In the next piece, a woman sergeant identifies what she sees as the principal cause of 'the male reaction'.

● *Kent WPS, age 41, fifteen years' service*

The problem is that (as far as the men are concerned) lesbianism is not seen as a threat because for many of them it's a macho sexual turn on – or supposed to be. However, they do feel threatened by male homosexuals because when they meet one who is open, for the first time in their lives perhaps, it makes them feel sexually vulnerable, and that's not something that men are used to feeling. They are potentially out of control and it scares them absolutely shitless. Although why they think the person concerned will fancy them is beyond me. Someone with attitudes like that is hardly going to appeal to a gay man or woman. These people have in their *assumptions about us, a tendency to flatter themselves to an extraordinary degree. Most of them wouldn't be touched with a bargepole. These people have to be made aware that we have the same likes and dislikes as everyone. We're just as choosy as they are and we're not sex maniacs. And if they don't want to go to bed with another man, then they have got to get used to simply saying 'No, thanks' just like us women have had to with men, and stop seeing it as such a terrible ordeal. They have to grow up a bit.*

By improving instruction in this area, then, attitudes might gradually be improved, and any institutionalized homophobia at training schools or tacit sanctioning of prejudiced attitudes by staff might also be dealt with effectively.

● *West Midlands WPC, age 35, twelve years' service*

I remember doing practicals at training school. Anything went there, so long as the probationer didn't win. I remember one practical I did was a simple case of littering, but the sergeant playing the part of the litter-bug decided to play it in the character of a stereotyped homosexual, for no reason, except to get some laughs – which he got. Having said that, I don't actually think that recruits join the police more homophobic than the rest of society. It's just that once they've been in the police for a while, they make more of a show of what prejudices they have, because the canteen culture encourages them to do so. In the police, the canteen is a sort of safe environment where anything goes. You can really say what you like and get away with it. It's a place where you can get support after you've had trouble on the street, where people will always agree with your point of view. New recruits coming in learn that this is the way to behave in the canteen.

When I was training at the Central Planning Unit in Harrogate recently, they were still doing the same limp-wristed role plays, and that made me really angry. Recruits need to be taught about it, so that they don't get that terrible prickly feeling when they come across it out in the real world. Most of them are incredibly ignorant about it. I've heard some unbelievable things in my time. You wouldn't believe me.

● *Metropolitan WPC, age 28,*
seven years' service

There was a girl on my course called Lisa who was from up north. She was quite open about the fact that she was gay – she didn't make it a secret. She had the rings on her little fingers and that. I think she must have clicked about me, although I never told her, because she kept coming up to my room and wanting to go out. Well, it all got a bit embarrassing for me because she looked a bit gay and I didn't really want to associate with her too closely knowing what the police were like with gay people. I didn't want any hassle at training school. I just wanted to make it through like everyone else. Everyone used to talk about her and she was aware of that. In the changing rooms the girls didn't want to change in front of her or go in the shower or anything. Just silly things really but it gets to you in the end. There were always comments about her getting into the hockey team as well because even at training school it was well known that all the hockey girls were gay. I also think that she was probably going through a difficult stage with herself. I mean she knew she was gay and that, but I think she was still not all that confident about it and was looking for some acceptance. That's why she wanted people to know, I suppose – because she wanted them to understand. She wanted to talk to someone. She didn't realize that they wouldn't understand and that as soon as they found out they would be horrible to her. She was a nice girl actually.

Anyway, in the end they all gave her such a hard time that she left; one morning I went up to her room and she'd just left. It's a shame. I feel a bit bad about not supporting her now because maybe I could have helped her through, but I couldn't afford to blow my cover at the time. I was even embarrassed to go to her room in the evening for a chat and when she came down to mine, all the girls would ask what she had come down to my room for.

● *Metropolitan PC, age 26,*
just passed out of Hendon training school

I got asked if I was 'a poof' at training school. We were
having a session where we went around the class asking each other
questions. Normally it would be on the law but it was our long
weekend and so we were allowed to ask each other anything we
wanted. Mostly just personal or silly questions. Me and this girl
were the only two in the class who didn't have girlfriends or boyfriends. Also I didn't mix all that much with them – I used to keep
myself to myself – and I didn't talk much about my social life
either. We were both automatically classed as being gay. So
someone asked me, 'Is it true that you're a poof then?' I didn't
really know what to say, so I just made a joke out of it and said,
'Yeah, come up to my room afterwards and I'll show you.' People
laughed and I got the occasional comment after that about my
sexuality, but nothing really bad. If you want to be in the police
then you have to learn to laugh at yourself. And if it gets out of
order, then you just laugh at them instead. It's like they say: If you
can't take a joke, then you shouldn't have joined.

When it comes to training, not all officers are convinced
about the merits of special training on lesbian and gay lifestyles,
and of those who are in favour, a number harbour reservations.

● *Metropolitan WDC, age 29,*
seven years' service

I'm not sure that training on homosexuality would do any
good because people have strong views on the subject which are
unlikely to change overnight. It could cause a backlash if it's not
done carefully, but then they said that about ethnic training so
that's no excuse not to do it. But I remember when I was in the
sixth form at school, when I still thought that homosexuality was
unnatural and I didn't understand it, we had these two dykes come
in and give a chat on homosexuality. At the end of the day, they
gave out a sheet and we had to return it to them with feedback. I

remember I was so angry, I said that I thought the day was a complete waste of time and that I'd wanted to walk out halfway through because I didn't want to know about those things – that I knew about them already, and that I came to school to learn about things for life and not about some dyke and her other half. So I know how it might affect some people, but then maybe that's because they are insecure. I guess I was.

● *Metropolitan WDS, age 30, four years' service*

I think the stuff we did on race at training school just made people more racist because people don't like having it rammed down their throats, if you'll forgive the expression. Of course I'd like to see more done on homosexuality but I'd hate to think that it was affecting people adversely. That kind of training needs to be backed up on relief as well, otherwise it all goes down the drain just like everything else you learn up there. I also think that by recruiting more experienced people into the Job, people who had seen a bit of the world, who were a bit more open-minded and had had other jobs, intolerance would be lessened. Most of them have never done anything else except be police officers and they don't know what the big wide world's all about, so when they get out on relief they're so young and vulnerable and keen to impress, that they try and emulate the big-mouth assholes on the relief. So few coppers have got a mind of their own and they all end up the same. They're like a bunch of sheep. I didn't know the police would be as bad as it was before I joined. I didn't realize how shallow they would be. I've never known a group of men to be so bitchy and childish. I found it hard to believe at first because you don't expect it when you first join, do you?

But you won't ever change the police. Giving them training on gays will just cause antagonism. I mean women still aren't equal in the police after all these years. You're still just a 'trout' or a 'Doris' to most of them, and a potential fuck. I came off some special squad having worked my tits off not long ago and when I got back to the CID office to do normal duty again, there's these fat DCs who don't ever do anything, and who assume that you are useless just because you're a woman. It really pisses me off because

I work far harder than most of them and I think I deserve a bit more credit than that. They've no idea what you're capable of doing; most of them have got no idea what I was doing before I got back to the office and they think all I'm good for is taking statements off of rape victims. I was working twenty-four hours a day before I got back there. So no, I don't suppose training will achieve much.

● *Metropolitan PC, age 23, four years' service*

Homosexuality is really only the basic human emotions of love and affection transferred from a man and a woman, to a man and a man, or a woman and a woman. I don't think our culture is really that different to straight people's, so I don't really know what they can teach about it, except that gay men love, live and have sex with other men, and lesbians love and live and have sex with other women, and we all want to be accepted into society more readily because there's nothing wrong with that. That's it.

Notes

1. As a result of recommendations by the Select Committee on the Armed Forces, the Conservative government announced in June 1992 that homosexual activity of a kind that is legal in civilian law will cease to constitute an offence under service law (bill to follow). The provisions of the 1967 Sexual Offences Act had not previously been extended to the above bodies. The Merchant Navy had also been excluded and will require separate legislation in order to be brought up to date.
2. The 1967 Sexual Offences Act does not proscribe same-sex relationships between females, thus there is no statutory age of consent for lesbians.
3. The minimum age of consent for both homosexual and heterosexual activity in Holland has recently been renegotiated from sixteen to twelve.
4. J. Q. Wilson, *Varieties of Police Behaviour*, 1968, p. 7. Emphasis in the original.
5. W. Hazlitt, 'On Prejudice', 11–18 April 1830, *The Complete Works of William Hazlitt*, Vol. 20, p. 316.

Chapter three

Cruising, Cottaging and Queerbashing

One of the classic stories about Clapham Common is the one where this PC on night duty leaps out of the station van and chases one of the local 'poofs' right the way across the Common. The guy eventually gives up in exhaustion at the other side, puffing and panting as the PC catches up with him. Instead of arresting him, this PC just stares at this guy who is absolutely terrified. Then the PC touches him lightly on the shoulder and says, 'You're it now. You have to chase me ...' and he turns around and runs back across the common towards the van.

● *Metropolitan PS, age 29, seven years' service*

OVER the past five years or so, the delicate issues of cruising, cottaging and queerbashing have continued to dominate the headlines in the conflict between the police and the lesbian and gay communities. Whilst many forces continue to organize specialized squads of officers to deal specifically with gay sexual offences in public places, gay and lesbian pressure groups continue to demand an end to public toilet and cruising area surveillance, and a greater attention to apprehending those persons who attack and murder homosexuals because of their sexuality. In his article 'Divided loyalties',[1] Sergeant Michael Bennett of the Metropolitan Police

Federation aired a concern that because of the hostility between the two communities, homosexual officers are liable to suffer a conflict of allegiances during the course of their duties and might, therefore, be selective about the type of laws they are willing to enforce.[2] This chapter, then, briefly examines the (sociological) basis of such conflict before exploring a few of the thorny issues which confront the non-heterosexually identified police officer.

Most individuals in society inhabit more than one *role category* and are able to behave in accordance with each category without conflict. Take, for example, the woman who effectively combines the roles of 'mother' and 'wife'. However, when two or more simultaneously occupied role categories contain conflicting expectations or values, the result can be difficulty in satisfying all the *role expectations*. The result is a mixture of emotions such as guilt, despondency, frustration and anxiety known as *role conflict*. The concept is well documented. Burchard's study of military chaplains provides a good example of the conflicting expectations to be found within one profession of Her Majesty's Forces:

> ... a good leader must be accessible; he must not be too distant from his flock; he must be on good personal relations with those he is leading. A military officer, however, must not be familiar with his men. His ability as a leader is presumed to depend, in part, on his ability to keep at a distance from his men. The chaplain, being both a military officer and a clergyman, must somehow come to grips with the problem of carrying on an effective religious ministry for enlisted personnel and at the same time of retaining his status as an officer.[3]

Likewise, Curb and Manahan's study of lesbian nuns highlights a similar, and perhaps more analogous, plight to that of the homosexual police officer:

> Religious women who happen to be lesbians live behind two closet doors. The one called religious life keeps us protected from the world, that sinful entity that we are taught we should be in but not of. The other door hides our sexual

orientation. I lived and loved behind those two doors for twenty-nine years ... As the years went by, my personal affairs became more physical and therefore more demanding. I found myself wanting more and more. Finally I wanted someone to love me, and only me, forever. My vow of celibacy made my desire for a personal love illicit and illegal. I knew that some choices would have to be made. I felt as long as I remained in one world, I could not be true to the other ... It came down to personal integrity and the old cliché of waking up each morning and liking the person in the mirror. I am not saying that it is impossible to be gay religious: I am saying that for me it was not possible. I could not keep the two worlds apart. Not being true to either world was causing havoc within me ... Finally, I knew that the only way to be the person God called me to be was to open both doors and walk away free.[4]

The problems associated with role conflict notwithstanding, the homosexual police officer is liable to suffer from a more general difficulty, that of *marginality*. Marginality is more closely linked with the concept of the multiple *culture* than with the multiple role, and is generated by the dislocation of a person from a single culture and their affiliation to a second without the loss of the first. It seems that those most at risk from experiencing extreme marginality have spent most of their lives intimately involved with the dominant culture. This scenario is one which frequently typifies the instance of the non-heterosexual. Unlike members of ethnic minorities, who usually spend much of their time involved with their 'subordinate' culture before entering their period of *marginal consciousness*, the young man or woman coming to terms with his or her homosexuality is unlikely to ever have mixed with others of a similar orientation. They have usually assimilated the heterosexual values of dominant society without question until that moment when they realize that they are unlikely to conform to the 'ideal' that they have been tendered. Realizing that their true orientation is likely to lead to ostracism and rejection, gay men and lesbians often find themselves in a state of severe crisis, completely overwhelmed and unable to cope. An awareness of marginality begins to define

... his [*sic*] place in the world in a way which he had not anticipated. It delimits his present and future in terms of his career, his ideals and aspirations, and his inmost conception of himself. And it is a shock because his previous contacts have led him to identify himself with the cultural world which now refuses to accept him.[5]

Able to see themselves from a heterosexual viewpoint, individuals may experience a 'double consciousness'. W. E. B. Du Bois describes this (in the context of black consciousness) as 'always looking at one's self through the eyes of others, by measuring one's soul by the tape of a world that looks on in amused contempt and pity'.[6] In this way, both worlds will constitute at the same time both a refuge and a prison; places that are longed for in one instant and yet despised in the next. Thus, the marginal is frequently

> poised in psychological uncertainty between two (or more) social worlds; reflecting in his soul the discords and harmonies, repulsions and attractions of these worlds, one of which is often 'dominant' over the other.[7]

Whilst the concept of the homosexual police officer has been little studied in this regard, it is clear that the predicament of these men and women represents a further example of two roles which frequently compete for dominance. Certainly it is commonly the case that, like the black officer, a gay- or lesbian-identified police officer possesses two primary identities – one which may be described as 'police officer' and one as 'gay man' or 'lesbian' (or bisexual). In isolation, either of these identities may, or may not, prove burdensome on its own merits. In combination, however, this dual citizenship – the occupation of two conflicting role categories and the consequent entertainment of two sets of role expectations – might reasonably be expected to result in some degree of conflict. As law officers, it is the responsibility of the police to enforce their country's legislation, yet as lesbians or gay men there is an equal moral duty to protect their communities from society's prejudice and discrimination (including that of the criminal justice system). The results of such conflict are numerous. Alienation and resentment are often felt towards heterosexual colleagues, since such officers will find themselves distressed both by the homophobic attitudes they are confronted with and by the judgements they believe they would be subject to if colleagues knew of their orientation. At the same time they may feel some inner sense of shame for not speaking out against such prejudice. With regard to their police identities, officers may also feel a sense of disloyalty to their profession for having to disguise their occupation when passing as 'security guards' in the gay communities. Ultimately, then,

> The marginal man ... is one whom fate has condemned to live in two societies and in two, not merely different but antagonistic, cultures. Thus, the individual whose mother is a Jew and whose father is a Gentile is fatally condemned to grow up under the influence of two traditions. In that case, his mind is the crucible in which two different and refractory cultures may be said to melt and, either wholly or in part, fuse.[8]

The word 'fuse' is important here since despite the difficulties the marginal faces, this dualism need not prove disastrous.[9] The acuteness of the marginal personality is ultimately dependent on a number of factors, including the development of individual 'coping strategies' and the overall effectiveness of adjustment/maladjustment roles which can be utilized to greatly reduce the effects of marginality. In the meantime, however, devaluation by the dominant culture may lead to the development of inferiority complexes, where the individual comes to see him- or herself in the same way as the majority group. 'The group definition precedes the individual's definition of himself. The individual may or may not consciously accept this definition; it influences him none the less.'[10] In other cases, the hatred marginals have been taught to feel for themselves may be redirected towards the dominant group seen as responsible for the process of marginalization. In the case of the non-heterosexual, this might take the form of gay activism, often referred to as 'homosexual militancy'. The effects of role strain and marginality (or 'divided loyalties') which may result from this type of situation will remain until the individual has evolved a new identity which takes account of his or her dilemma. This may involve assimilation into either the dominant or subordinate group, or, more usually, some form of compromise.

● *Thames Valley PS, age 29, six years' service*

I'm very loyal to the police but if I were pushed, I would have to say that I see myself as a gay man first, because being gay isn't a choice. Nobody came up to me and said, 'Hey, Andy, you can be gay, you can be bisexual or straight, which one do you want?' I didn't choose to be gay. It's the way I've always been, and probably always will be. I remember a Chief Inspector asking me when I told him about me, 'Why did you choose to be gay?' My response was simply, 'Why did you choose not to be?' He said, 'I didn't.' I said, 'Well, there's your answer.'

If the police started placing restrictions on my private life then I would probably leave the police. I have no intention of being restricted outside my working hours and if the police said to me, 'Here are the things you can and can't do', then I would have to seriously reconsider my career. And if the issue was forced, I know which one I would choose. Being gay is more important to me than anything else these days. It's a way of life. And I've had to hide it for too long to give it up now. The police is just a job. It won't be there for ever. Even so, I protect the police when gay people criticize them. I prefer the criticism to come from my own mouth rather than other people's, although sometimes I think that my being an apologist for the police is rather misplaced – after all they're big enough and ugly enough to look after themselves.

● *West Yorkshire WPC, age 26, four years' service*

You've got to have rules by which to live and my loyalties are in enforcing those rules, because gays break the law as well. They're not perfect. They commit burglaries and assault each other and steal like the rest of the community, and without those laws, there would be chaos. I have been charged with the responsibility of seeing that the rules we have decided to have in this country are obeyed. Having said all that, whilst I believe in law and order, it's not at any cost of course. The police have this tendency to think that they are the moral protectors of society – that they are on some kind of mission to uphold the moral standards of the country – and so they frequently end up taking on board more than they are blessed with.

● Metropolitan PC, age 19, one year's service

At the moment my loyalties lie with the police. But then it's all new to me now. And it's all I've got that means anything to me. I'm starting at a central London station on Monday with a Street Duties course. I've already heard that there are five other gay PCs there at that nick. I hope it's true!

● Suffolk PC, age 32, seven years' service

As far as my identity is concerned, I suppose I see myself as a gay man first – because that's me first of all. But I think my primary loyalties lie with the police. And that's because I believe in the concept of policing.

● Devon and Cornwall PC, age 39, fourteen years' service

When I first joined the Job, I was very committed to it. At that stage being gay was very much a guilty sideline if you like, but then I wasn't happy with being gay initially. But as time has gone on, I've developed more as a personality and as a gay man, and now I find that that's often at odds with, and has very much harmed, my work. The two just don't exist very well together. As one develops the other suffers, and so my commitment to the Job has deteriorated a great deal since my primary loyalties are to myself. Whereas once I was prepared for promotion, now I think why commit yourself to something that might not last very long? It could all be a massive waste of time. Now the Job's just a meal ticket, and even that might come to a sorry conclusion if they find out I'm gay.

● *Nottinghamshire WPC, age 28,*
six years' service

The only loyalties I have in this world are to myself. When it comes to the crunch, I wouldn't trust the gay community or the police to look after my interests, and so I look after them myself. That way I don't owe either of them anything and that's the way I like it best. Nor do I feel that I have to take sides with any of them against the other. They're both incidental to me. Both of them are OK for the most part, although both of them have their hangups. As organized bodies I dislike a good degree of both.

It is clear that many gay and lesbian officers do feel some degree of alienation both from their heterosexually identified work colleagues and from those with whom they feel obliged to disguise their occupation. In general, however, the ambivalence would appear to be fairly even and it would seem that the gay or lesbian police officer is frequently unable to singularly furnish either community with the exclusive rights to his or her allegiances. This theme is returned to shortly.

Cruising and Cottaging

In the following pieces, officers specifically discuss the legislation relating to indecency in this country. The first piece continues the sketch of Clapham Common which appears in the extract at the beginning of this chapter, and the account is corroborated by an ex-Clapham officer in the second piece.

● *Metropolitan PS, age 29, seven years' service*

Clapham Common has been a cruising ground for gay men since the second world war, and it was the haunt of prostitutes before that. The locals know all about it and on the whole it doesn't cause too many problems. It's just a part of Clapham Common. The standard approach for dealing with it up until recently has been to patrol the area by driving through the Common in cars and shining headlights around the area. The gays still complain about that but as I've already explained, before I got there they used to play this game where they would jump out and chase the men, who would always run away towards their cars. Then, when the police had gone away, the gays would just come back again. It became almost a ritual. That's about the level of it really.

This whole issue has always been a difficult one, as cruising and cottaging are not the sort of activities which elicit much support or sympathy from people be they gay, straight, police or public. Even so, it would probably surprise most people just how common it is, and for those that are caught, the majority of whom would seem to be middle-aged, married men,[11] there is the prospect of their lives being wrecked by a court appearance, with little chance of beating the charges, and their name and address in the paper once they are convicted. More than a few cases end up as suicides.

I have to say I've done it – nicked someone for that kind of behaviour – but I've felt distinctly awkward, because I understand what forces a man to go out and look for sex in a park or wherever. Others don't understand at all, and that makes it that much easier to condemn. The way I try and work these days is, if the offence wouldn't be an offence for a heterosexual couple in the same circumstances – which is frequently the case – then I don't get involved. If the law is an ass, then I'm quite prepared to ignore it.

● *Metropolitan PC, age 35,*
resigned with seventeen years' service

I didn't much like working at Clapham on night duty, the reason being that if there was nothing much happening crime-wise, then about two o'clock in the morning, cars from Lavender Hill, Wandsworth and sometimes Brixton would converge on the Common. It wasn't really arranged – and it never had any official sanctioning – but it used to happen quite a lot. The cars would all descend on the Common from different directions and arrive at a point known as Gobbler's Gulch. Then the officers would jump out and terrify all the people who were there. Normally they weren't nicked, unless they were caught in flagrante delicto – *we just gave them a hard time*. That normally meant blocking them off with a police vehicle as they tried to get away and verbally abusing them, but on a couple of occasions I saw people physically abused as well, but as I say, rarely arrested. The whole exercise was one of 'Let's go and have a bit of fun with the poofs'. It was really quite humiliating. I found it hard to distance myself from it at first because if you're operating on the area car and the driver decides that that's where you're going, then it's very difficult to do anything about it because he normally has far more service than you and so he's in charge. At first I felt like I had to go along with it but then as I became more competent I refused to get involved. If a message came over the radio that we were all going to the Common, I would just say to the driver, 'Oh no we're not!', and we didn't. Later, when I was section sergeant I used to drive up there myself and direct officers away.

● Metropolitan Crime Squad WPC, age 29, three years' service

I don't agree with cottaging and I don't have a problem with enforcing the laws relating to that. I've kicked down toilet doors and pulled people out before. I've done that loads of times. There was this young retarded black guy who used to use the toilets where I used to work. He was only sixteen and they used to pay him a pound to go in there. So whenever we used to see this kid hanging around we knew something was going on. It was just a matter of watching the traffic going in and out for a few minutes and then we'd go in and normally catch them in the act. It didn't bother me doing that because I used to feel sorry for the kid. Nobody liked the fact that he was being used. You need permission to do observations there now,[12] but all that means is that you just go in and look under the doors whenever you're passing by without doing any special observations first. If there are two people in there then you can go in anyway and they are always at it. Once a plain-

clothes guy at our nick was in one of the cubicles taking a shit when a dick appeared through a hole in the cubicle wall. He was so shocked that he got his truncheon out and hit this dick with it. I mean, what do you expect? It's a bit chancy sticking it through a hole in a wall when you don't know what's on the other side, isn't it? I mean, women don't do it. I've never been in a toilet when a boob has come through the wall for my attention.

● *Kent Robbery Squad PS, age 38, thirteen years' service*

As far as the subject of the 'pretty police' is concerned, whereby a pretty young probationer is sent as bait to the local public toilet to catch the cottagers, I feel no sympathy whatsoever for those 'cottage queens' who fall foul of these police officers, although at the same time I do not in any way condone the tactics used. Those gays who go to public toilets to pick up a 'quickie' do the gay community in general a great disservice and merely serve to reinforce the stereotypes of the gay man who hangs around pestering men and children in toilets – not to mention the question of health, of Aids and other sexually transmitted diseases. As far as the Sexual Offences Act comes into play, I feel that it should not be altered. Some of these cottage queens would say 'We've got our rights as human beings' and yes, I would agree with that wholeheartedly. But I would also say that they forget that heterosexuals also have their rights and one of those is to be able to go into a public toilet to relieve themselves without having some guy hanging around and giving them the one-eyed squint along the urinal or having an unwanted proposition made to them. As for myself, I have never nicked anyone for cottaging but I have given a very strong caution on more than a few occasions.

● *Metropolitan Home Beat PC, age 36, eleven years' service*

I would definitely have problems enforcing some of the sexual offences legislation – and I wouldn't bother. I don't see that as having divided loyalties. I don't bother getting involved with traffic offences either. It's not something that interests me. That's what specialization is all about. And if I came across a situation which required me to act then I would simply use my judgement. That doesn't mean I would ignore it, I just wouldn't automatically go into arrest mode, because I don't see it in the same catastrophic terms as a heterosexual might. What's the point in wasting police resources in a park at night when the only people to be offended are police officers who are hiding up trees like schoolboys waiting to catch who ever happens to come along? 'The primary aim of the police is the prevention of crime. The next, that of the detection and punishment of offenders where crime is committed.' That's what Sir Richard Mayne said in 1829. Everybody learns that at Training School. Those aims have not changed. Where does hide-and-seek come into it; waiting in the hope that crimes might be committed, not so as to prevent them, but so that the 'perverts' can be caught and humiliated? I don't remember that bit in the manual.

For many heterosexual police officers homosexuality remains a fear. And like many fears it is at the same time an immense attraction because the fear makes it exciting. Coppers also like the power involved and the thrill of the chase, because they have to skulk around in the dark with flashlights and night sights and it's all very exciting because they don't know what they'll find. For many of them it's the closest they get to being a real 'detective'. The fact that the offences are explicitly sexual also makes the whole thing very arousing. I'm sure some of them have hard-ons by the time they nick the poor bastards they manage to find. Like I say, they're attracted and repelled at the same time. They express their repulsion verbally. Their attraction is not expressed verbally of course but is expressed by the fact that they get involved in that sort of thing in the first place. They're fascinated. It's always the same (usually guys) that do it. And they tend to be well known for their interest in the area. The fact that women officers don't get so worked up about it suggests to me that it's all to do with men's personal sexual hang-ups and insecurities about their sexuality. The other problem is that because the police reflect the more conservative aspects of society, they are more homophobic than most and they just can't tolerate it. It's a purely personal thing for most of them.

● *Metropolitan Mounted Branch PC, age 31,
resigned with eleven years' service*

*I was posted to Hampstead Heath when I first joined
Mounted Branch and everyone knows what goes on up there. We
used to use horses to patrol the heath because we can't use cars and
it's too big to walk around. I was there eight months and then I
asked for a transfer because the only reason we were there was to
watch out for gay men, and I saw it as a total waste of police time. I
felt like shit when I found out what I was supposed to be doing
there but I couldn't get out of it because I was on six months'
mounted probation. After a while, I used to just ride around and
chat to people. If I saw someone doing something 'naughty', which
I did numerous times, I wouldn't arrest them, I used to talk to them
and find out why they were doing it and whether or not they had
somewhere else to go. Then I would read them the Riot Act and
send them on their way. That was when I was on my own. When I
was with another mounted officer it became more difficult. One
day it got quite embarrassing because I was with a colleague on
patrol when this gay guy who I'd stopped and spoken to a few days
before came up to me and said, 'Hi, how are you?' I just said, 'Fine,
thanks.' Then after we rode on a way, my mate looked over at me
and said, 'So who the fuck was that then?' I just said that I didn't
know.*

*Fortunately for me, I never actually caught anyone doing
anything serious when I was on patrol with a colleague, although
we caught plenty of people coming out of the bushes pulling their
trousers up, still with big bulges in them. It's tacky up there, very
tacky, but I think we've got better things to do than patrol it all
day.*

● *Surrey PC, authorized shot, age 34,
twelve years' service*

*Although I've never actually had to do it, I suppose that
there is always the chance that I might be selected to go on a 'Bog
Squad' at some stage in the future. If I was, I know how I would
like to deal with it. I'd like to think that I would refuse – but I don't*

know if I would have the courage to do that. It's not easy to go against the grain in the police or come out as a liberal. But that doesn't mean that I would submit to it either, I might have to take an alternative exit – some might say the coward's way out – and develop a mysterious and terrible illness and go uncertificated sick for the week. But I couldn't go through with it. My conscience wouldn't let me. I wouldn't mind if they put out units to deal with all the heterosexual bonking that also takes place in the cars on the heath where I work, but they don't. It's all highly selective and that's the problem I have with it.

● *Metropolitan WPC, age 42, seventeen years' service*

What happens if you're recognized as gay yourself whilst nicking someone for having a quickie in the park late at night by someone who knew you from a club or whatever? Apart from shopping you to your mates right there which could be embarrassing if they don't already know, they might also allege things against you. I would definitely try and get out of an operation like that if I could.

● *Thames Valley PS, age 37, seventeen years' service*

There are numerous police operations carried out each year by my police force against gay men who go cottaging or commit sexual acts in some not-so-public places. I know that some of these operations have been instigated by police without there being any legitimate complaints from the public despite what the police say. Police are quite aware which toilets are being used as cottages on their ground and a quick word with a park-keeper who has a cottage in his park, for example, could result in a letter being sent by the local authority to the police, as the grounds for mounting a police operation against that particular convenience. In this way police operations are instigated by police where there was no genuine complaint. The complaint is fabricated.

Such operations are regarded as successful by police because as each crime is recorded, it is also recorded as being 'cleared up', as the offenders are always arrested. The more 'clear-ups' there are, the better the police are perceived to be in the eyes of the general public. Many thousands of hours of police time are devoted to these types of operations.

However distasteful one finds the activities of this small minority of homosexuals one has to remember that indecency is a victimless crime, unlike, for example, assault, robbery, burglary or theft, and I feel that the victims of 'real' crimes would be incensed if they knew how much police resources were devoted to indecency offences whilst real crimes are at record levels. In all my long service, I have never heard a member of the public complaining 'What are the police doing about the men in the toilets?', unlike the oft-heard 'What are the police doing about catching all the muggers, burglars, thieves and vandals?' I do not believe that indecency features at all in the public's idea of crimes that the police should be paying attention to and I am convinced that unless a genuine case can be made out for such police operations, the resources deployed on this kind of operation can most definitely be redeployed to detect serious crime, crime which the public want and would expect police to be making efforts to detect and solve.

With regard to the way in which these operations are undertaken by police, I believe that the use of agent provocateur tactics is deplorable. I say again this is usually a victimless crime – the only real 'victim' is the person or persons who get arrested. Because in addition to the phoney complainants, I know from conversations with colleagues who have been engaged in these operations that, in many cases, the police evidence is also fabricated. Many men are arrested for just loitering in or near a cottage and the evidence is then 'embroidered' to prove that the men were engaged in an illegal act, i.e. masturbation, indecent exposure, etc. The men plead guilty at court as they are too afraid to challenge the police lies and do not want the publicity that a full court hearing might bring. In this way, gays are regarded as a soft touch by police; they do not struggle when arrested and in most cases plead guilty.

The Sexual Offences laws are too harsh for behaviour which is distasteful but basically harmless. If someone is caught having sex in a public toilet there are adequate and appropriate laws to deal with this type of offence without resorting to 'gross indecency', for example the offence of 'Harassment, Alarm or Distress' under section 5 of the Public Order Act. The offence of gross indecency should be used only in cases involving children or non-consenting adults.

For those caught who are under twenty-one, there is the additional problem of charges relating to under-age sex. I feel that the age of consent for gay men in the UK should be brought into line with that for heterosexuals. I say this because I knew before I reached puberty where my sexual inclinations were taking me to but because of an unfair law, I was supposed to wait until I was twenty-one before I could fulfil my sexual expectations. It's not unlike apartheid. Parliament should remember that good laws will be obeyed, bad laws won't.

● *Metropolitan Inspector, age 43, twenty-one years' service*

I don't agree with the way certain laws are used against gays and lesbians which weren't specifically designed for that use. Like nicking two men for kissing in the street under Breach of the Peace laws. I've no particular wish to enforce rubbish like that and fortunately you have a certain amount of discretion, so it's not as if you have to. You end up enforcing the laws that you feel are worth enforcing in the end, and whether that's right or wrong, it's human nature. You can't enforce all the laws all the time. Nor can you enforce them all with the same amount of energy. I mean there's one that says you can't beat your carpet out of the window with a stick before 8 a.m.! Who the hell enforces that? It depends on the legislation and officers should be encouraged to use their discretion. For example, those that get caught for acts of gross indecency where complaints are not received – the vast majority of cases – could have cautions and verbal warnings – that's still enforcing the law. There's nothing that says you have to arrest them, and nothing that says that if you do, you have to charge them at the station. Again, they can receive a caution. It means being more creative about the options open to you. I see no point in sending two blokes to court and wasting taxpayers' money if there's no bloody victim.

It's ridiculous. If there is a victim, then fair enough, but nine times out of ten there isn't.

As for divided loyalties, you could make the same allegation about ethnic officers of course – they come from two communities as well – I'm sure they experience the same difficulties from time to time. I'm sure everyone does, whoever they are – you face moral dilemmas every day. It goes with the job. That doesn't mean you don't do your job properly or don't do what you think's right. I think anyone who thinks we'll be significantly selective on the grounds of our sexuality is selling us short.

The notion of 'discretion' is mentioned by several officers and in the next two pieces, the officers concerned demonstrate alternative means of dealing with the situation.

● *Metropolitan PC, age 25, four years' service*

We've got a bit of a problem with some of the toilets on our ground and one day my governor, who knows that I'm gay, actually pulled me aside and said to me: 'Look, we've got a problem here – but I don't want to start prosecuting these people for it. I don't want to set up an observation and waste police time on victimless crimes like this between consenting adults, but the thing is, we're having complaints about it so we have to do something, and I think that we should sort it out between ourselves, on this relief, in whatever way you suggest.' I have to say I was impressed. So what I suggested was that I go into the toilets in full uniform and give them all a bollocking. And that's what I did. The way I dealt with it was like this: If I caught someone doing anything out in the open which could be seen by the public, then I would nick them because if I can walk in and catch them, then so can a little kid, or the local vicar. But if it was all discreet, and most of the time it is, then I would just give them all a lecture and clear them out quietly.

● *Metropolitan PC, age 40, twenty-two years' service*

A straight colleague and I were patrolling together and had seen a young teenage youth hanging around outside a toilet we knew was used for sex. He went inside, and when he did not come out after several minutes had passed, my colleague suggested we go in to investigate why he had not come out. We went inside but the youth was not at the urinal. There was a line of cubicles behind the urinal and we found the youth inside one of them, by himself. He must have had a sixth sense that we were coming as he was in the process of pulling up his jeans, but not quickly enough as we saw that he had an erection. The first thing we did was to ask the youth, who could only have been about fifteen years old, what he was doing and he naturally gave the answer that he was going to the toilet. It was obvious to anybody, including him, that he was lying. My colleague asked him to tell the truth and the youth said that he'd come into the toilet for sex. I asked him what was in his jeans pocket and he pulled out a small tub of vaseline. The youth admitted that the use he intended it for was sexual. My colleague or I could have arrested him as being a young person 'in need of care and control' under the Children and Young Persons Act. However, I did not believe that this course of action would solve anything and in fact would probably render life impossible for both the boy and his family. I felt that the police juvenile procedure would be inappropriate for him, as it would not change him from being gay and would only lead to his domestic circumstances and school being investigated and the reasons for the investigation being known to the family, school and social workers. I felt that what he really needed was a good reprimand for cottaging and a warning of the dangers, including arrest. I was about to put this line of thought to my colleague, when he pulled me aside and virtually gave me the same reasons for not arresting the youth. He also proposed just a telling-off and naturally I agreed and was very relieved. So the youth was given a severe ticking-off and went on his way. My colleague and I agreed that it would be better for the youth to tell his parents on his own terms rather than have a police officer calling at his house to inform his parents that he had been arrested in a toilet and was gay. My colleague was not gay, but he showed a good understanding of the problem. He obviously gave the situation some serious thought which was more than the average police officer would have done. I believe that we dealt with the situation in the best way possible. I also believe that the laws on indecency in public places are all right in their present form. They just need to be applied with discretion and enforced with honesty.

It has been alleged that the lesbian or gay officer will suffer from divided loyalties when it comes to enforcing certain sections of the 1967 Sexual Offences Act. The research evidence suggests that in some cases it may be true: a number of officers interviewed were found to disagree with certain sections of the Act. For others, however, it was a case of 'the law is the law' and the sexual orientation of the offender failed to enter into the matter. However, all officers recognized their dilemma. Most also recognized that their ambivalence was (a) largely theoretical, sporadic and navigable, and (b) not peculiar to gay or lesbian officers. It is recognized that the constant fight for the preservation of impartiality when dealing with the public is simply another feature of police work that has to be managed by all officers, and one which is unlikely to prove itself any less burdensome than most other aspects of their work.

Queerbashing

Earlier in this chapter, an officer suggests that as soon as the police leave a cruising area, the cruisers (and presumably this also holds for cottagers) return. Whilst some of these may be arriving unawares for the first time during that day/night, it is often alleged that the risk of being arrested constitutes part of the thrill.

● *Metropolitan DC, age 36, fifteen years' service*

I'm sure some of that lot up the Common actually enjoy the risk. The danger enhances the fun of it – the thought of getting caught – and some of them actually admit this. It's a bit of a thrill for them. The trouble is that when they're out there sometimes they get beaten up by local thugs, and when that happens they expect police protection, even though they shouldn't be out there doing what they're doing in the first place. Not that they deserve to get beaten up for it. But that's what happens when the police aren't there. And the reason we aren't there is because they've made such

*a fuss about our presence that we aren't supposed to patrol the area
any more. They want to have their cake and eat it. What they
actually want is for you to patrol the area in order to protect them
whilst they have sex – but they don't want to get nicked if you catch
them bonking in the bushes. In effect, they want police protection
to commit offences. And you can't have it both ways. Either the
police are there and they do their job – both ways – or they're not.
You pays your money and you takes your choice.*

If it is truly the element of danger that excites the cruising enthusi-
ast, then perhaps that makes the allure more comprehensible, for
there is certainly no lack of danger in their activities. Apart from
risking harassment or arrest from the police, they also risk the most
serious of physical abuse from both the drunken and the premedi-
tated queerbasher. And whilst some might find it tempting to judge
that those who make a nuisance of themselves on the common or in
public conveniences deserve all they get in the way of torment from
delinquent thugs, the seriousness of the queerbashing problem
should not be underestimated. Yet despite the steady flow of
assaults and murders over the past few years, it seems that both the
police and the men who take such risks continue to misjudge the
gravity of the problem: whilst gay and bisexual men continue their
cruising and cottaging activities, most police forces are refusing to
monitor the attacks which are regularly taking place.[13] Sadly, each
year several men experience at first hand the reality of the dangers
of cruising and at least one police officer now also appreciates the
real extent of the problem. Unfortunately, the tutelage he received
proved costly.

● *Derbyshire DC, age 37,*
seventeen years' service

*Back in 1974, I joined the Derbyshire Constabulary as an
eager nineteen-year-old intent upon setting out before me a career
which I hoped would last until the day I had to retire thirty years
later. I knew when I joined the Job it wouldn't be easy. I also knew*

that if I made my sexuality public, my hopes for a career would be dashed. Nobody in the force had the slightest idea I was gay, not because I was ashamed, far from it. I just didn't feel the Job was ready for guys like me and so I deliberately kept a low profile. As I progressed I was recommended for a two-year tour of duty with the Derby Vice Squad. I went through the standard selection panel which consisted of a Detective Superintendent, a Detective Inspector and Uniform Sergeant. Having been selected, I was engaged on many varied and interesting cases and I got on well with the other members of the squad. Most of the time was spent on pimps who were caught living off the earnings of the local prostitutes.

As a matter of standard vice-squad work, the public toilets in and around the city would be visited, usually just to show a police presence and on other occasions to clamp down on homosexual behaviour if it was deemed to be getting out of hand. Until I joined the squad I never really gave the subject of gays going cottaging much thought. I'd certainly never done it myself and to be honest I couldn't ever imagine picking someone up in a toilet either. The whole subject of cottaging was alien to me. I admit that when engaged on some of our observations, usually at the well-known Markeaton Park toilets, some of the men whose activity was notably homosexual were absolute stunners but I always kept the professional side of policing in the front of my mind, always aware of being compromised. I think it's fair to say I did feel distinctly awkward when on 'homosexual activity' tours of duty and where possible, I'd try my best to get out of doing them, but it wasn't always possible, plus I didn't want to raise any suspicions in my direction.

My personal opinion is that if vice squads or anyone else wants to do gay vice work, they should use Breach of the Peace laws or something else instead of the 'gross' laws which are too serious for consenting behaviour between two adults. But as I say, I've done observations for gross before. I felt bad in a way but I've never had, and don't agree with having, sex in public toilets anyway. We wouldn't tolerate that from the heterosexuals either on our Vice Squad, so I didn't lose any sleep over it.

The worst thing ever to happen to me occurred when I was on a 'four to midnight' tour of duty. My partner was Richard. We had worked as a team for the past six months. We got on well together and each of us understood how the other liked to work. However, there was one thing Richard didn't know or suspect, and that was that I was gay.

Normally on a late shift we'd patrol the red-light district picking off the prostitutes and their clients whenever they dared to emerge, but for some strange reason none of the girls and very few prospective clients appeared to be out this particular evening. After four hours or so, Richard and I were completely bored stiff. It happens that at times such as those we'd sometimes slope off to the local and grab a quick pint, waste away half an hour or so and then go back to the red-light district. We did just that, except when we got back to the area it was just as dead as before. In total and utter desperation Richard suggested we nip down to the Markeaton toilets to see what was happening there. Richard took his car and for the four miles or so to the park I sat in the passenger seat. The time would have been around 11.15 p.m., which is pretty late, but these toilets were constantly busy, fronting the main inner and outer ring road junctions. It wasn't unusual to find the toilets full at midnight. I've been there before at that time and seen upwards of eight men at the urinals and all three cubicles engaged. So it is true to say that Markeaton is famous, albeit for homosexual activity.

As we pulled up outside the toilets, no cars could be seen parked up and it looked as though the toilets were going to be as quiet as the streets. Richard and I left the car and entered the toilets together and as we suspected they were empty. It was a lovely, still-type of evening so I said to Richard he should drive out of the park onto the Ashbourne Road. I'd walk across the grass to the exit and meet him there. As we were talking, Richard noticed two figures, obviously men, walking through the trees from the direction of the toilets. Neither of us could understand where they'd come from, but from the way they kept looking back at us I genuinely believed they were two guys going into the trees for a bit of mutual wanking to put it bluntly. I suggested to Richard that I follow them on foot and he said he'd park up outside the park and join me if I signalled something funny was going on.

The two youths aged about eighteen went behind this very large tree and as I slowly skirted around it they would from time to time look out from the tree to see where I was. Although my eyes had become accustomed to the dark I didn't appreciate that Richard was having difficulty spotting me. Suddenly as I reached the tree the two youths pounced on me from behind. Before I could identify myself, the taller of the youths screamed, 'Queer fucking faggot!' and produced from his side a four-foot-long wooden stick which he struck out at me with, hitting me on the right shoulder with all his might. The blow knocked me back a good six feet and I tumbled to the ground racked in absolute agony. I knew immediately my shoulder had been broken. As I struggled to get up I was struck another blow with the stick across my chest with as much force as the first. Doubled up with pain unable to catch my breath or shout to Richard for help, I lay an almost willing victim to my attackers. Disturbed by another man in the park walking his dog, my attackers ran off towards Richard, chased it seems, by the man's boxer dog. The man was a guy I had met a while back on the Vice Squad. He knew who I was and realized what had happened to me. He screamed for help and I heard Richard shouting back, though what he said I don't recall. I knew I was badly injured. Frothy red blood was coming from my mouth, I couldn't breathe and I kept passing into states of unconsciousness. I feared I was dying because I had no control over what was happening to me.

In the meantime, my attackers, it seems, had escaped, though not before they'd struck Richard in the mouth and knocked him to the ground. Once he'd recovered he ran over towards me, looked at me and once he realized how badly injured I was, additional police assistance was called for on our personal radios and also an ambulance. Within minutes the park was alight with blue flashing beacons and I could hear voices in the distance. When the ambulance men arrived they immediately recognized signs of severe internal injuries. They decided not to move me and requested that the police turn out the Accident Flying Squad. These are a team of doctors who attend only the most serious of incidents. It seemed like hours as I lay on the cold damp grass of the park. As I lay racked in pain I felt the warm hand of someone near me but I couldn't see who it was because my eyes had stuck closed with the dried blood on my face. I felt him very close to my face, and in my left ear he whispered, 'Don't give in, you've got so much to live for.

Don't give in.' Soon his words were drowned out by the sirens of the Flying Squad.

I can't recall much more because after that I was injected with morphine and removed to hospital. Later that morning I was operated on for severe internal injuries which were as follows: broken right shoulder, three broken ribs, punctured left lung, bruised spleen and bruised kidneys. I spent a week in the intensive care ward and a further six weeks on a general ward, and an additional eight months off work.

My attackers were caught the day after. They pleaded guilty to wounding me, they accepted they were queerbashers and at Derby Crown Court were sentenced to twelve months' imprisonment. With one-third remission for good behaviour they'd do eight months. Hardly a fair exchange. Little did my attackers know that on the night of the incident they had scored a rare hole-in-one. Not only had they bashed a cop, but a queer one too. They would have been very proud.

I've since returned to work, but my attitude towards gays who are queerbashed has changed dramatically. I can sympathize more easily now and understand how they feel. I've learned a lot from the park experience – enough, let's say, to change my life for the better.

Notes

1. M. Bennett, 'Divided loyalties', *Police Review*, 25 January 1991, pp. 164–5.
2. Such views have been echoed more recently by Inspector Alan Folkes of the Bedfordshire Constabulary, who asserted: 'A homosexual officer's impartiality could easily be seriously compromised if called upon to deal with offences in public toilets or elsewhere, especially if one of his sexual partners was involved' (*Police*, December 1992, p. 26).
3. W. W. Burchard, 'Role conflicts of military chaplains', *American Sociological Review*, 19 (1954), pp. 528–35.
4. Charlotte A. Doclar (served 1952–81) in R. Curb and N. Manahan, *Lesbian Nuns: Breaking Silence*, 1985, p. 175.
5. E. V. Stonequist, *The Marginal Man*, 1961, p. 144.
6. W. E. B. Du Bois, in Stonequist, *The Marginal Man*, p. 145.
7. Stonequist, *The Marginal Man*, p. 8.

61: *Cruising, Cottaging and Queerbashing*

8. R. Park, in his introduction to Stonequist, *The Marginal Man*, p. xv.
9. The experience of marginality, whilst often presenting difficulties, may also carry certain benefits. See Chapter 11.
10. Stonequist, *The Marginal Man*, p. 149.
11. In the celebrated study (*Tearoom Trade*, 1970) by Laud Humphreys, 54 per cent of those observed in 'cottages' and later followed up were found to be married.
12. In the Metropolitan Police, official observations must first be sanctioned by a Commander or above for specified areas, for a limited period (usually two weeks).
13. There is a tendency on the part of some police officers to feel that queerbashing victims contribute to their assault by way of their activities and may, therefore, be inclined to be rather unsympathetic. For this reason, many victims who report their assault disguise the circumstances of their injuries, and many fail to report the assault at all for fear of harassment or prosecution. It is therefore not surprising that most police officers do not appreciate the true extent of the problem. However, owing to the continued pressure of recent years by gay campaigning groups, the Metropolitan Police began, for the first time in August 1991, to monitor attacks on homosexuals at trial sites around London. These areas include Clapham Common and Hampstead Heath.

Chapter four

Lovers

MAKING a success of a relationship is rarely a straightforward matter. Even with the countenance of society and the blessing and support of family networks and friends, heterosexual relationships usually require a good deal of effort if they are to survive any length of time. Homosexual relationships, on the other hand, are not endowed by society with the same status as their heterosexual counterparts. In the case of males, sexual activity may still constitute a criminal offence, and this results in many relationships being conducted in secrecy. Because same-sex relationships frequently lack the props afforded to opposite-sex relations, the odds are stacked against their succeeding even before they have begun; hence, the labour required for the success of a gay or lesbian relationship may be considerable.

The pressure of modern-day policing coupled with shift work has given the police divorce rate an almost legendary status, and no canteen conversation would be complete without a discussion of who is currently 'over the side' with whom, and which of their colleagues is next in line for the divorce court. The situation is such that there may even be some loose parallels between the status of heterosexual relationships within the police and the status of same-sex relationships outside of the police: Both are burdened with vexatious pressures that can result in a significant degree of unnecessary stress, and the consequent instability of many relationships means that a disproportionate number end prematurely. When the professional hardships of police work that destroy so many heterosexual relationships are added to the stresses and strains of a gay or lesbian relationship, then that relationship will require a very considerable degree of effort if it is to see even its first anniversary.

● *Metropolitan WPS, age 36, eight years' service*

If you have a problem with a relationship, or if one breaks up, or if your partner dies, then, in the heterosexual world, family and friends rally round and do everything to help. If you're gay, then their attitude is 'Snap out of it.' It's as if it wasn't for real, and they want to know what the big problem is. Once, on my brother's birthday, we said that we would have a celebratory get-together and that it would be a family affair. I asked my parents if I could bring my girlfriend, whom they liked. They said, 'Oh no, it's just family.' You see there's this total exclusion; everyone is with their partner except you. They're all judged as family but your partner isn't. That's one of the things I don't like about being gay. I don't think they even realize how much they hurt you with attitudes like that. But I don't want to hurt them. I already feel that I've let them down already – I know that that's basically my problem – but it's like there is an invisible wall between us sometimes, and so I'm not as public as I otherwise might be. But it's only for their sake.

● *Sussex PC, aged 26, seven years' service*

I wasn't a very suitable candidate for a boyfriend for a long time – not until I learned to push the police side of my life into the realm where it belonged. Before that, it affected me very badly indeed. Like going shopping with your boyfriend in Sainsbury's and being terrified about being spotted by colleagues in every aisle you go down. I persisted together with one of my boyfriends for four years but in the end it couldn't last, and now I've come as far as I have, I feel that it was the police force that was responsible for fucking up what was potentially a very promising relationship, and that makes me sick. The thing is, I had too much respect for the police in those days and not enough for my boyfriends. But that experience changed me quite a lot, although it's too late for him now. These days if it happens, it happens. Getting seen I mean. I can't help that, but I refuse to let it affect my relationships. You have to try and balance living a normal lifestyle with surviving at work. But it's not easy.

● *Metropolitan PC, age 38,*
resigned with ten years' service

My first relationship in my younger days was very sad. I was seeing a very attractive young man who was mad about me – and I was mad about him but I just couldn't be seen in public with him, and should we ever be unlucky enough to be caught in police presence I effectively treated him (and all my partners) as second-class citizens – not like people I loved or cherished. For example, if for some reason, we should end up in a car together with a colleague of mine, then my boyfriend would always have to sit in the back of the car while my colleague sat in the front, although having said that, I suppose that happens with police wives as well – but that doesn't excuse it. I couldn't let them answer the phone if they were at my house, I even had to draw the curtains when we were in, so that the neighbours didn't see us together.

Because I was a police officer, I tried not to let it affect me, but of course it did. It really affected my work. The whole thing also affected him very badly and he's never really forgiven me. Needless to say, he's not with me any more, which is a great shame and I'm sorry I let it happen.

● *Metropolitan woman Detective Inspector,*
age 36, fourteen years' service

It's difficult to give any relationship 100 per cent if you have to exclude your partner from half of your life. It's little things that most people take for granted: girlfriends can't pick you up from work, and when it comes to phone calls, if I was at work I always made sure I called them and I discouraged them from ever calling me. If they had to call me, then I gave them all kinds of rules: times they could call, times they couldn't. And no more than a certain number of calls in a week. If they had to call, then they should say *that it's Mrs, Miss or Ms Brown and not their first name, and if they leave messages they should leave it for the DI, again not me by my first name. It sounds complicated and silly but people pick up on that kind of thing really quickly if you're not careful.*

I've never taken a partner to a police event because I wouldn't want to embarrass either of us, although I really wish I could. I suppose I could really, but I think part of me still feels that I'd be rubbing their noses in it by bringing a girlfriend along. I've taken straight girlfriends to these things, after I came out that is, and everybody automatically thinks that they're gay as well, just because they're with you. In fact if you're ever seen with anyone of your own sex in a social context, they assume (a) that they're homosexual and (b) that you're probably having a relationship.

● *Metropolitan Mounted Branch PC, age 28, resigned with nine years' service*

I often used to meet nice guys when I was out places, and I'd start seeing them, but then after a couple of weeks I would get so paranoid that someone would find out that I would stop calling them up and eventually I'd give them the elbow. I never used to let any of my boyfriends meet me from work, and if I'd had a bad day I would take it out on them and stuff like that. The stress of keeping everything a secret can make you really bitchy.

In the end I left. One of the reasons I left is that I'd met a boyfriend whom I was really serious about and it used to piss me off badly that I could never talk about it at work. You have to be so careful. I could never say that I did this with Pete and that with Pete, or we've been here or there, or whatever. And we used to do so much – we had three holidays a year and I could never talk to anyone about it. It used to piss me off that I couldn't be honest because a lot of the conversation in the canteen revolves around what people have been doing at the weekend. I used to read the paper instead.

Despite an officer's best efforts to hide his or her partner or sexual identity from police colleagues, unanticipated events can sometimes thwart any strategy.

● *British Transport Police PC, age 26,*
three years' service

I'd been going out with this guy for about six weeks, when, unfortunately for me, he turned out to be a bit of a nutter. We went to this party one night, and he suddenly started to get nasty with me. And then when we got home and I wasn't looking, he hit me over the back of the head with something and started attacking me. I was bleeding all over the place and eventually I lost my temper and fought back because I couldn't stop him any other way and I was starting to get scared. I had to scream to the neighbours to call the police, which they did. Once the police eventually arrived they calmed us both down and squared the whole thing up and then left. They knew I was a copper and so we let it all drop. But then, a bit later, this Inspector turned up and nicked us both for assault – which I couldn't believe. It probably did me a favour in the end though because otherwise if this bloke had decided to take up an assault charge himself (I'd given him a few injuries in defending myself), then the Job could have been accused of doing nothing at the proper time and being biased because another police officer was involved. In the end though, we both ended up going back to the police a couple of days later and making withdrawal statements so that it could all be NFA'd.

In the meantime, I thought I was going to lose my job of course, and so I went and got advice from the Federation, a Chief Inspector and a Superintendent, who were really good. All of them were just concerned about my welfare and my feelings and how things could be sorted out for me best. They asked me if I wanted to change reliefs, or maybe keep the whole thing a secret, but none of them were really looking to get me out of the Job, and I was quite chuffed about that.

● *Metropolitan PC, age 32, eight years' service*

I had a boyfriend who used to come down from Scotland and stay at the section house when I was there. I was actually trying to dump him at the time and so I used to make sure that when he *came down, he had his own room. But he used to bang on my door in the middle of the night to cause a fuss. He used to use the fact that I wasn't out at work to get me to sleep with him, which I hated but there wasn't much I could do about it at the time.*

● RUC *officer, age 30,*
resigned with seven years' service

I remember one time I picked up this guy at a cruising ground. I was so blocked – *I could never do anything unless I'd had a skinful.* My parents were away at the time and so I brought him home to our house. The one thing I hadn't noticed was that there was a police shirt hanging up drying in the kitchen. He clocked it straight off. After a while he started hinting around it, although I didn't realize at the time because I was so pissed. I didn't know what he was trying to say, and so I just got suspicious and took the number of his car when he left. When I checked it, it came back to another police officer.

He couldn't believe it when I called him at work. He wanted to know how I'd gotten his number. We saw each other about once a month for six months after that. One weekend a month. It was all we could manage between us. That was the first time that I thought I was in love.

● *Metropolitan WPC, age 23, five years' service*

Whilst I was in the cadets there were these two girls who were having a relationship together. A lot of the cadets had sussed what was going on and eventually even some of the staff began to make comments. In the end, someone obviously decided that some-thing had to be done before it got out of hand, and so they were both hoisted up for a 'chat'. They didn't know about me at the time and so I also got called in as a kind of character witness, which I thought was quite funny under the circumstances. What was even funnier was that the person who was conducting this mini enquiry, so to speak, was also on our side, if you see what I mean. She just said, 'Look, I know what it's like and I know what you're going *through.' She told us all to take it easy and keep a low profile until we were out of the cadets. So we all calmed down for a couple of weeks and flirted with the boys for a while. In fact, we all had boyfriends by the end of the week! I've never felt like I was the only one in the police because I've known from the beginning that I wasn't.*

Police officers are acutely aware of their lack of popularity within many sections of society, including some segments of the lesbian and gay communities. In the case of homosexual or bisexual police officers socializing on the gay 'scene', the stigma attached to being a police officer can be a significant problem. It will be noted in Chapter 7 that many officers disguise their occupations for fear of rejection. Many continue that process of concealment when interacting with gay friends with whom they are close and, in some instances, within relationships. In such cases, the fear of rejection would appear to be secondary to the problem of potential blackmail by a disaffected lover. Some police officers, however, believe that the knowledge of their profession can bring them increased attention.

● *Surrey PC, age 24, five years' service*

When it came to telling boyfriends what job I did, I tried all sorts of things but I rarely told the truth. My last three relationships broke up when I finally told them what I really did for a living. I'd told a couple that I was an accountant, I think, and the other that I was in insurance. They didn't like it. I'm not sure if it was the fact I'd lied they didn't like, or the fact that I was a police officer. The longest I've managed a relationship for was six months and it was a lot of pressure because it snowballs. The lies, that is. One lie leads to another and before you know it you're out of your depth. It's not fun.

I used to worry a lot that I might be forced out of the closet by one of my exs. I sent him some call up papers for the Gulf, as a joke – I'm a bit of a practical joker – but by the time he'd received them, we'd split up and he didn't really think it was very funny. He threatened me and told me to keep away from the pubs and clubs or he'd 'out' me, which was a bit worrying at the time, although it never happened in the end.

● Metropolitan PC, age 32, seven years' service

Once when I lied, it backfired on me quite badly. I met this guy whom I really liked and I think I told him that I was a security officer or something. When he found out what I really did he left me, so I decided that I would never lie again, because I liked him a lot. I never saw or heard from him again, which really hacked me off.

Even though I was honest after that, I still didn't tell people my surname or which station I worked at, just to be on the safe side. The most common reaction though, once I'd started telling people in the gay community what I really did, was wanting to jump straight into bed with you, which I thought was pathetic really. Others were really surprised. They thought the only bent coppers were the ones who took bribes.

● Thames Valley PC, age 25, four years' service

Two of my lovers guessed – because of my hours – and they practically told me in the end. One of them gave me a really hard time over it. Once he found out, the whole relationship changed and he made all kinds of threats about calling up the station and telling them about me. He never did, but I was scared shitless. I'd only just joined the Job, and it was a real worry. I was always waiting for that call from my Chief Super to ask me what the hell was going on. I'd also asked this guy not to tell all his friends about me, but he did. He had me thinking and acting as if nobody knew, but all the time they did, which really annoyed me. Even when the relationship was all over for me, I kept on seeing him because he wanted me to, and I was worried what he might do if I said no. He gave me a really hard time. That was my first real male lover and it nearly put me off for life!

Chapter five

Heterosexual Homosexuals

THE fact that a person is currently engaged in a relationship with a person or persons of the same sex does not mean that they have always been homosexually attracted, nor that they will continue to be so in the future. Many of those who eventually decide to settle down with a partner of the same sex have had heterosexual relationships, been engaged or even married, and a considerable number have children.

That individuals who are ostensibly gay or lesbian should decide to get married may seem bizarre or even perverse at first, yet there may be several reasons why someone who is predominantly homosexual might get involved in a relationship with the opposite sex. A great many men and women get married in good faith, and only in later life resolve that they are more intensely attracted to their own sex, or that they are so attracted at all; many remain totally incognizant of their homosexual capacity for a significant portion of their lives. In such cases, their naivety may be due to an act of unconscious repression – a refusal to recognize the truth; others sublimate or suppress their attraction for the same sex and become espoused only half aware of their homosexual potential. In such cases, there is rarely any concern over orientation since the mechanisms ensure that reality is kept flickering beyond, or at the very edge of, consciousness. The latter case differs from the former in that in the case of suppression the deceit is not unconscious but rather subconscious. That is, their sexual orientation is actively ignored, rather than not observed at all.

In other cases, individuals may harbour a desperate desire to have a family and may, in spite of their primary gender preference, marry in order to fulfil that need. Some even marry for financial gain, or for the legal convenience not afforded gay couples in the UK. Such marriages are often termed 'marriages of convenience' – although they may eventually prove anything but convenient.

Finally, marriage may reflect a simple shift in sexual preference and in the instance of the bisexual, wedlock may represent the consummation of a successful heterosexual relationship. Should that relationship ultimately end in divorce, however, then the fact of the marriage will not act as a precedent for the succeeding relationship which might be with a person of the same sex. For many bisexuals, it is the nature of the individual which is most important in determining sexual attraction. Biological sex is purely incidental.

Perhaps most, though, are fully aware of their true orientation from an early age, most typically, it seems, from the onset of puberty. These people may just wish that they were not homosexually inclined and may attempt to modify their desires through marriage in the hope that forcing themselves into a heterosexual lifestyle will precipitate some kind of orientational metamorphosis. And whilst there are those who find that they can successfully acquire some taste for the opposite sex, more often than not their primary homosexual preference prevails, and most, realizing the failure of their re-education plan, eventually take up gay or lesbian (or bisexual) lifestyles.

This chapter presents experiences of lesbian or gay officers with significant heterosexual experience. Such experiences are not exclusive to the police; on the contrary, they are rather common. Their value lies in that they illustrate well the result of the 'heterosexual assumption' and the desperate need to conform, both of which are perhaps more urgent amongst police officers.

● *Surrey WPS, age 31, twelve years' service*

I first started to think that I was different at around twelve I suppose, so I knew that I was attracted to other women before I joined the police, but there was never a handle put on it before then. I joined as a cadet when I was only sixteen and I certainly didn't identify as homosexual back then. When I was in the cadets someone called me a lesbian for the first time and something must have struck a chord because for the next ten years I denied to myself that that's what I was. I tried to pretend to myself that I was straight. I had several boyfriends after that and I also got engaged.

Looking back on it with the benefit of hindsight, it should have been obvious to me what I was doing, but there's none so blind as those who won't see. If anything on the TV involved two women, I turned over; if a book had a scene even slightly lesbian, I stopped reading it – I didn't really want to know. Then I got involved with an older man kidding myself that I loved him. It was a sort of an on-and-off relationship, and it was during that relationship that I got engaged. He was married but he left his wife for me. But I couldn't really keep it going, and I just used to put up with the sex. After four years we finally broke up. The thing was, I had security with him, I was safe, and so after a while I started seeing him again, twice a week, fooling myself that that was what I wanted. But it wasn't. I was constantly searching for something, but I didn't want to know what that something was. We lasted eight years altogether.

It ended when my first real relationship started with a woman – another police officer – but not from my force. Once that started, it was like a huge weight had been lifted from me and overnight I changed. I changed my wardrobe, my hair, my outlook, and at last my real personality was allowed to show itself.

● *West Yorkshire PC, age 31, four years' service*

I got engaged once, whilst I was still in the army. I met this nurse whom I really liked a lot. We were really compatible; we had the same interests and we used to have a good laugh together. And at that time I wanted to put the gay side of my life out of the picture. I knew I was gay, but I was convinced that I was able to subsume that side of my life and carry on leading a totally straight life without any adverse effects. I needed to do that because I thought that by being gay my whole future would have exploded, and that frightened me a lot. I just wanted to have a normal life like everyone else and I thought I could only have that by leading a straight lifestyle. My intention was that I would get married at some stage and so I got engaged to this girl who I got on really well with. I wasn't getting married to try and change myself – I knew it was a part of me – but I thought that it could just remain dormant. I told her fairly early on about my feelings and things, and she more or less accepted it. I explained that I still wanted to get married but I told her that she would have to accept the way I was. I had no intention of acting on it though – I wasn't planning to run off or anything – I thought I could be totally monogamous with her, even though I knew that I was gay, and that it wouldn't matter or make any difference. So we agreed to carry on with the relationship and started making plans for the future. The engagement lasted for two years.

During the engagement period I got posted away from home for several months, and it was during that period of separation that I had a chance to think about the whole relationship more closely. I decided eventually that to get married would be wrong – that it wouldn't work out and that it would be a big mistake. Besides, my girlfriend had begun to notice that I was becoming less affectionate, less intimate, and towards the end we were beginning to have arguments. So I made the decision that I should end it. The problem was that by then it was quite difficult because the wedding plans were quite advanced. The date had been set, the church had been booked and wedding presents bought, etc.; I was being propelled along by the momentum rather than by what I really wanted. Anyway, just before the wedding, we arranged to go on holiday together and it was on that holiday that I actually told her what I had been thinking – that I thought we shouldn't get married after all, and that in the long run we'd probably only end up getting divorced. Although it was a bit traumatic initially, and we both cried a lot, she agreed with me and after that we broke up amicably. In fact, within minutes of breaking up it was like a great burden off both of our shoulders, and we were laughing and joking and getting along much better than we had up until that point. We've stayed good friends over the years and we still keep in touch now.

● *Essex PC, age 29, twelve years' service*

When I initially joined the police and went to my first relief, I got involved with another female officer. What neither of us knew at the time was that we were both gay, but we were both so confused, and we actually liked each other so much as friends, that we tried to get it together sexually. It didn't work too well for obvious reasons, I see that now. We just loved each other as friends and did the rest due to pressure from society I suppose. After that episode finished, I still didn't do anything about my homosexuality – I remained totally confused and I still ended up getting married. The sex was very good with the girl I got married to, but deep down I was still unhappy with the whole thing. Over a period of time I became progressively more unhappy, not only with the sexual side of things but with the living and social environment as well, and I decided I had to do something about it.

I started out by going to gay bookshops and things, hoping that I might catch someone's eye that I liked. That went on for a while and eventually, I reached the point where I felt I had some serious decisions to make about my life. I felt like I would burst inside if I didn't do something soon. And then suddenly, I ended up having a sexual encounter with this guy I met on the tube. I couldn't believe it. It was just wonderful – I felt like I just wanted to move in with him and stay with him for a few days, just to get away from the situation I was in at home. I realized then that that was what I wanted, and now was the right time to do something about it. I hadn't done anything until then because I didn't know where to start, and meeting this guy started it off I suppose.

In the end, I dealt with the whole thing in five days. Very calmly. The day after I met the guy on the tube I told my wife. She'd half guessed anyway as it happens, and within a week the whole thing was sorted out and we had a very quick divorce. We still speak and what have you, and although we still get on OK I suppose it's only natural that she holds it against me a bit. I've been living with my boyfriend for several years now and I'm much happier.

● *Metropolitan PC, age 42,*
twenty-one years' service

I was married for nearly twenty years. And during that whole time I had no idea that there was such a big gay community out there. It seems incredible to me now, but I was so busy with my family that I really didn't have time for much else. Not for years. My whole social life was tied up with kids and relatives, etc. Sometimes I wonder if I'd found the gay scene at eighteen if I'd ever have got married at all – perhaps there would have been no problems – I might have fallen into being gay quite easily. But I never found it. It just wasn't an option. And besides, I never really accepted I was gay anyway at that stage. I sometimes thought I might be bisexual because I found men attractive; I used to find myself fancying men, yet I never saw it as gay – although I never fancied other women either; I mean I slept with my wife but I never thought of going with another woman sexually. It just didn't interest me. Even my own marriage was never that great sexually, it was never a strong part of the marriage, but I was married, I had kids, and I'd never slept with another guy at that time so I didn't think I could really be gay as such.

I first started going to a gay club once the kids had grown up because I wanted to meet other people like me. That went on for five years. My wife and I had stopped sleeping together by that time anyway – you know, the old 'separate beds' syndrome. I just can't understand why it took me so long to realize everything because I feel so strongly now that I am 100 per cent gay. I find it difficult to understand how I went through all that. It was a waste of a lot of years in some ways but I don't regret it. On the other hand I feel a lot happier now and I enjoy my sex life much more.

● *Woman Inspector, age 37,*
seventeen years' service

I had a boyfriend at training school. He always said that there was something different about me but that he could never quite pin it down. Bearing in mind that I hadn't been with a bloke for about five years until then, it was hardly surprising really. I think I'd forgotten what I was supposed to do and I was a bit uneasy about it all. I wanted to get it all off my chest and tell somebody and so I eventually told him. I think he was hurt at first, although I tried to break it to him gently. I told him bit by bit. To start with I said that I'd had a couple of experiences with women – 90 per cent heterosexual and 10 per cent gay. Then I gradually lowered it until it was fifty-fifty.

I'm still seeing him. Now I think he just finds it fascinating and although he knows I still sleep with women, at least he knows he's the only man I sleep with and I think it would hurt him far more if he thought I was sleeping with other men.

Chapter six

Pubbing and Clubbing

MANY folk declare that they do not understand the need for exclusively gay and lesbian venues. They see no reason why homosexuals cannot enjoy 'normal' establishments like everybody else. Such reasoning, whilst seductive, betrays the thinker's naivety. Minority groups do not ostracize themselves; rather their expatriation is the accomplishment of a society that scorns their persistence. Those who have read the preceding chapters will already have some understanding of the way in which gay men and lesbians suffer the bigotry of certain sections of society; hence the space afforded by alternative establishments provides an invaluable sanctuary. Gay venues provide a host of preliminary and ongoing opportunities including: (a) a simple means of introduction for those who are just 'coming out' to large sections of the lesbian and gay community where they can find support and draw strength, (b) a secure, social environment where simple tactile affection with a same-sex partner or friend will not result in assault from other patrons or ejection from the premises, and (c) a safe and pro-social way to meet others of the same sexual orientation, thereby helping to mitigate the need to seek partners in less salubrious and often dangerous circumstances.[1]

Most gay men and women have vivid memories of their first visit to a gay pub or club. It is often remembered as a liberating experience, and some undergo a total and extraordinary metamorphosis thereafter, delivering themselves from their previous isolation or low self-esteem and beginning new lives. By 'going social' as Kenneth Plummer calls it, the individual moves from a world characterized by secrecy, solitude, ambiguity and guilt to a subworld where homosexual-role models are available, where homosexuality may be temporarily rendered public ... A highly diffuse, unstructured experience, somewhat akin to anomie, becomes translated into one that is more clearly socially organized and ultimately stabilized.[2]

However, for those whose nocturnal ventures are a closely guarded secret, their delight at having 'come home' is tainted by the ever-present concern that they will be seen whilst inside or whilst entering or leaving the locale. For this reason, many find themselves unable to visit such venues at all. Media celebrities, politicians, police officers and members of the armed or security services are amongst their number. The cavalier and the desperate may elect to bear the risks but live instead in constant fear of recognition and exposure.

● *Derbyshire WDC, age 31, nine years' service*

I used to go right out of the county to do my gay socializing, just to avoid coming into contact with colleagues from my own force. You see it's so much easier to get caught out doing things in a small force because you know everyone. Despite my efforts, I once bumped into a colleague at a gay venue some miles away. He probably had the same idea as me about getting away. Anyway, we'd both been in this place for about fifteen minutes before we suddenly passed each other coming from the bar, and our eyes met. I nearly dropped my pint. I shat myself and immediately thought about leaving, and so did he as it turns out, but for some strange reason we both stayed. On the next circuit of the bar, I made an effort to go and speak to him to find out what was going on because the thought had occurred to me that he might actually be in there on duty. Again, he'd thought the same thing but probably with more reason than myself since I'm in the CID. In the end though everything was fine – we were both in there for the same reason.

● *Metropolitan Mounted Branch PC, age 33, resigned with fifteen years' service*

I used to be scared shitless about the Job finding out about me in a raid on a gay bar or something. One night I was in what used to be Silks in Shepherd's Bush, when I saw about half-a-dozen plain-clothes coppers stood over by the door. I was based in Hammersmith at the time, which covered this bar, and I recognized them, but I couldn't get out of the place because they were right by the door. I was totally paranoid and I stood by the far end of the bar the whole night just watching them. They didn't see me but the following week the place was raided and it was closed down for quite a while. It scared the shit out of me.

Another time I was coming out of the same club at about midnight and as I came around the corner I walked head first into a patrolling Inspector that I knew. We apologized to each other and I don't know if he even had time to get a good look at me, but by then I was so flustered and nervous that by the time I got back to my car and tried to get into it I realized that it was the wrong one – my car was two in front – and of course then I got followed by this Inspector and another guy all the way to Chiswick roundabout in a police car.

After that incident I was so worried that I used to send friends out of the pubs and clubs before I left to make sure that there were no police outside because I knew a lot of them in the area where I used to socialize – especially in Earls Court. I knew that they'd be parked up in a car or van outside Copa's, or around the corner, watching what was going on and who was coming out. You have to be so careful because they'll see you and you probably won't even know it until you get into work the next day.

On a couple of occasions whilst I've been in clubs I've actually bumped into other coppers whom I didn't know about before. Once at the Hippodrome, when they used to do gay nights on Mondays, I bumped into two in one night in separate incidents. I couldn't believe it! I nearly died. I was out with this other PC from work who had recently come out to me. When we got there, we saw one guy who I knew from Mounted Branch – who was married with kids – and I totally freaked out when I saw him in *there, all over this guy on the dance floor. Then later, I saw another guy whom I actually joined the Job with – who is also in Mounted Branch. My friend and I went up into the balcony to watch where they both were so as we wouldn't bump into them. It sounds silly now because they were obviously gay as well but we were both so paranoid at the time that we weren't thinking straight. My friend was more paranoid than I was and he wanted to leave but I said that the club was big enough for us not to bump into each other if we kept a look out. In the end, after we lost track of them, he went to see if either of them had left. Whilst he was gone, I was leaning over the balcony with a drink in my hand, when I felt a tap on my shoulder and it was one of these PCs. I nearly fell over the balcony with fright. I couldn't believe it and I just looked at him. What had happened was that whilst my mate was wandering around the disco looking for, but at the same time trying to avoid, these two blokes, he walked right into this one. They had a quick chat and he brought him upstairs to me. Anyway, he wasn't really surprised to see me there because apparently he'd seen me at Heaven a couple of weeks earlier – only he'd left as soon as he saw me. He hadn't approached me which was just as well because I'd have denied it anyway if he had, because I wouldn't have known for sure that he was gay – even though he was there. I'd have denied it to the hilt.*

The other guy we didn't see at all the rest of the night and so I thought I'd got away with it – only I bumped into him in Banana Max a couple of weeks later. Eventually, this guy left his wife and came to live with me as a lodger. But he's left the Job now.

● *Merseyside WPC, age 26, eight years' service*

I've only ever been in a club once when the police have attended. Somebody had passed a counterfeit note at the bar and the bar staff had called the police. The staff knew about us being in the Job and they told me and my friends they'd called the police so as we could stand away from the door when they came, in case we were recognized by them. As it happens, I didn't know any of them. They arrived in plain clothes, very discreetly, spoke to the person concerned and escorted him out. I doubt anybody was even aware

*of what was happening except for the bar staff. And us of course –
you can be sure we were watching.*

● *Metropolitan PC, age 34,
resigned with twelve years' service*

At clubs I was normally let in and out the back door if the
staff knew me. I was also totally and utterly paranoid about picking
up people in gay clubs and being stopped on the way home by
officers on my own patch with them in the car. As time went on, I
realized that I wasn't actually doing anything wrong and as the
paranoia dissipated, the burden decreased and the imaginary paper
bag which I had carried around in my pocket for so long was no
longer required and was eventually disregarded.

Now that I've left of course, I've got nothing more to worry
about, and one night after I'd left the force I even spent some time
outside a gay club talking to a carrier on my old ground and when
I'd finished, I just walked straight towards the club in front of them
– and they knew where I was going. Then later, they came in to deal
with a serious fight and I assisted them by pointing out both the
victim and the assailant. They just said, 'Thanks, Andy' and I
carried on drinking my pint.

● *Surrey PC, age 32, seven years' service*

At one time I was very, very cautious about going into gay
pubs and clubs. I was frightened to death. Totally paranoid. I felt
like a criminal, even though I hadn't done anything wrong. When
'time' was called I used to finish my drink immediately, something
people don't normally do – I wouldn't dream of doing that in a
straight pub but I wasn't taking any chances in case the place got
raided. But I've come to realize now that although the police is a
well-paid job and I'd probably be absolutely gutted if I had to leave
for any reason other than my own choice, paranoia is a very destructive thing, and if I spent my entire life afraid to go into gay
pubs, and then afraid to go out again when I wanted to leave, I'd
probably end up very bitter and twisted. I'm a lot happier now that

I've learnt to do what I want, in that I feel I'm able to lead a fairly normal gay lifestyle.

● *Metropolitan PC, age 29,
resigned with eleven years' service*

As far as I was concerned, going into a gay establishment was too risky to even contemplate, due to the fear of being seen coming or going. I needed to be straighter than straight, or else that would be the end of my career – or so I thought. I never ever went into a gay establishment whilst I was in the police, although I would have liked to – it would have provided me with the valuable form of social contact I so badly needed. I knew something about the structure of gay society but that was about it. My contact was zero.

Not all the risks of attending gay establishments come from off-duty fraternizing. Police officers working in large cities with numerous gay venues may also have to visit pubs or clubs in the course of their duties. There, they risk meeting friends who may unwittingly allude to their acquaintance, blowing the officer's cover. And where anti-police clientele were previously unaware of the officer's occupation, they may even attempt to 'out' them in front of their colleagues.

● *West Yorkshire PC, age 36, ten years' service*

My nightmare is going to one of our gay pubs and being recognized. Like having some screaming queen come running up to me and putting her arms round me and telling me how wonderful I look in my smart uniform. But it has its advantages as well. It's a bit of a novelty for lots of people and you can become a minor celebrity in a way. I get invited to dinners and things quite a lot. For a lot of people it's someone for them to show off to their friends – it's a talking-point.

● *Metropolitan woman Inspector, age 36, thirteen years' service*

If I were to arrive at a gay pub on duty and be faced with people who knew me socially – who knew that I was gay – and yet I was still surrounded by colleagues who had no idea, I would feel more than a little uncomfortable. That was my greatest fear before I came out at work. And that I would be put in a compromising situation or accused of being biased as a result. I consequently kept well away from those kinds of situations – as far as I could manage. You're bound to feel vulnerable when two carefully segregated sides of your life are about to collide. I felt particularly vulnerable in case I was recognized by someone whom I knew disliked me and who might take exception to me.

● *Metropolitan PC, age 26, four years' service*

If I ever had to go to a gay pub or club on duty these days, all my friends there would recognize me and I'd get dead embarrassed. They all know I'm a copper. The ones who didn't know me would probably hate me as soon as they saw me because of the uniform, but sometimes you can have some fun with them if you can break the ice. A couple of years ago me and another PC were in a Job car and we went to the Royal Vauxhall Tavern at around kicking-out time to deal with something or other. When we got there, people were milling around in groups outside the pub. As we pulled up, I jumped out of the police car, slammed the door, put my hands on my hips, minced up the road towards the pub, and screeched, 'Any of you girls touch my shiny new police car and you're dead!' My mate was kind of stunned and embarrassed at the same time, but he thought it was quite funny. Most of the people outside the pub thought it was funny but some of them probably thought I was taking the piss. But they made that assumption simply because of the animosity between the police and the gay community. They wouldn't have thought for one minute that I could actually be gay as well.

When I'm off duty, I don't go to any of the clubs on my

ground to avoid being seen, not so much by the police as by the local slags, because then I would lose the respect of the uniform. I don't want to have to deal with that kind of crap when I'm trying to nick someone.

Notes

1.   The importance of this latter point is illustrated by a Metropolitan Police constable who explained:

> When I was young, I knew that there must be other people like me around but I just couldn't find them. I was outside of London in a very rural town and I didn't know what to do. There was nothing for people like me there – they probably thought they didn't have any gays. Then one day, quite by accident, I discovered that I could get sex in certain public toilets. The first time I went I was about sixteen and a half. I went several times after that.

2.   K. Plummer, *Sexual Stigma*, 1975, p. 148.

Chapter seven

Two Communities, Double Lives

I'm very aware of the fact that I belong to two different
'families', neither of which are very fond of each other.
It's like being married and having your mother and
mother-in-law with you in the one house when they
hate each other's guts.

● *South Wales WPC, age 34, six years' service*

BECOMING a component part of a lesbian and/or gay
community and spending vast amounts of time fraternizing on the
gay scene is not an automatic corollary of recognizing one's homosexual orientation. Many people are not interested in what a
(largely commercial) scene has to offer, whilst for those who live
outside large towns the nearest gay retreat may be many miles
away. Others may have still to reach the stage where they feel
confident enough to explore their new-found territory. A recurrent
theme of previous chapters (see especially Chapter 3) suggests,
however, that those homosexual and bisexual officers who *do* make
it onto the gay scene may then find themselves simultaneously
attached to two very different communities with divergent subcul-
tures and opposing values. The animosity between these two bodies
frequently causes police officers to pursue the two facets of their
lives separately and in the second section of this chapter, the
obstacles and intricacies of living a 'double life' are explored. In this

first section, the difficulties of this dual citizenship are discussed and in particular, the ways in which the two populations are perceived as relating to each other are considered.

Two Communities

Some officers believe that it is primarily lesbians and gay men who are responsible for the friction that exists between the two groups.

● *Metropolitan PC, age 39,*
nineteen years' service

Although most gays are law-abiding and respect the police there are a few radicals who are always protesting against the police. That may be because they have been arrested at some stage themselves. They want this, they want that, and they hate the police because they can't get it – even though the police don't make the laws. They can't open their minds up to see the police side of things. They need to sit back and think about what they're doing instead of always just attacking the uniform. If they tried to get through to the human being instead of always going on the offensive and deliber-ately winding the police up, they might find that a lot of the police can actually be sympathetic. In the end people react to people, whoever they are.

● *Metropolitan Traffic Division PC, age 28,*
ten years' service

I think a fair amount of the criticism from the gay com-munity is unfounded. Most of them don't have any direct experi-ence with the police, be it good or bad, and they just share a handful of second-hand stories and experiences that are constantly passed around. It's a kind of hand-me-down philosophy where gays coming onto the scene are taught that the police are homophobic and nasty before they've met one, which is analogous to heterosex-

uals being taught that homosexuals are nasty, effeminate child molesters before they've even met one. For example, I've been out on the gay scene for years and I've never been in a pub or club that's been raided. It's always 'my friend' had such-and-such happen to him or her and half the time you know from personal experience that it couldn't possibly be true. And they only tell you half the story anyway. They don't tell you what they were doing to deserve the treatment they got – that they were standing there taking the piss and blowing kisses at the police and making a nuisance of themselves. Then they make out it was all for nothing and that they just got picked on for no reason. In my experience the ones that get nicked normally deserve it. Some of them are real assholes.

Others suggest that the majority of the blame lies with the deep-seated conservatism and consequent intolerance of the police.

● *Metropolitan PC, age 34, nine years' service*

I think there is this tendency for the police to distance themselves from anything to do with homosexuality – they don't want to have anything to do with it. There was this time a couple of years ago when these two male strippers had been invited to a straight party to do their stuff, but when they arrived they were duly beaten up and kicked out again. When I came on for early turn at 6 a.m., they were still sitting in the station office waiting to be dealt with, and still waiting to see the Divisional Surgeon re their injuries. They'd not been offered a cup of tea, or even first aid – quite deliberately – in the hope that they would go away. I wanted to help but I couldn't, because it was nothing to do with me. You can't get involved in somebody else's job.

● *Metropolitan PC, age 21, two years' service*

Once I got called to a gay nightclub in Deptford where these two guys had had an argument and one had hit the other with a bottle and GBH'd him. I went in there with about six other officers but as soon as they realized that it was a gay club and that they were dealing with 'queers', they visibly took a step back. You could see that none of them wanted to have anything to do with it. So I started to deal with it and they just left me to it. Some of them actually left the pub and as one of them walked out I heard him say, 'I'm not waiting around in here.' I wasn't impressed.

Several officers propose that there are in fact good and bad elements on both sides, and when it comes to the bad, both are equally mischievous.

● *Essex Training School WPC, age 34, seven years' service*

I think the police are often fearful and very mistrustful of gay people because they don't understand them, and so they tend to treat them a bit differently. They're also very wary because the gay community is associated with the loony left and the police hate that. The police react very strongly to the left and once you're even left of centre, they tend to tar everyone with the same brush. The people I work with know about me and they want to know who I vote for and things like that. They think all gays are automatically left-wing Marxists. I can understand it sometimes because some of them do go over the top. But I think it's a bit like being chased by a dog: if only they were to stand still instead of always running away, they would find that they didn't get bitten half as often. Of course, a large part of the gay community is equally mistrustful of the police because they equate them with fascism and oppression and they automatically think that all police vote Tory. Bad police officers are imagined to represent all police officers and when a hand is held out by the police it just gets bitten. So then it gets retracted and it's kept retracted. It all works both ways. It's a shame because there is mistrust on both sides and then the situation becomes hopeless. It makes me want to do something about it because the constant lack of understanding makes me very uncomfortable at times to say the least.

● *Metropolitan PC, age 33, nine years' service*

I don't think that on the whole the gay community have tried very hard with the police. They tend to give up quickly and resort to aggressive tactics. *Their politics are very confrontationary. Generally speaking, that is – there are a lot of conservative homosexuals out there – but the loudest mouths are the ones we all hear. They are, as usual, a minority of radicals who are not at all representative of the wider community. They certainly don't speak for me. The gay radicals think it's the rest of the world that needs educating but there are a few things they also need to learn. The gay movement is very immature in some ways.*

Of course, the police can't see the gay side of things. Half the time they don't listen, they don't understand, nor are they prepared to listen or understand, although they are starting to pay lip-service, and I guess that's a start. But actions speak louder than words, and when they're still raiding gay bookshops and confiscating 'obscene' material which you can buy in ordinary bookshops, then either they're not doing their homework properly, or something else is wrong. It gives the impression to the gay community that they're being persecuted. The whole thing distresses and upsets me a lot. The problem is that radicals react to policeman and policemen react to radicals. They both need to calm down a bit and try and understand each other's point of view. It can be done because I do it every week with friends of mine, some of whom are gay but not police and some of whom are police but not gay. You just have to talk to them.

● *Metropolitan WDC, age 31, seven years' service*

It's not so much that the police respond badly to the gay community – they don't respond to them at all in my opinion. They've responded to women's issues, domestic violence, rape, child abuse and issues of race, but for some reason, issues surrounding sexuality have largely been ignored – at least until recently. That may be partly because the homosexual community haven't done themselves any favours by constantly attacking the police instead of liaising with them, or lobbying the relevant bodies. They'd rather throw temper tantrums and be thoroughly nasty, which endears them to no one. They want to drag the whole world to their perception of it overnight – even though it may have taken them years to understand who they were, and even longer for their parents. Some of them refuse to be reasonable or go step by step – they want it all yesterday – which I can understand but in the end they get nothing that way. Because the noisy ones would rather attack the police instead of taking the time to sit down and show them why what they're doing is wrong and helping them to see things from a different point of view, the police continue to misunderstand the homosexual community. The radicals don't help the police to understand them or their predicament, so the police simply see their actions as aggressive and tend, therefore, to ignore them. Sometimes I think that there are some people (and organizations) who just do not want the police to succeed, they bash the police whatever they do and never give an ounce of credit. But they are the minority, and the police should not use them as an excuse to cease persevering with the real issues.

That's not to lay all the blame at the feet of the gay community. For a start, the police do nothing to inform themselves as well as they might, due to a conservatism which prevents them from seeing and judging these kinds of issues with a clear head. Most forces' community liaison branches don't take the gay newspapers like Capital Gay and Gay Times. I mean, it's not as if it would even cost them anything. Most of them are free. No wonder they don't know what's going on; the police are reported on week in and week out in the gay press and they don't even know about it, so no wonder they are unable to keep abreast of the many lesbian and gay issues which involve them. It might also be useful if there were gay officers in community involvement branches who knew what the score was. It is equally important that the rest of the force be kept up to date with the developing relationship between the two communities. At the moment only a handful of specialized officers who are involved in it all the time know what is happening. Half the time the arrangements are only at a divisional level anyway. What that means is that no one gets to see the whole picture. Each division is doing its own thing. The police in Hampstead for example have got little idea what is happening outside of their division. Few divisions bother to communicate with the central gay liaison officer over this at NSY. So how can any meetings be of use *if none of the content is disseminated to the people that matter throughout the force? How are the troops supposed to know about all this supposed attitude change if they never hear about it? They're the ones who need to know. They're the ones who are out there doing the job and causing the problems, not the people in the offices whom we continually see and who are OK.*

Double Lives

Unlike many other government civil service departments, most of Britain's police services still have no equal opportunities' statements relating to sexual orientation as they do in favour of race, colour, creed, etc. (see also Chapter 12). It is therefore not surprising that police officers may be loath to (a) reveal their identity as 'homosexual' or 'bisexual' to other police officers (who are exclusively heterosexual), or (b) reveal their identity as 'police officer' to homosexuals (who are not also police officers). Gay officers may find themselves stigmatized in both of their major roles in life: they may be rejected by the community at large, and especially by a hostile gay community, as (fascist) 'pigs', and they may be rejected by their colleagues at work as 'queers' or 'lezzies'. In this way, institutional heterosexism, coupled with the competing expectations brought about by the dual citizenship of non-heterosexual police officers and celebrated levels of antipathy between the police and gay communities, means that inception of the 'double-life syndrome' for fear of rejection by both cultures is an unusually common corollary in the gay police career. The most notable such example in recent times was the well-publicized case of the Queen's Police Officer, Commander Michael Trestrail, whose resignation as head of Royalty Protection was accepted after his tabloid exposure in 1982. Lord Bridge, who was subsequently tasked with the investigation of Trestrail's original appointment, noted that 'until the disclosure made in July last, no one ... entertained the slightest suspicion of Commander Trestrail's homosexual inclinations, let alone of the secret double-life he was leading'.[1]

The case of sexual stigma is not analogous to those other stigmata like race, since unlike skin colour, sexual preference is not visible. It was Irving Goffman who originally made the distinction between *discredited* and *discreditable* identities. In the case of the former, identities are already discredited by some visible stigma like skin colour, whereas the latter identities are only *potentially* discredited, and this is dependent upon seepage of the stigmatizing information, for example one's sexual orientation. In this way, the stigma carried by most non-heterosexuals is, in a sense, optional and many elect to conceal their deviance and 'pass' as heterosexual. Passing has the advantage of allowing 'discreditables' to discover the true feelings of others towards issues of homosexuality in safety, enabling them to make informed decisions regarding the kinds of situations in which they ought to continue passing. In each case the question is:

> To display or not to display; to tell or not to tell; to let on or not to let on; to lie or not to lie; and in each case, to whom, how, when and where.[2]

Living a 'gay police' double life involves exercising two roles – owning two identities – one of which is always 'spoiled' or 'discredited' (and therefore camouflaged) depending on the company one is in. There develops one life at work, where an officer's organizing identity is that of 'police officer' and his or her sexual orientation remains undisclosed and disengaged, and another 'off-duty' life, where one's identity is either 'gay', 'lesbian', 'bisexual' (or simply 'confused') but where occupation is a closely guarded secret. Others may be out in one sphere but not in the other. Some officers live double double lives. They are those men and women whose identities are constantly camouflaged; who are both 'heterosexual' at work and 'bank clerks' in the evening. Thus, there are degrees to which police officers may, or may not, entertain the notion of a double life.[3] The effects of this double-life syndrome can be both disruptive and destabilizing. The stress caused by an artificially constructed schizophrenia may be extreme and in some cases, may lead to a violent disruption of normal psychological functioning (see also Chapter 10).

● *Metropolitan YACS PC, age 44,*
twenty-two years' service

    *I maintain a heterosexual identity which is quite easy really
since I'm bisexual anyway. The people at work don't recognize me
as gay because their paradigm of homosexuality tells them that
homosexuals are effeminate. I'm not effeminate, so as far as most
people are concerned, I can't be homosexual. When you're surrounded by people like that, sometimes it's hard not to be con-
temptuous of their naivety.*
    *If they found out about me, they might move me to another
station for a fresh start. But I'd probably leave anyway if they
found out. I don't think I could take it. I couldn't cope. I wouldn't
want to leave because I've been in the police a long time and I'm
proud of being a police officer, but if they gave me a really bad time
then that would make it easier for me to do, I suppose.*
    *Leading a double life is a constant conflict within myself and
it affects me quite badly sometimes. I don't really know what I
want at the moment and it's begun to affect my health. I drink and
smoke to excess and sometimes I can't sleep at night. I don't know
who I can talk to about it, so I'm seeing a psychiatrist next month.*

● *Metropolitan Detective Chief Inspector,*
age 45, fifteen years' service

    *Since I've been in the Job, I've never told anyone that I'm
gay. Not in fifteen years. But there's a constant fear of being found
out. So at work I make the odd remark about large-breasted
women and I used to go out with a girl every once in a while, but
my efforts were rather feeble. It affects career decisions as well. I
even left SB to avoid vetting and in the end I had a nervous breakdown, so it has probably put a lot of stress on me over the years,
although I haven't always realized it. And that may even have
affected my judgements from time to time. It's a shame that so
many straight police officers have such a problem with it. The
organization ends up by losing a lot of good people that way, and
the funny thing is, they don't even know why.*

● *Staffordshire WPS, age 39,*
resigned with eleven years' service

When people asked me what I did, I used to say that I put the bones in corsets. That hurt because I'm proud to be a police officer and I used to hate myself for lying but if you're not out, sometimes you have to lie to protect yourself.

All that closetedness used to make me cringe, absolutely cringe. The thing about being gay and not out in the open about it is that you feel second class and second best. When there were jokes about dykes in the police canteen, I felt that I had to laugh because if I was the only one who was not laughing then they would soon pick that up. But under the charade of the laughter I felt hurt. To be honest, they used to make me feel ashamed of myself. The worst thing was that I knew that their jokes relied on things about being gay which I knew weren't true. Those years were awful.

● *Metropolitan Inspector, age 34,*
twelve years' service

When it comes to hiding my sexuality at work, the pressure is not on me at my rank to constantly prove my manhood to the same extent that it is in the junior officers' canteen. In fact, people don't expect me to talk about that sort of thing or behave in the same way as PCs do, swearing like them and so on, so I escape most of it. My private life is not so much under the microscope; people are less inclined to notice what I do and they can't grill me about my love life the way they would do on relief. You just don't go asking senior officers who they got their leg over with last night – even amongst each other. It's not the done thing. Also, I often have my own office, so my boyfriend can call me direct. That way, I don't get people calling me up on the PR and making sarcastic comments like 'It's Mr so-and-so on the phone for you ... AGAIN.' So you get a certain amount of privacy as a senior officer. Even so, I think the deception is sad. I would still like to be more open because that's the kind of person I am. I don't like having to deceive people.

I don't go out on the gay scene that much but when I do, I rarely lie about my job. I just tell them because I don't want to live a total double life. Once I was in this club chatting somebody up, and he asked me what I did for a living, so I just told him that I was a police officer. He just looked at me and said, 'That's funny, so am I.' The strange thing is I used to lie more at straight clubs, where I often said that I was a traffic warden. I didn't like saying that I was in the police because I think it's such an antisocial thing to be. Sometimes I feel ashamed to be a police officer and I thought that if they could take my being a traffic warden, then they could probably take anything!

● *Strathclyde WPC, age 27, six years' service*

Being gay in the police can cause a strain in many areas of your life. For me, once I'd actually accepted my sexuality and started to have proper relationships, the whole thing put a tremendous strain on me at work. I ceased to trust those close friends I had trusted implicitly before, and my relationships with just about everybody I knew became strained simply because I was constantly worried about saying something that might give me away. I felt I had to watch absolutely everything I said, and was ultra-careful not to let out any double meanings. It was a real effort. Looking back, I think I was too careful because I actually started to avoid some people totally, just in case I should slip up and they guessed. I had nobody I could turn to or talk to, and it got very lonely after a while. It's difficult not being able to talk about your love life like everybody else. I'm quite a private person in some ways but at the same time, what I don't like is when you're sitting in the canteen talking anecdotes or whatever, and you want to say something about yourself or what you've been doing lately, but you hang back because of the reaction you might get. It's very unnatural. It must make you come across as really strange. My partner, who was also a police officer, had stressed the need for me to live this double life but because I'm naturally a more open person than she is, I found it more of a strain. She used to get paranoid about it and told me that I should wear a dress at least once a week, and not walk around with my hands in my pockets, because that was 'dykie' and it would give me away. But I did, and we would end up having arguments about it. The need to keep the whole thing secret caused a lot of unnecessary stress.

● *Sussex PC, age 27, four years' service*

Although I'm not open about my sexuality at work, I don't go about inventing girlfriends and things because I think that would just damage me, more than anything else. Besides, I feel that I'd be demeaning myself to go about telling facile lies just to put people off the scent. I do my best not to lead a double life and so I try to avoid deceiving people as much as possible. So I just don't talk about my sex life a lot. The strange thing is that because I spend a lot of my free time socializing away from my colleagues, I've gotten the reputation for being a bit of a Casanova. For some reason they assume that when I go away for the weekend, I'm working my way through the female population of England. They think I'm a bit of a dark horse who just doesn't say much, I think.

Although I try not to fabricate things, I can never be totally honest and I find that quite upsetting. I not only don't like lying to people but I don't like deceiving by omission either; like most policemen I'm a great believer in honesty. I would like to be more open – I would like to be able to take my boyfriend along to police functions and that sort of thing but it's just not a realistic proposition.

I also used to be very cautious about letting people I met on the gay scene know what I did for a living. I used to be the archetypal civil servant, but then you always get the smart-ass who asks you what grade you are and what department you work for and then you're totally buggered. (No pun intended.) Sometimes, if I'm in a more extravagant mood, I might think of something a bit more bizarre. Because I can't tell the truth, I can be whatever I want to be, which can be quite fun.

On the whole, I tend to think that I'm a fairly good judge of human character these days, and if I like the look of someone and I think we might become friends, then I just tell them. That way I don't have to come clean later, which can be difficult. The rest of the time it doesn't bother me too much that I'm not entirely honest, since it's a case of looking after yourself sometimes. In any case, some of them might just want you for your uniform once they find out, or take an unnatural interest in your handcuffs and truncheon...

● *Metropolitan Special Branch PC, age 37, eleven years' service*

I have partners of both sexes. I actually have quite a lot of girlfriends – I suppose I could even end up getting married. I'm not trying to change myself or anything, but I suppose maybe I do it sometimes for the benefit of other people. I don't have any problem with having sex with women, in fact I quite enjoy it, but if I had a straight choice I would always go for the guy. Yes, I join in the banter in the pubs and put up a front. I think that's what they all do. It's 'Hey, look at me. I'm a big macho man and I hate poofs.' Most of them think that they don't know any gays but of course they do. Nobody knows or even suspects about me, I'm pretty sure of that. I'm your typical East End type. The whole thing makes me laugh really. It's a big joke. When I'm at work, I often relate experiences that were homosexual and make them heterosexual: Chris grows a pair of tits and becomes Christina. That way, I can still join in the conversation.

I don't care that I can't be open – it's none of their business anyway. I suppose in an ideal world I would prefer to be myself but I don't see that as realistic in the present climate; I don't want to be parading at a station twenty miles from where I live, thank you very much.

● *West Yorkshire WPC, age 27, five years' service*

I don't normally tell anyone about my true sexual orientation because I'm frightened of the consequences. I wouldn't get my CID board for a start. The other thing is that if you don't go for a drink with the others after work, then since they always end up talking about you, I can see me being on the end of everybody's jokes. I don't want that. And I don't want to be treated like a leper by other women or for them to think that I fancy them. They should be so lucky.

I don't have a boyfriend but I often invent them and I also have a friend who comes to all my dos, and I go to all his – he's gay – and it works quite well. Most of my colleagues think we're about to get engaged because he's been turning up to things for about two years now. We have a right laugh about it. We might even have a false engagement one day just for the hell of it.

When I go to gay clubs I have to make up stories about my job as well. It started before I'd really considered what to say and someone asked me at a club and the first thing I could think of was a sandwich round, so now when I'm with people I don't know, I say I have a sandwich round which is really good because you can talk about all the different fillings that can go into sandwiches and they can't catch me out. I don't know why I thought of that one.

The problem is, I find myself getting caught up in so many lies purely because I'm trying to get out of awkward situations in the Job, that I end up tripping myself up in the end. It would be so nice to be able to go in and tell everyone who you are and where you go of an evening.

● *West Yorkshire PS, age 34, eight years' service*

When people talk shit about fags and stuff, I normally join in, I've even said a few bad things myself and made derogatory remarks about gay prisoners to give the impression that I'm as straight as the next man. I remember the clause 28 campaign – I went along with the straight point of view in order to deflect any suspicion about me, although I don't go out with women or anything like that. I can't say I'm proud about it but I never challenge assumptions. I just make a mental note about who says what for the future. My worry is that if they ever found out I might be disowned by my shift. And I might not get back-up if I needed it in a hurry.

● *Metropolitan PC, authorized shot, age 34,*
fourteen years' service

I've lived with my lover for four years now and the police
know about it – but they just think I've got a lodger, although some
of them suspect. Sometimes I make a joke of being gay as a way of
dealing with it and then I can actually say what I mean and feel, like
they might point to someone on the street and say, 'Oh, I bet he's
your type, eh?' and I can just laugh and say, 'Oh yeah, he's really
cute' or whatever. I can reply however I want and because it's
supposed to be a joke, it's OK. Yet at the same time it's a real way
of allowing me to say exactly what I really feel which means at least
I'm not holding it all in.

I think the situation's totally unfair but I've learned to
accept it because I've chosen to stay. The whole thing can be a bit of
a palaver sometimes because when colleagues come round to the
house, I have to take down certain pictures which might give the
game away and collect up any gay news magazines, etc. It's so easy
to leave stuff lying around when people come because you are used
to seeing it there and you forget what it is. It's like having to
remember to put away the Radio Times *every time; it just doesn't*
come naturally.

● *Metropolitan PC, age 24,*
resigned with six years' service

I knew two guys at my station who were supposed to be gay
and both had the piss taken out of them behind their backs. Hardly
a good reason for me to be open. I hated them for what I thought
they would do to me if they knew and it made me a bit disruptive.
When they made their nasty comments I said nothing but used to
despise them for it inside. In the end, I hated them all.

Eventually, I started going out to gay social groups, but I
found myself in a similar situation because I didn't want to come
out as a police officer in case any of them ever got nasty and told my
station. I used to say that I was a security guard. One day though, I
told one of the facilitators at the group what I really did, in confi-
dence. It soon got around, although everybody pretended that they

*didn't know, which was really annoying. I felt a right asshole when
I found out.*

*It seemed like whichever group I was with I couldn't be
myself and the pressure really started to build up over the next
couple of years. I wanted to change, just so that I didn't have to
hide all the time. One night I was in this gay pub in Camden with a
friend from the group, and I'd had quite a bit to drink and then
suddenly I just started crying at the bar and couldn't stop myself.
Over ten years of pressure and anxiety came out at once. The guy I
was with wanted to know what was the matter and I ended up
telling him that I was a copper and immediately regretted it and
told him that if I ever found out that he'd told a soul I'd blow his
fucking legs off and I meant it.*

● *Metropolitan WPC, age 29, one year's service*

*My big worry is recognition outside the police. If I was put
down to do the Gay Pride march or something I would have to
either take the day off or go sick. There's no way I would do that.
It's just too risky. I would even avoid transferring to a division
where there was a high concentration of gay pubs or clubs so as not
to be recognized by anyone I know. Not that I go out to gay places
much these days. Since I've been in the Job I haven't had a relationship either, which is largely because I'm living in the section house
and I don't really want women traipsing in and out of here for
everyone to see – that would be a bit of a problem – but once I
move out of here then all that will change!*

*Before I joined the Job I used to be out but then when I
joined I went back into hiding, which is a bit strange but now I
want to do things for myself rather than for the cause. I've done all
that already. But what I do tend to do now is just be very liberal. I
think that by showing the flag of liberalness I can still do quite a lot
of good by setting a good example.*

● *Devon and Cornwall PC, age 28,
resigned with six years' service*

*It would probably be OK with the people that you know
well on your shift – it's the people who you don't know on other*

shifts that will talk about you, and I would find that difficult to handle. 'Oh yeah, that Dominic on A shift is a poofter, didn't you know?' and I would just be known as the poof on A shift. I didn't want that. I think it would have been OK with the guv'nors, provided I didn't flaunt it. The problem is, it's always a bit of shit that they can throw back in your face if you put a foot out of line. You might think that it's not worrying people but it's always there at the back of their minds.

● *Metropolitan PC, age 35,*
resigned with fourteen years' service

After I'd left the police, I discovered that everyone knew about me which was really annoying because I thought nobody knew. I wish they'd told me so I didn't have to suffer by pretending all that time. You see, you have to make a decision based on what you think would happen if you came out. The reality of the situation might really be quite different but you have to make a decision based purely on what you know. The dilemma is, do you admit to your homosexuality and risk the career, or do you submerge it and get on with being a police officer: Am I going to be myself or am I going to pretend that I'm straight? I chose the latter; I chose to pretend.

Fears regarding the possibility of discrimination are widespread, particularly amongst officers seeking promotion.[4] And as the officer points out above, perceptions are paramount. As Thomas and Thomas have noted, 'If men define situations as real, they are real in their consequences.'[5] Hence, if an individual *reasonably believes* that he or she will experience prejudice or discrimination then the reality of the situation is irrelevant.

The role of the police has never been an easy one – that much has always been accepted. Indeed, for many it is the challenge of police work which makes the career such a satisfying one. But impartiality, benevolence, and above all steadiness are called for when dealing with both the public and colleagues, and major events in a person's life inevitably affect their efficiency in their employment. No one can expect to bring their problems to work with them and continue to remain objective and unwavering under pressure. The tension caused by having to constantly negotiate one's way through a complex maze of lies cannot be underestimated. As the Chief Constable of South Yorkshire noted, 'Police work is difficult enough already without extra pressures of that sort.'[6] One means of exit from the maze is achieved by coming out and this is considered in the next chapter.

Notes

1. N. C. Bridge (Baron Bridge of Harwich), 'Report of an enquiry by the Right Honourable Lord Bridge of Harwich into the appointment as the Queen's Police Officer, and the activities of Commander Trestrail; to determine whether security was breached or put at risk, and advise whether in consequence any change in security arrangements is necessary or desirable', HC 59, London: HMSO, November 1982, p. 11.
2. I. Goffman, *Stigma: Notes on the Management of Spoiled Identity*, 1963, p. 129.
3. It is conceivable that in the case of the gay police officer, more than one double life might be entertained. It is clear that an officer who is married but not out to their spouse will be adding a further dimension to their 'double life' and to their difficulties.
4. In a recent study by the author, 78 per cent of respondents ($N = 36$) reported their conviction that an 'out' homosexual officer would not have the same career prospects as a heterosexual officer (see M. Burke, 'Homosexuality in the British police', Ph.D. thesis, University of Essex, 1993).
5. W. I. Thomas and D. S. Thomas, *The Child in America*, 1928, p. 51.
6. R. Wells, *Police Review*, 18 January 1991, p. 105.

Chapter eight

Coming Out

I'm out at work and I get on with most of my
colleagues really well. One of my mates at work
always calls me a poof and I always call him a fat
ugly bastard. The relationship works really well.

● *Metropolitan PC, age 35, five years' service*

THE sociologists Gagnon and Simon defined coming out as
'the point in time when there is self-recognition as a homosexual,
and the first major exploration of the homosexual community'.[1]
However, since self-recognition and social exploration do not
always occur simultaneously (they are not logically contingent),
other definitions have been offered. Yet these have often characterized coming out solely in terms of either the former or the latter
portion of the above definition. The term is also employed to refer
to the process of homosexual identity formation and this adds
further to the confusion. The expression 'coming out' was originally used in the élite circles of the 1920s, and referred to the entry of
a débutante onto the social scene. It was borrowed by the contemporary homosexual subculture and has come to embody a number
of meanings today, including the similar entry of the neophyte
homosexual onto the gay scene. Thus, all and none of the above
definitions are valid. In this chapter, however, the term is employed
chiefly as a reference to the process of disclosure.

Whilst it is certain that the entire spectrum of sexualities
is represented in all professions, within many of them only the

heterosexual is visible. The police, until recently, have been an example of such a profession. There are many reasons for this, most of which will be covered by police officers themselves in the pages that follow. I will, therefore, make only a couple of observations here.

Despite the provisions of the 1967 Sexual Offences Act, homosexuality is still synonymous with criminality in the minds of many police officers, particularly those who may have been policing before the 1967 amendment came into being. Like high-ranking government staff, police officers have long been considered open to blackmail and, thus, possible threats to security. In cases where a homosexual orientation could be identified, they have traditionally been deemed as generally unsuitable for police work and denied office.

The double silence which surrounds an officer's occupational and orientational identities can result in serious difficulty in the accomplishment of an affirmative self-image both in terms of police officer and more consequentially perhaps, in terms of sexual orientation (see also Chapter 10). Research on the acquisition of sexual identity suggests that one of the central processes in acquiring a positive lesbian or gay identity is coming out. Part of that process involves the gradual disclosure of one's sexual orientation to family, friends and colleagues. This act of disclosure is valued and much fostered as a means of self-affirmation and this is illustrated in the pieces that follow. However, to come out in certain occupations is to court serious difficulties at best and dismissal and criminal proceedings at worst – as in the case of the lesbian or gay teacher, priest, youth worker, soldier and police officer, for example. And yet whilst such self-exposure is often regarded as occupational suicide in the light of the negative homosexual stereotypes which prevail in our society and the tragic repercussions that can follow such a revelation, coming out has endured because of its consummative and therapeutic effect. For some, disclosure is a means of reducing the tension in their lives caused by the almost incessant need for deceit. For others, the perceived inevitability of eventual discovery means that coming out is more of a pre-emptive strike than an act of self-affirmation. Examples of both strategies are represented in this chapter. In nearly all cases though, individuals begin by being highly selective about who they tell, coming out to those they feel they can trust and gauging reactions carefully before moving on. In cases of sensitive professions or positions, disclosure may be limited to family or a few close friends for reasons of security.

The following represent a broad cross-section of coming out experiences, not all the elements of which are regulated by a police backdrop.

● *Metropolitan CPS PC, age 45,*
twenty-six years' service

I've nearly finished now but if I were to join again today, I think I would announce from day one that I was gay so I didn't have to hide. Hiding used to be compulsory because it was all about blackmail and compromising security. That kind of thing was OK in the days when it was impossible to admit being gay for fear of being slung in prison because it was still illegal, but today plenty of people would be quite happy for it to be known that they are gay. Where's the problem then? How can you be blackmailed if every- body already knows and nobody particularly cares? It's a classic piece of outdated thinking. The problem is a manufactured one. I'm older now and it's easy for me to say that but I don't see why I should go around pretending to be something that I'm not just to please others. In that sense I guess I'm more political about it than I used to be, and wiser. I think the more people that come out and surprise others who know them, the more people will realize that we're everywhere and that we're just the same as they are. Eventu- ally there wouldn't be any surprises left and nobody would give a shit about it. When you first join of course it's less easy to take that attitude. You're younger, and particularly when you first join the Job, you are very much a small fish in a big pond; you are part of a huge world that doesn't really belong to you and you're not free to do what you want, even if you're straight. Now I'm older and more experienced, I see the world as belonging to me and I'm going to do in it whatever I want to. I'm a bigger fish now and I'm less likely to be intimidated. That's one of the pleasures of getting older. Age brings with it a kind of natural authority, whatever your rank, both to others and to yourself. But from your lowly position as a probationer, it can be difficult enough for you to fight your way through to confirmation, without having to worry about other things.

● *Metropolitan WPC, age 24, three years' service*

So far I've had to tell two people in the police: one guy, because he was coming on a bit strong but I knew I could trust him 100 per cent; the other was a WPC who lives in the same block as me and she used to see the traffic coming in and out of the flat, so I had to tell her in the end as well. She came to one of my parties once where most of the people were gay and this woman whom I'd invited spent most of the evening trying to get off with me, so I had to tell her before she started talking to the people at work about it. She's been really good, I trust her completely and now she confides in me about things as well.

● *Surrey PC, age 36, seven years' service*

I've only ever told two other people in the Job about my sexual orientation and fortunately, I've had positive responses on both occasions. Both asked me in fact. The first one was a WPC, and I tend to think they're a bit more astute than the blokes anyway, but this one had also made an unsuccessful pass at me and I think it was that that'd got her curiosity aroused. Also when we were patrolling together, she used to watch who I was looking at in the high street and then from time to time she would hedge around the subject. Eventually, she plucked up the courage and asked me. The second was a PC who was a lot older than me, and who outwardly was a very aggressive character indeed. I was getting a bit nervous about him finding out because I thought if he discovered then I could expect a lot of problems – like a rearranged face. And he slowly began to realize. Typical policeman's nosey mind. I think he gradually put two and two together, and then one night he got pissed and asked me. Luckily, in the end I had a very positive response from him, very supportive, and that was a weight off my mind I can tell you!

I haven't come out generally though because I think I could go from being quite popular to being the lowest form of human life. I'm still well liked at the moment, and I don't really want to be responsible for my own demise. I think the whole thing will eventually come to a head on its own. I'm living dangerously enough as it is – I make some very unguarded comments at times. I used to keep my mouth shut about the whole issue. Then I developed to making fairly weak, ineffectual comments and now I have slanging matches and live dangerously. I still laugh at jokes if they're funny – so long as they're not malicious. But I worry about how the discipline regulations might apply. Maybe they will get me for 'bringing the force into disrepute' – I don't know how they'd twist it.[2] There are enough people who are violently homophobic to make my life unpleasant, and being in a small force it would spread like wildfire and I probably wouldn't even be in a position to move stations. I might just be able to survive at the station I'm at now once everyone knew, but it's not a very pleasant prospect. Policemen have got nasty minds and they always want to believe the worst about people, especially their colleagues.

● *Metropolitan PC, age 34,*
sixteen years' service

About half-a-dozen PCs and I were having a cup of tea after 6 a.m. parade one early turn. The conversation was about nothing in particular, when all of a sudden the conversation just stopped and one of my colleagues turned to me and said, 'We've been discussing you and we want to know if you are gay.' I was totally taken back – it was so sudden – I was caught totally off guard. I didn't know what to say. I had never given the question of coming out any real thought and was quite unprepared for this kind of confrontation. I couldn't afford to say yes, because I could not know how they would respond, but nor could I bring myself to say no. I just didn't know what to say. It reminded me of a night in the cadet corps when I was with a group of cadets who were on a night-duty security patrol of the police training estate. We were in a small *office, by ourselves, discussing our sexual experiences. One of the group said that the only sexual experiences he had had were at boys' boarding school. There homosexuality was evidently rampant amongst the pupils. The others had been boasting of how many girls they had had sex with. When this cadet came out everybody was dumbfounded, including myself. There was a deadly silence for a few moments before one of the other cadets thanked this cadet for being so frank and honest. The matter was then closed and I never heard it raised again. When my turn came around, which was last, I did not have the courage to admit that I was gay. I lied and said that I was still a virgin. And here I was caught out again. After a few moments of dumbfounded silence from me, the previous conversation just resumed and the subject of my being gay was never brought up again. I guess they made up their own minds.*

● Metropolitan WDS, age 36, fourteen years' service

Before I came out I had graffiti about me written on the toilet wall. I had vibrators given me at Christmas and other sexual aids put in my tray. A lot went on behind my back as well. It was very unpleasant. Some of my friends would tell me what was said when I wasn't there. It's worse when they don't know about you for sure. Once you come out then it's all over. I haven't had any of that stupid stuff since I've come out and that's why I think it's better for officers to come out. If they suspect for any reason, whether it's because you don't respond to being chatted up, or because you don't have a boyfriend, or because you don't behave just like they do, then you're up for derision. They go for you in a big way. Once you're out, the whole world comes off your shoulders and the pressure just goes. It's incredible. You don't have to look over your shoulder any more, and after fourteen years it's just such a relief. I had two distinct lives, police and private. I was two different people. The thought of me being discovered made me paranoid. Now I'm out, I see it all slightly differently. It's a bit like the fear of crime, in that the fear is usually worse than the reality.

The reaction to me has been generally good. But I was at a

police function not all that long ago and this very senior officer came over to me and said to me that he didn't want people like me going up the ranks, which was a bit ironic since he'd just left his wife for another woman after twenty years. I thought it was a bit rich coming from him and very hurtful but he had had a few gin and tonics. It also made me wonder if I'd ever get promoted although in the meantime I have been, thank God. We'll have to wait and see exactly how far I get. So far my appraisals haven't deteriorated but if I should ever fail a board, I would like to think that it has nothing to do with my sexuality. But I'll never forget that incident and I doubt I'll forgive him for it, which is a shame because I used to respect him immensely until that day. I found it very disturbing. The hypocrisy of it pissed me off, but you see, if you're heterosexual you can get away with having vices. It doesn't matter what he does, I'll always be seen as lower than him, just because I prefer to sleep with women. It doesn't matter how good I am at my job, I'm always second best.

I was at a party the other week and I remember having a conversation with three other gay women who were also in professional occupations. One was a barrister, one was a senior army officer, and one was a public school teacher. The only one who was out was myself. The barrister felt that because she was in such a male-dominated, public-schoolboy-type occupation there was no way she could come out. The army officer knew she would be dismissed 'services no longer required', and the teacher was in an all-girls public school and felt that if the parents or board of governors found out that she was gay, there would be uproar and she would lose her job. So out of all those professions, I was the only one who was out, which is a credit to the police in a way. If you look at other professions, there is often more pressure put on women in management positions than there is in the police, so I guess it could be worse, although that's no excuse for not improving our lot.

● *Thames Valley PC, age 23, three years' service*

Two other policemen know I'm gay. I told one friend while he was driving me to a job in a police car. He was so shocked he nearly crashed the vehicle. Anyway once he had calmed down he was very sympathetic and now I understand both his initial reaction and his support, as two weeks later he invited me round to his house, where he introduced me to his boyfriend with whom he has been living for a number of years! He has managed to keep it a secret from work all this time – quite an achievement I thought.

The second policeman that knows about me found out after a group of us had been out on the town one evening. I stayed the night at his place to avoid driving and we ended up having sex and have done so on a number of occasions since. He has a girlfriend, but she doesn't know about us.

● *Metropolitan WPC, age 29,*
seven years' service

I was taking part in the Gay Pride march a couple of years ago when I saw this WPC I knew from my station. She was on duty lining the route, so I went over for a chat and playfully put my arm around her and she put her arm around me, and we gave each other a hug. She didn't know that I was gay until then and so we had a chat and a laugh about it and then I caught up with my friends. When I got back to work I left a note in her tray saying that I hoped I hadn't embarrassed her or anything. She said, 'No problem.' Later that day she told me that the Sergeant on her serial had asked her who I was and that there might be a problem after all. Apparently, this Sergeant had gone upstairs and told the Superintendent what had happened. Another Sergeant on my relief managed to find out what was going on for me, and told me that I would just be getting 'words of advice' – told that I was out of order and basically given a bollocking – but apart from that, everything would be OK. But when the Chief Superintendent came back from where ever he'd been, he called me up to his office, gave me his 'words of advice' and then threw me off the Crime Squad.

When I went in the next day for normal duty, everyone had already heard that I was coming back on relief. I knew they would all start asking questions, so I thought I might as well come out with it and get it over with. I didn't want all those unsubstantiated and exaggerated rumours flying around the station so I thought I might as well lie in the bed that I'd made for myself. But if that was going to be the case, then I was at least going to have my say. So when everyone was on parade I said, 'Before we start, you've no doubt heard what's happened with me and I want you to know that it's all true. That's me. If you don't like it then I'd rather you spoke to me about it – said it to my face. You've known me a while, I've worked with you long enough and I haven't changed overnight; I'm the same Rachael I've always been and I hope there won't be a problem.'

Afterwards people said that they didn't mind. Some of them had guessed anyway and they congratulated me on what I did. Everyone was really good about it. A week later, this Chief Superintendent said that he thought I'd learned my lesson and that I could go back on the Crime Squad. I guess he'd had a chance to calm down by then. I said I didn't want to because I was happy where I was, and in any case, the relief had been so good to me. Besides, I really didn't want to be bounced all around the station. He also told me that it wouldn't cause any problems as far as courses and promotion were concerned, and so far it hasn't.

Although I was really pissed off at the time, in a way I'm glad it happened, because it seems to have worked out for the better. I'm much happier now and I can be myself. When we're talking about what we've done at the weekend, I can honestly say where I've been and we can talk about it. It's great. And when you're alone with them, they're actually dead interested. Everyone at work knows now but my family don't and I think that's sad. I've never had to lie to them before but when you go home at Christmas and everyone asks you if you've got a man yet, then it can be really hard. Why should I have to lie? I meant to tell them last Christmas but the right time never came.

● *Metropolitan PC, age 25, five years' service*

Pretty much everybody knows about me at work these days. A friend caught me in bed with another PC at the section house a few years ago and I think that's what started it all off, but I was starting to tell people around that time anyway. But as you can *imagine, it didn't take long to get around once a few people knew. If anyone asked me outright, I would just say, 'Yeah, so what? It's boring. What did you do with your woman last night?' I found that that kind of attitude helped, because I didn't try to hide it.*

I think it's important to get known and respected for being you before anyone finds out. I want people to know and respect me for being me before they know I'm gay. I want to be known because I'm a good copper, not because I'm gay. I think you have to make your name first by nicking robbers and burglars before you come out, so that you're not labelled and stereotyped as a poof. The more they know about you as a person, the less they feel the need to stereotype you. With me, people are generally blasé about it now because everybody knows anyway. It's not hot news any more so they don't really talk about it. I also think that it's because I'm a good policeman and I love the Job that I don't get any flack. But on the other reliefs they don't know me so well, so they're more inclined to gossip.

A lot of people want to know all about my love life. I think the people at my nick have got a good attitude towards homosexuality because they know me and they've learned a lot from me. Most of the reactions I've had are good; in fact the only bad reaction I've ever had was from my mum.

I believe that gay people in the Job should lose their fear of coming out. Let's face it, there are far more gays in the Job than bigots. Nobody likes a bigot and they'd soon get sorted out by the others on the relief.

● *Metropolitan PC, age 31,*
resigned with seven years' service

I had a police colleague lodger at my house and although I didn't initially suspect him of being gay, there was one week when I took a lot of strange messages for him from a guy whilst he was out, and obviously, being gay, I began to wonder. Later in the week I asked him if he was gay and he told me to fuck off. Two nights later, I got in late and there was a note out to wake him up when I got in. So I went upstairs and woke him up to see what the problem was. He told me that he had lied before and that he was actually gay and he cried a bit. I said don't worry about it but I still didn't tell him about me, just in case he was testing me out. That's how screwed up I was about it at the time. I'd known him for years and I never had any idea that he might be gay – I'd never even heard any rumours – and we'd been on the same relief for years so I wasn't sure whether or not I could trust him. We talked about the whole thing over the next week and then, when I was satisfied that he wasn't winding me up, I told him about me whilst we were watching TV one night. He nearly fell off his chair.

After that, we plucked up the courage to go out to a gay pub together. Neither of us had been to one before and so we went to the Brief Encounter near Trafalgar Square. Once we'd got there, we took twenty minutes to actually go in, because he was supposed to go in first and he wouldn't. Eventually we did it together. We stayed in there for a while and then we went to Heaven. I couldn't believe it when we got there. It was a Saturday night and it was absolutely heaving. I never knew there were so many gays in London. I just didn't realize. I was totally gobsmacked.

● *Metropolitan PC, age 32, four years' service*

For me, coming out at work is almost routine – but not quite. I assume most people know by now. Everybody knew when I was at the section house because of an incident which happened there. Then one day in the station yard, the area car driver said I should just come out with it to stop the rumours that were flying around. I said that I wasn't against the idea but I could hardly walk into the canteen and announce it, so he offered to do it for me. So in he went and told all, and shortly after that officers came out into the yard to shake my hand and say well done for being honest. I remember one of the little hard guys on the relief came out and said, 'I just want you to know that I think you did a really brave thing and I think it's really good.'

It was all quite easy really because this guy did the hard work for me. I'm glad now because there had been a lot of rumours, and stuff had gone on the toilet wall. Now that doesn't happen so much. Nothing's really said these days as far as I can tell.

Some people think that I should lie low because although they can accept it, they think others won't be able to. And yet that's what everybody thinks. They think that they're liberal-minded but they don't think that others will be. But more often than not, that's to do with their own hang-ups. What they really mean is, 'I can't handle it.' And yet I've had no problems so far. One guy at the nick actually breaks out in a sweat when we talk about it. You can draw your own conclusions about him. I think that some of these people actually identify an element of homosexuality in themselves which they can't accept. That's why some of them take it out on you. One guy in particular that used to badmouth me and say that gays shouldn't be in the Job (although never to my face) ended up seducing me, which suggests that the main reason he'd acted the way he did was to put up a smokescreen, which wasn't really necessary because nobody suspected him anyway, although he was a public schoolboy, so I suppose he should have been a prime candidate. But after it happened he couldn't speak to me and he avoided me until he left the station.

When I've come out as a police officer to people at gay pubs and things, the reaction has been unfailingly positive. They think of us as their own police officers and they're very protective because they feel for us.

● *Kent Chief Inspector, age 40, twenty years' service*

I first came out to a WPC at a Christmas social; I just came right out and told her. She was quite surprised – said she didn't have any idea – but she was really supportive and it seemed like she was proud of me in some way. I don't know why she should be but she was. I've come out to most of my friends outside the Job as well and they were great. I guess I knew they would be, that's why I chose to tell them. Most of them were just intrigued and asked lots of questions. If you ask me, that's the normal reaction, because people are fascinated by it. But in the police, the need to appear repulsed often prevents that from happening, but they go away every bit as intrigued I'm sure.

115: Coming Out

When I'm out at gay pubs and clubs I try to come out as a police officer to gay people because they all think that we're all bastards and we're not. That's why I tell gays that I'm an officer, so they can see that we're not all bad.

● *Metropolitan Sergeant, age 41, twenty-one years' service*

When I split up with a bloke that I had been living with for seven years, I suddenly found that I couldn't cope, I really couldn't. So I went and told my duty officer. I had to tell someone because I needed time off work. He said, 'Fine' and I took a couple of days off. When I came back he said that he'd been thinking about what I'd told him, and had been advised to tell the Chief Superintendent. I couldn't believe it. So at nine o'clock the next day I found myself up in the Chief Superintendent's office. After that I knew it wouldn't take long for it to get around because there's no such thing as confidentiality in this job, so I thought I might as well get in there and start spreading the gospel myself before Rumour Control took over. So I told a few people and they did the rest. It didn't take long.

I actually feel far happier now everyone knows. You put so much energy into hiding because you don't want people to find out, and then once it happens, you find it's not so bad and you never have to worry about hiding again. It's a real weight off your mind. And so long as you're a worker, a lot of people actually respect you for it. If I were to join again, I'd come out a lot sooner. Provided I didn't want promotion of course. Promotion is so tight these days that any blemish is a reason not to promote, and unfortunately, being gay is a blot on your copybook. You might cause the Job a bit of embarrassment and that's the last thing they want.

People that know me never take the piss out of me. They wouldn't dare ... I'm about as far away from the gay stereotype as you can get. Unfortunately, other people on the area, who aren't on my relief but who have heard about me, tend to be more prejudiced. A couple of days ago the charge room was empty and I put a message over the radio that we had space for drunks and robbers and what have you, and a voice that I didn't know came back, 'What about homosexuals, Sarge?' It wasn't someone from my station because I'd have recognized the voice and besides, they wouldn't think that kind of thing was funny or clever. It was someone on the area who had heard about me – probably a bunch of PCs on the area carrier who had plucked up enough courage between them to make a clever comment, so I just put on my campest voice and said, 'Oh yes please!' and that was that.

If more police officers would come out, then the rest of the Job would realize that we're not all off-duty hairdressers. More should come out. That's the way forward. If we would all stop hiding then they would see that we're not weirdos.

● *Derbyshire DS, age 34, twelve years' service*

I got invited to a gay friend's party and as I walked through the door I saw this individual I knew from work and thought, 'Oh God!' He obviously thought the same thing because once I'd got over the shock and went and talked to him, he said that he'd come with a friend and didn't know that it was a gay party until he arrived. I couldn't be bothered to lie so I said that I knew it was gay and tried to play the liberal without giving too much away. Eventually, after we'd had a few drinks out of the punchbowl in the kitchen, he succumbed to old mother alcohol and admitted it. After that we didn't stop talking the whole night.

Another time, I was giving this PC on my shift a lift home after work and I stopped at a petrol station to fill up. Whilst I was paying for it, I suddenly realized that I'd left a copy of the Pink Paper *on one of the seats of the car. Under the lights of the fore-court, this guy had seen it and by the time I got back to the car he'd picked it up and was reading it. I just went crimson and as I got back into the car my heart was beating nineteen to the dozen as I tried to think of a way out. He said, 'Do you take this then?' I said, 'No, it's a freesheet and I just picked it up' and left it like that. Then he said, 'Only I've not got this one.' I said, 'You what?' He said, 'I haven't seen this one yet.' 'Do you get it then?' I said, and he just replied yes. I said, 'Shit, you had me scared stiff!'*

● *Humberside WPS, age 34,*
twelve years' service

When you meet someone who you think is the best thing since sliced bread then you want to tell everyone about it and you can't. Only if I were in a full-time relationship that I could be proud of would I be totally open. Then I wouldn't care what anyone thought anyway. I think I might refuse to continue with the pretence and so the Job might have to lump it.

● *Metropolitan Chief Inspector, age 38,*
fifteen years' service

People ask me why I tell them that I'm gay. They tell me that they don't go around telling people that they're straight. Well, there are lots of reasons: they don't need to tell anyone. It's assumed. And once I've told them that it's not that way with me, I don't have to pretend any more. And I don't see why I should have to pretend. It's that simple. Being gay is such a very important part of my life that I want people to understand it, and I want them to understand what it means. If I had the choice tomorrow to be straight or gay, I would be gay – every time. I never used to feel that way, but I feel that way now. Because of my sexuality I've become a deeper person, more caring, a more profound thinker, less subjective, and I wouldn't want to lose those qualities. I wouldn't want to be heterosexual any more. I don't go mad about it though because of my family. They know about me but they don't really understand, so I try not to embarrass them.

The experiences related in the chapters thus far help to elucidate a number of issues surrounding the question of disclosure of sexual orientation, and provide an effective answer to the question or charge concerning the reasons behind homosexuals 'constantly advertising' their sexuality.

Although sexuality is a private matter, as so often argued by those who do not wish to see or hear about alternative sexualities, it is clear that many people find the implicit assumption of their heterosexuality in every aspect of their lives – in their anticipated marriage, in magazines, records, radio and television, in applying for a mortgage, in advertising, and so on ad nauseam – is a major feature of the frustration they face. Coming out can kill off much of that oppression by actively changing assumptions and expectations. Such initiatives are not designed to force anything down anyone's throat.

The second theme has to do with meaningful partners. For those gays, lesbians or bisexuals in serious or long-term same-sex relationships, disclosure is seen as an important part of validating and giving strength to that relationship and there may be a strong temptation to put a stop to endless prevarication by coming out. For others, the stability, strength and security of a relationship may be a prerequisite for coming out, since once part of a team, the jibes of others become endurable.

Thirdly, coming out can be terrifying: it is an experience that can challenge and test to the limit in a process that is normally irrevocable. Yet at the same time it is seen to emancipate; it is both therapeutic and self-actualizing. Coming out pertains to the affirmation of identity, to the recognition of a 'real' self as opposed to what others imagine one to be or would have one be. It may be the only means of liberation from an intricate web of duplicity woven and sustained over many years. Coming out, then, symbolizes the intention to grow towards a more honest, self-fulfilling and less restrictive lifestyle. (See, for example, the anonymous piece beginning on page 137.)

Lastly, coming out challenges popular prejudices by demonstrating in the most dramatic way possible that the person concerned is very ordinary, and it is this course of action which would seem to lay the best path for effective and long-term change.

A further feature of coming out noted by many officers is that the fear attached to the experience would appear to exceed the degree to which that fear is warranted. Its analogy with the fear of crime has already been made and this parallel is tempting, yet there may be several reasons why the lack of conspicuous aggression towards officers might be misleading. Most obviously, what is said behind one's back will always go unobserved. More optimistically, it may be the case that when a person discovers that a friend or colleague that they have known for some time is not heterosexual, they find the fact easier to deal with because of their acquaintance and consequent first-hand experience of that person's lack of degeneracy. This is sometimes verbalized: 'I normally hate poofs/ dykes but you're OK.' Alternatively, it may be that potential candidates for the disclosure effort are so carefully selected as to reduce the risk of rejection or other hostile reaction to a negligible degree. In other cases, the ostensible lack of belligerence displayed towards them may simply be a corollary of the fact that the hypothetical homosexual is easier to discriminate against than is the homosexual face-to-face. Finally, there is the prospect of internal discipline as a deterrent measure for overt offensiveness.

The interview data indicate that officers are most likely to suffer prejudice and discrimination whilst their sexual orientation is strongly suspected yet unconfirmed, and in general, the act of disclosure would seem to put an end to the speculation and the rumour which can so easily run unchecked in the police canteen. Coming out, then, would seem to be an effective method of reducing the conflict between roles. However, one must take care not to oversimplify the problems of identity reconciliation with banal solutions. The success of coming out may be dependent on a number of factors. It has already been noted, for example, that coming out may prove a more effective tool for those individuals who are considered to be 'good coppers' or whose personalities could be described as 'charismatic' or 'dynamic', than those who are considered to be lazy 'uniform carriers' or whose personalities are more insipid. One officer suggests: 'I think you have to make your name first by nicking robbers and burglars before you come out.' Chief Inspector Robert Anthony of the Metropolitan Police describes the problem as the 'Good Copper Syndrome'. This refers to the tendency to accept and even respect individuals who may be in some way 'odd', so long as they are perceived to be effective police officers. But he notes the limits within which even the 'good copper' is restrained:

> Provided an officer passes the good copper test, he or she may be allowed to have one odd characteristic, such as being homosexual. Because homosexual officers have used up

their allowance by being homosexual, they must not have any other characteristic which may be seen as deviating from the cultural norm. I believe this may apply to an officer who has an unusual religious faith, has unusual dietary requirements or voices unusual political views ... An officer who fails to demonstrate that expertise must comply with cultural expectations in every respect.[3]

Whether the advantages of being open about one's sexuality outweigh the disadvantages is a matter for the individual. Yet it is not always a straightforward matter of choice. Coming out normally represents the climax of a self-acceptance process which may require a period of several years. Accordingly, those persons who have still to make their first 'confession' regarding their orientation are likely to be at a stage where they are still dissatisfied with their orientation and their status as 'deviant', or are having unsatisfactory personal relationships. Consequently, coming out may require a number of preconditions before it can be said to constitute a viable proposition. The freedom to mature in self-acceptance at one's own pace and then procrastinate on the matter of disclosure may be just one of those preconditions. There is seldom adequate justification to out someone against their will.

Notes

1.   J. H. Gagnon and W. S. Simon, *Sexual Conduct*, 1967, p. 181.
2.   See page 222 on discipline.
3.   R. Anthony, 'Homosexuality in the police', MA dissertation, University of Exeter, 1992, p. 182.

Chapter nine

Prejudice and Discrimination

I thought the mounted officers' reactions at
Hammersmith towards homosexuality were as bad as
I've ever seen. That's partly because they cover the
Earls Court area I suppose, which is very gay, and they
would come back after late turn, saying things like
'Fucking queers. We should put a bomb in the
Coleherne [pub]' and stuff like that. Also, whenever
they read about it in the paper I used to hear them
talking about what they would like to do to them –
how they should be shot or hung. I dread to think what
would have happened if they'd found out about me. I
know a sergeant who is openly gay, and a Chief
Inspector once said to me that if they had known about
him, he never would have got as far as he has. Needless
to say, he didn't know about me.

● *Metropolitan Mounted Branch PC, age 28, resigned
with nine years' service*

ALTHOUGH there is little research examining police attitudes towards homosexuality,[1] there are many studies that enquire
into the question of whether or not the police are racially prejudiced. The answer to this question according to one such study is:
'... yes, but only slightly more so than the community as a whole.

Policemen reflect the dominant attitudes of the majority of people towards minorities.'[2] It is the latter sentence which is of chief significance here, since it expresses a popular police justification when it comes to the rationalization of prejudice and this idea is represented in the writing that follows. However, despite similar levels of prejudice in wider society towards minority groups, police officials should take no comfort from the fact that they mirror society's prejudices in this way, since, whilst it may be reassuring to know that the police are not significantly more prejudiced towards minority groups than the rest of society, the degree of prejudice found in society is sufficiently high to cause concern that such levels are potentially being translated into performance on the streets. There is, however, little evidence to prove that attitudes are necessarily transposed into behaviour – indeed, the research by the Policy Studies Institute suggests that prejudiced attitudes frequently *do not* affect behaviour.[3] There may be several reasons for this. It may be that sanctions for those officers who are found to act in a prejudicial manner are severe enough to prevent the behaviour; equally, it may be a result of police professionalism denying prejudice its place, or, more plausibly I believe, it may be the case that much police 'prejudice' is simply another symptom of the machismo and bravado of police culture; derogatory sentiments that are espoused beyond the extent that they are believed in order to appear to be 'streetwise' and not 'soft', 'green' or 'wet behind the ears'. Nevertheless, it would be naive to suggest that in some cases, prejudice is not directly responsible for a less than satisfactory street performance on the part of some police officers.

With specific regard to homosexuality, it seems that in the United States at least, homosexuals are ranked amongst the most disliked categories of people by police on both coasts of the country.[4] The present author's research did little to repudiate those findings, with many gay police officers believing that the police were particularly prone to high levels of homophobia.[5] However, not all gay officers agreed; indeed, some believed they were more tolerant.

● *Metropolitan Inspector, age 37, sixteen years' service*

I actually think that the police are less prejudiced than the rest of society because they're used to dealing with all kinds of shit and so they are more tolerant. They might put on a lot of bravado, but underneath I think they're quite tolerant, understanding and worldly-wise. After all, the only crime of these people is being gay, whereas most of the nastiest crimes you ever see are committed by straight men on women. There's just no comparison to my mind.

● *Metropolitan PC, age 31, five years' service*

I don't think that the police are bothered about sexuality or colour. They do their job regardless. The thing I wish people would realize is that so long as the police force is recruited from the general population, it's bound to reflect all the prejudices (and sexual orientations) of that population, no matter what the training. You can't expect an unprejudiced police service from a prejudiced society.

● *Metropolitan WPC, age 22, one and a half years' service*

Once I went to this burglary with a PC and when we got there it was obvious that the flat which had been burgled was occupied by two gay men. Afterwards, this PC said he thought the two blokes were 'a bit ginger' but they were dealt with the same as we'd have dealt with anyone else. Exactly the same. Also, on Pride day, another PC that I was with saw these two women in a car – they were absolutely starkers – but he just went over and told them to put their clothes on. He could have dealt with it differently, I would say there's definitely a power of arrest for nakedness in public, but he didn't. So you see it's all about individuals.

● *Leicestershire WPC, age 32, fourteen years' service*

If you're not liked or good at your job then it's only human *nature that when someone slags you off they pick out the things that stand out, like your colour, because when you're having a go at someone it's normal to pick on anything that's different about them. That doesn't mean that they're really racist or homophobic, it's just a way of getting at someone. What people assume is an example of prejudice is frequently just the vocabulary that people commonly employ to run other people down. It doesn't necessarily reflect their views, or mean that they will discriminate against you. When you're at school for example, you get called a queer before the people that use it even know what it means. It's just a way of being nasty to someone. It's a term of abuse. There's this guy at work who is gay and he takes a bit of shit for it, but it's difficult to say whether or not it's because he's gay because his manner is aggressive and offhand and it's hard to know whether people are nasty to him because of his manner or because he's gay. I think he's a pain in the ass and a real rude bastard. When people slag him off they sometimes say 'That queer bastard' or whatever, but if he was Scottish they would say 'That Scots git' and if he was black then they'd probably bring that in as well. It just happens that that's the way they identify him.*

It would seem that where prejudice against homosexuals – both in the police and in society – does arise, it does so for a number of reasons. Two of these reasons are identified here.

Prejudice and Religion

Uneasiness with the idea of same-sex attraction is not an innate but a learned phenomenon and the ancestry of our education in this matter should not be forgotten. The Judaeo-Christian heritage of Britain and in particular fundamentalist forms of Christianity are largely responsible for the condemnation of homosexuality, and much of the misunderstanding witnessed today on all matters concerning sex and sexuality is the legacy of Christian teaching. *Police Review* (11 January 1991) published the following letter by Brian Morgan, an officer from the Humberside Constabulary, in response to one of the magazine's gay-positive editorials:

... one of the most important [responsibilities of ACPO members] is that they are expected to conduct their lives within the Christian ethic. If they cannot, or choose not to do so, they must be accountable for that failure.

Furthermore to state as you do that 'a police officer's sexuality has nothing to do with his or her colleagues, supervisors, juniors or employers' is so incredibly erroneous (and naive) as to beggar belief. After all why stop at lesbianism (and by reference homosexuality)? Shall we now extend acceptable deviations to police officers engaged in bestiality, or how about being chairperson of the local paedophile ring?

... may I remind you that engaging in homosexual acts is still a criminal offence and only fails to be so in certain specific circumstances; even then it remains offensive and contrary to Christian teachings and beliefs.

But perhaps times are changing. Morgan's letter resulted in a stream of protest. Amongst the published replies were a letter from Ian Westwood, Chair of the Greater Manchester Police Federation,[6] and another from Chief Inspector Roger Webb of West Mercia police.[7] Both of these officers noted Morgan's display of those 'well-known Christian virtues of intolerance, hypocrisy and double standards' as well as his summary dismissal of the values of his Jewish, Islamic, Hindu, Buddhist and atheist or agnostic colleagues. Finally, this letter from an anonymous officer of an unnamed force appeared in *Police Review* (1 February 1991):

I am a gay police officer. Within myself I am happy to make this statement, but reading the comments of Brian Morgan's letter reminds me how much prejudice does exist.

Does being gay make me a bad person? ... I've been called a lesbian, a whore and a queer bastard by individuals I have worked with. Comments such as these I find upsetting, but I now have a strong enough sense of self to distance myself from it all.

I am neither sick, perverted nor 'one of nature's mistakes'. I am the same as anyone else. Sadly and from experience, though, I advise other gay officers to stay in the closet, keeping the door ajar only for your close friends. The 'spoiled identity' which is part of being seen as different, tends to stick, and at a time when opportunities within the Job are scarce, you will be limiting your opportunities further by admitting to same-sex attraction.

There may be 'no discrimination' clauses in Job selection procedures but this is not in my experience, to say that one is not disadvantaged, however subtly, by being openly gay – not just in employment but in many areas of social life.

As a police force we serve the public and should be made up of a cross-section of it ... As a police officer I see myself as making a valuable contribution to society, and the contribution is not lessened by my being gay.

Prejudice and Stereotyping

Prejudice also arises from the employment of false stereotypes fuelled by gutter-press hype. It is important to state before tackling an emotive issue such as stereotyping, that in its most basic form, such classification is not simply concerned with the attribution of negative attitudes with respect to certain societal groups but is a way of breaking up a large and complex world into more easily manageable parts. It is, crudely speaking, a system of simple classification. By constantly analysing our surroundings and grouping similarities in our everyday situations and interactions together, given a particular set of circumstances or set of conditions, we are more able to predict the outcome than if we had never before encountered a similar situation. In this broad sense then, stereotyping is a tool that we all employ.

However, stereotyping is also a well-recognized phenomenon which works at a more specific level, and this has been of particular interest with regard to police work.[8] Like societal prejudice, police prejudice is something that is acquired both by teaching (direct or indirect) and by experience. Such stereotyping need not always be pernicious; indeed, cautious stereotyping by an experienced officer allows that officer to reasonably predict the behaviour of all kinds of people in a wide variety of circumstances, often with a remarkable degree of accuracy. This 'perceptual shorthand' allows the identification of what Skolnick refers to as 'symbolic assailants'[9] and on occasions, this may save the officer from serious injury.

Nevertheless, stereotyping is harmful to the extent that when it is applied to human beings, it does not readily allow for deviations from expected patterns. As a Lancashire Inspector has noted, it involves

> attributing to a category of individuals a group stereotype which does not take into account individual variations within the group. This reveals the negative aspect of stereotypes which contributes towards prejudice.[10]

The popular homosexual stereotype that the majority of the police readily accede to is the antithesis of the 'machismo' that is so strongly embraced within the force.

It may be a corollary of the limited exposure the police have of many minority groups, often in unfavourable circumstances, coupled with a lack of relevant training and affirmative experience that leads some police officers to be gratuitous in their stereotyping. Officers may never learn to recognize that such 'working rules' are no more than that, and many eventually come to believe that the stereotypes are accurate descriptions of the groups in question. In *Catching Criminals: Some More Basic Skills*, the Met's Superintendent J. R. Robinson actively encourages stereotyping, but he also offers a warning: 'By all means therefore "stereotype" people and put them into "categories", as long as you always appreciate the dangers.'[11] Unfortunately, the proviso is not always heeded and is by no means as simple to put into operation as Robinson suggests, once the insidious categorization process has begun.

Stereotyping and Homosexuality

The stereotype of the homosexual is well known, although where males are concerned, there is a choice of at least two: the effeminate, limp-wristed, mincing, ambisexual, handbag-carrying, weak and rather pathetic 'queen', or the butch, leather- or denim-clad, heavily moustached and closely cropped 'clone'. For many heterosexuals, such stereotypes are likely to have become synonymous with child molestation, drug abuse, hanging around public toilets, prostitution, and more recently, with Aids. In a similar fashion, lesbians are imagined to be large, aggressive women in dungarees, with short haircuts, who rarely wear bras and who hate men (and society in general).

Contrary to these popular and pervasive images, homosexuals, unlike coloured minority groups, are not commonly visible. However, those that do fit the playground stereotype can sometimes be spotted by the lay person, reinforcing the belief that all homosexuals fit the same mould. In reality, the above descriptions, like all stereotypes, are applicable to only a small proportion of homosexuals, whilst the straight-looking or acting majority remain *ipso facto* hidden from view. As Kinsey noted, 'Inversion and homosexuality are two distinct and not always correlated types of behaviour.'[12]

Unlike in their dealings with ethnic communities – where the police are constantly aware of that community's existence, even when they are not brought to police notice – gay men and lesbians may frequently only be recognized as such where they choose to be so recognized, or where their activities define them as such. For the most part, such circumstances are unlikely to be 'police friendly' and will include occasions where the police are arresting those caught committing acts of 'gross indecency', or policing events like the annual and rather flamboyant Gay Pride march. Accordingly, the police rarely have the opportunity to see the homosexual community in an ordinary light owing to the fact that unless they are 'causing trouble', they tend to go unrecognized.

For the police, like the rest of society, there is an inherent tendency to accept the common homosexual stereotypes because they see little in either their home or their work lives which challenges these stereotypes.

Perhaps the advent of the openly gay or lesbian police officer will change that. When an officer comes out at work, it allows other officers to see that the colleague that they have long respected and with whom they have enjoyed working is not deranged, and in this way the distortive stereotype is effectively challenged. In so doing, prejudice towards the lesbian and gay communities outside the station is also questioned. Most police officers are already sensitive to the problems of being indiscriminately tarred by the public with a dirty brush for the misdemeanours of a few, and are able to apply that principle to non-heterosexual populations once they have evidence that those lesbians and gay men they routinely deal with are not representative of the whole.

Discrimination

Unfortunately, however, practice does not always operate according to theory. In the vignettes that follow, the first three pieces reflect one of the most common forms that discrimination can take at rank-and-file level: that of the refusal to accept a beat or vehicle posting with a gay or lesbian colleague. The following are typical of the reports involving the opposition of such postings each year.

● *Metropolitan PC, age 24, four years' service*

One day I came on parade and was posted operator on the RT car by the section Sergeant. When the driver heard I was posted with him, he refused in front of everyone to work with me. There were about twenty other people right there in the parade room waiting to be given their postings for the day. I just looked down at the floor and thought, 'Oh God, here we go.' I knew that a lot of people knew about me by then and it was obvious that this driver had also heard. But then, whilst I was trying to get myself out of the stupor I was in, the Sergeant, much to my surprise, said: 'I've done the postings for this month and that's the way they're staying. If you have a problem with that, then you can walk and I'll find another driver.' At that point I said that it was OK and that I would come off the car if it was going to cause problems. The skipper refused to take me off, saying that the area car was a prestige posting and that he would rather find another driver than take me off just because this guy didn't like me. So then the driver said that if the Sergeant did that he would go to see the Federation rep and complain about being removed from his proper posting. But the skipper just said, 'I'm not taking you off anything – you're doing it yourself. If you refuse to work with this officer then I'll find a replacement for you. I'm not replacing this officer.' Then a few of the others asked him what his problem was, and told him to shut his big mouth. Some of the women asked him if he had something to hide, at which point he backed down, but they found me another driver anyway.

The whole thing was very humiliating. If that had happened to me a few months earlier when I was feeling really insecure about myself, I don't think that I would have been able to handle that kind of pressure in front of so many people. Being accepted was so important to me then. But if it happened to me again now, I'd just laugh and tell him to go boil his head.

● *Metropolitan PC, age 22, three years' service*

When I finally got my monthly posting on the area car, the driver said he wasn't having me. The reason he gave was that I was unreliable as a police officer. Everybody knew that was trash, it was because I was gay – and open about it – but because he was the only RT driver available, I got taken off. The guv'nor said to me after that had there been another driver on the relief then I would have stayed on and he would have come off but there wasn't anyone else, so I had to walk. He put me back on the car the following month and everybody told me not to worry about it – that it was just typical of this driver and that he was a dickhead. The sad thing was that he was also the station's Federation rep and it was his job to protect you in exactly those kind of instances, so I don't know if he thought I had Aids or what.

Aids

Although the refusal to suffer a gay officer as 'operator' is not new, the justification has been bolstered in recent times by reference to the Aids pandemic. In the next couple of pieces, the importance of Aids as a new and persuasive tool for discrimination is considered.

● *West Midlands PC, age 31,*
resigned with nine years' service

One guy got transferred to our station after a supposed affair at his last station. Of course Rumour Control had things organized long before he arrived, so the poor bloke didn't stand a chance. They probably called it a clean start for him – I had one of those – but actually it's normally the beginning of the end. Anybody with a bit of service will tell you that. He was a decent bloke in fact, early twenties, but he ate shit right from the start. People used to talk about him behind his back in the canteen all the time. The whole thing used to make me sick because I couldn't do or say anything very much without blowing my own cover. I'd have liked to have spoken to him on the quiet about it, just to tell him that at least I was on his side, but I never got around to bringing the subject up. I didn't want to embarrass him by bringing up something that must have caused him so much grief over the past months and that he was probably trying to forget. Anyway, some of the blokes refused to go walking with him on night duty, and when it came to his posting on the area car, the driver refused to take him out on the grounds that if they were to become involved in a messy RTA he might get some of this bloke's blood on him and catch Aids. Pathetic. The whole affair made me pretty sick. I think a lot of people thought this driver was being a prick, but in those days nobody bothered to argue with the area car driver. He was God. So what the hell do you do?

● *Metropolitan PC, age 41,*
thirteen years' service

It's easy to see how anti-police sentiment is spread through the gay community. One of the latest worrying developments in the police is the practice of wearing surgical gloves when attending incidents where those involved are known or discovered to be gay.

While this is standard practice when dealing with anyone who is bleeding, it isn't policy to wear gloves for other reasons. The Aids rationale is just an excuse. Most PCs now know how Aids is transmitted and that the risk to them is minute during the course of their duties. I can't help but feel that it is only done as a deliberate insult to the people concerned. So what do the supervisors and senior officers do about these breaches of policy? Not a lot is the answer. They are also part of the Job's institutionalized canteen culture. And in my opinion, it is this same weak and ineffectual management that is the root cause of most of the police's problems.

● *Essex PC, age 23, four years' service*

Everyone is still up in arms about Aids – they just don't listen to Aids education in relation to their work. We've had these new resuscitators for about a year now, where you put this plastic stuff over their faces and this short tube in their mouth to blow through. It all makes them a bit paranoid you know. If I had the choice of resuscitation on a body that was HIV positive or even had full-blown Aids, or on a dirty smelly vagrant crawling with lice, I'd take the HIV one any day, but I doubt if any of the others would – and that's the difference.

Notwithstanding the latter observations, I would suggest that in the main, officers are able to contain the personal feelings they may have about matters they personally find distasteful and deal with the public in a reasonably professional manner, saving their comments and observations for their colleagues and the canteen. However, an officer's 'impartiality remit' is often perceived as ending at the station door, and this might partially explain why the same 'civility, forbearance and good temper' normally afforded to the public are not always extended to colleagues.

● *Metropolitan PS, age 39,*
twenty-one years' service

Over the years I've had a bit of abuse; most of it rather half-hearted I suppose, but nevertheless hurtful. I think the first time was when I opened my locker at the station one day to find that somebody had slipped the lock and left a jar of men's sex cream in the locker. There was a rather explicit note attached which referred to anal sex.

Several years later at a different police station, I was posted on night duty to the control room for a tour of duty. The room had three computer terminals linked to the police communications CAD system. All of the terminals could be logged off, bar one, as a safeguard; that way the control room was staffed at all times. This particular night, I was in the control room alone when I had to go to the toilet and could not log off my computer because it was the last one. I radioed to my colleagues on the streets that the control room would be empty for a few minutes while I disappeared. When I got back I continued my duties as normal and about an hour later I had to dispatch a message. The computer was logged on in my name and I had pre-programmed a number of the function keys for the evening's use. I pressed one of the pre-programmed keys to call up a message format. As I looked at the screen, instead of the correct format appearing, the word 'Gaylord' stared at me in the top of the screen. I pressed another key and the words 'Leave the little boys alone' appeared on the screen. Several of the programmable function keys had in fact been tampered with and it could only have happened when I left the control room to go to the toilet.

In a way, I was lucky that I had discovered the change without there being someone else there to see me find out. I was also lucky that the keys they had changed had not been ones I had programmed to acknowledge messages from New Scotland Yard as in that case, they and many other stations around the Met would also have seen the comments.

I found this incident the most distressing of my entire service. It showed me that some of my colleagues were juvenile in behaviour, insensitive to the effect their actions were likely to have on me, ignorant of what it is like to be gay and, perhaps, even afraid of me. The most upsetting feature of this incident was that I felt that I could no longer trust my colleagues or anyone else at the station. I had not come out to my relief and knew then that it would be unwise to do so. These were people whom I both worked and socialized with and upon whom my life might depend, and vice versa. I still cannot comprehend how they could be so cruel and insensitive.

● Greater Manchester PC, age 27, eight years' service

Whilst I was a PC at training school I was quite good friends with this guy in my class and then after training school we ended up getting put in the same section house together. Neither of us really wanted to stay in the section house but neither of us could afford a place of our own, so since we got on really well, we decided to buy a place together. I'd already told him that I was gay and he didn't seem too bothered about it. In retrospect, I don't know if he really believed me because once we'd moved in together he started to take exception to it. He started by telling a few people at work that I was queer and it all escalated from there really. Within a few months everyone had heard the rumour that I was gay. For a while I denied it because it was really causing me problems. It was at a time in my career when being a police officer was much more important to me than being gay, and so I'd pushed my sexuality into the background.

Anyway, one night I brought someone back to the house. It was quite innocent – we weren't going to sleep together or anything because by then I was aware of my flatmate's feelings and I didn't want to upset him. So I showed this guy into my bedroom and I was walking back out of the room with some bedding for the spare room when I was attacked. I didn't know who it was – I thought we had burglars – but once I got the lights on I saw it was my flatmate. I was so shocked I didn't know what to do. I mean I thought I was fighting for my life at the time, it was really vicious. Even once the lights were on he carried on and managed to injure me enough for me to be off work for the next two weeks.

He beat me up because he couldn't handle the fact that I was gay. He's never even apologized. I think maybe it was because everyone knew that I was gay at work and he felt that people were starting to talk about him – he was getting tarred with the same brush and resented me for it. My answer to that is that it's his own fault. *If he hadn't gone telling everybody in the first place then they wouldn't know. There was never any need for him to tell everyone. The other ironic thing is that he's black. I mean he really ought to know better than to act like that. After all, he ought to know what it's like to be treated like shit for no good reason. Another outrageous thing is that he has more sexual partners than me anyway – I mean he's no celibate puritan, and that really pisses me off. I thought it was us gays that were supposed to be promiscuous.*

After it happened, I went to stay with an ex-girlfriend for a while but I realized that because of my injuries, I would have to tell someone senior at work what had happened – that I was gay and that this was an ongoing situation. So I phoned up this senior officer that I thought I could trust and he came round straight away, saw me, and arranged for me to have two weeks' time off with no questions asked. Then to my surprise he proceeded to tell me that he was gay himself. It was a lot to handle in one night. He was married and I had absolutely no idea that he was gay. I had just picked the only person that I could think of at the time who I thought I could confide in.

When I got back to work, although not much was said, most people already seemed to know what had happened because my flatmate had apparently gone in the next day and bragged about what he'd done to me. A lot of people came up to me after that and said that they thought whatever my sexuality was I didn't have to put up with that and that I should do something about it. But I didn't have the courage at the time. It all happened at a time when although a lot of people had guessed or had been told that I was gay, I didn't really want it publicized.

It was only several months later that I decided I really didn't have to take that kind of shit from anyone and decided to tell a more senior officer. I explained what had happened and although I no longer had the injuries, I was able to provide him with a couple of witnesses, including the bloke who had come back with me that night. I said I wanted something done about it and that if nothing was done then I would take him to court over the property so that I could get out. I wasn't going to bother about the assault, all I wanted was to get out of the house – to force him either to sell his half to me, or for him to buy me out – I didn't care which. I just wanted to get out of the situation I was in. I mean it wasn't as if it was the first time he'd hit me. On another occasion when he was drunk he punched me in the face. But he wasn't interested in either of the two propositions.

This senior officer said that taking him to court over the property would involve bringing out in the open the incident where he'd attacked me. He said that if I took it to court and then all that came out, I could kiss my career and specialization prospects good-bye and spend the rest of my time doing foot duty. Apart from that he was very supportive. He was just worried about the 'Black PC Assaults Queer Colleague in Flat Share Rumpus' type of headline, which I have to say I sympathize with to a degree.

In the end the Chief Inspector had words with this PC which helped quite a bit. There's been no recurrence since, and I don't think that there will be. I would have him arrested and charged if he ever tried that again. Unfortunately, I'm still living with him now because we haven't been able to sell the place, although we've been trying for three years now. I just try to spend as little time there as possible and I spend most of the time at friends'. There's no other way out for me. We're just polite with each other these days and I don't bring anyone back to the house for any reason, because he just can't handle it.

Institutional Prejudice

The negative experiences of many officers reflect the prejudice of particular individuals and as such, discrimination is often overt. In the case of institutional prejudice, however, discrimination may be more subtle.

● *Metropolitan PS, age 30, ten years' service*

It's difficult to know if you've been discriminated against because they're not so stupid as to tell you why they're doing what they're doing, but I got moved from my last post recently and got posted to a station that I specifically said I didn't want to go to. I can't prove why they did it, although it got back to me later that one of those involved in the transfer had said, 'We're sending all the people like that to [my station].' I also had comments get back to me afterwards that when I found out what had been said, they were worried I would make a big fuss about it.

The next three pieces deal with incidents that are more conspicuous (although nevertheless anonymous). The chief identifying features of the institutional assault are that it tends to be: (a) unidentified, (b) multi-directional and (c) unremitting, in the hope that an officer will buckle under the pressure and tender his or her resignation. The anonymity which often characterizes the attack can magnify the sense of victimization whilst at the same time rendering defence impossible. This unpleasant means of procuring an officer's resignation will be considered in more detail in Chapter 10.

● *(Details withheld), age 37,*
seventeen years' service

The most difficult decision I've ever had to make as a police officer was not out on the streets but was one that affected my personal life. Trying to be a good cop and keeping your nose clean is hard enough, but when you're gay it's doubly difficult. I've lived almost every day of my seventeen years in the Job terrified somebody would find out I was gay, or that some spiteful individual would write in anonymously to my nick suggesting I was gay. To combat such an eventuality, I had devised in my head numerous plans to head off any would-be attacks on my sexual orientation by colleagues. It wasn't because I was ashamed to be gay, quite the contrary, it's just that I felt that the Job wouldn't understand or be prepared for people like me. The most terrifying thought for me was what my senior officers could do to me if they found out. Any policeman will understand me, when I say that when the chips are down the brass hats are very adept at character assassination, even though you've probably done nothing wrong. If you don't fit in, you're out.

So I conformed to the nth degree. I acted exactly as I thought they wanted me to be – your typical chauvinist male – and although I would never deliberately decry my own sexuality, occasionally I would laugh at the jokes. It's difficult not to be party to them sometimes, although often I was laughing at them because it was so clear that they knew nothing about what they were saying. My nightmare was that one day I would go into work and somebody would come up to me and say, 'Oi, are you gay? Because so and so reckons he saw you going into a queer club the other night and we want to know.' I knew that one day that would occur. So I used to keep such a low profile that at work, most of them thought I was a buddhist monk. I didn't want to give them any cause for suspicion at all. I was trying to keep the two worlds apart but it was beginning to get around that there was something odd about me: people wanted to know why I hadn't got a ticket to the genito-urinary clinic like every one else had. The other thing was that I used to dress strangely. If you don't dress in a dull, unimaginative and thoroughly conservative fashion, people immediately decry you as a poof. If your haircut is not a poorly cut short back and sides, people decry you as a poof. If you fail to conform in any way, you'll be decried as a poof and pulled down for it. I used to wear what I wanted – the same as every other normal person out there, be it colourful teeshirts, ripped jeans and bumper boots or whatever. Especially since I worked in plain clothes every day. But if you spend time on your appearance, or wear trendy jeans or (heaven forbid) aftershave, or spend more than ten pounds a year on clothes, it's 'What the fuck do you look like – you fucking queer!' and you never hear the end of it. Even if you wear plain clothes, you have to conform to a conservative dress code, which is why you can spot police officers even in plain clothes. Plain shirt, Marks & Spencer jacket, cheap ill-fitting jeans and plain black or brown shoes. The police are conservatism personified. The funny thing is they think it's everyone else who is strange. They're so wrapped up in their little world, and it was that little world that was pissing me off something chronic. It really was. It was getting to me day by day by day. I was being worn down by their total narrow-mindedness. I just couldn't be let to be me. I had to conform all the time and for me, to conform was to lie.

The Job likes nothing better than a juicy bit of scandal and a queer in the Job was just about as scandalous as you could get. I became aware of the sniggers in the canteen and the whispers behind hands. I tried to ignore them believing that it would probably be a five-day wonder, eventually blowing over. My hopes were soon dashed though, as tales began to be spread about me, all of which were totally untrue. I think I know who was responsible now. I thought it was just one person at first but it now seems there were a few in on it. I got really worried though about two weeks after the start of the rumours when I was approached by a close colleague of mine who was concerned enough to take me to one side and explain how he'd heard I'd been found in bed with a Superintendent of all people. I just said, 'Oh my God, you don't believe that, do you?' He said that he didn't believe it, which made me feel a bit better, but by then my guts were really churning over. I went into a blind panic after that and ended up getting married to a woman friend, who knew I was gay, just to stop the finger pointing. I really needed the security. Of course I knew I wasn't being true to myself and as time went on I felt an increasing need to be open. Once I'd heard about the Lesbian and Gay Police Association and realized that there were lots more like me, I decided to come out. I was already quite well respected as the longest serving vice-squad officer in the country but I wanted to be respected for what I was and not on the basis that I was heterosexual. Living a double life may seem exciting to those who have never done it, but after years of it you become weary and that leads to terrible tension both in and out of the Job, and it affects your personal relationships. In fact, it poisons everyone and everything if you don't bring it under control.

The time had come for me to be true to myself if not to the Job. In any case, it seemed that the Job was becoming more and more receptive. After talking with my wife, I decided to take the bull by the horns and speak to the Force Welfare Officer. She was just like I expected: she listened well, didn't jump to conclusions but suggested that I keep quiet about my homosexuality, not because it wouldn't be understood by the senior officers, but because of the canteen culture – the snipes and offensive remarks I could expect from so-called colleagues. My Federation representative accepted this line of reasoning, advising me that in my own interests I should keep quiet. Having spoken at length with these two people I decided to remain in the closet, although by this time I desperately wanted to come out.

Two days after my meeting with the Welfare Officer and the Federation I received a phone call at my station. The call was from a Chief Inspector at Force Headquarters. He summoned me before the Police Surgeon at 9.30 a.m. the next day. When I asked why I had to see the Surgeon I was told bluntly to just do as I was told.

The next day, I appeared before the Force Surgeon. I'd not eaten anything since getting the phone call from the senior officer the day before because I couldn't stop worrying about why I had to see the doctor. I walked into his office, and saw the doctor sat behind his desk. He was a balding example of a man aged between fifty and fifty-five years. He walked over towards me and sat on the edge of his desk. He stared at me momentarily, looking at me in a puzzled sort of way. Then he said to me, 'So you're suffering from stress then.' I couldn't believe what I was hearing. 'Stress?' I said, 'No, sir, I feel fine.' 'That's not what it says here, officer. It states you're under lots of stress.' I couldn't even begin to imagine who would write such a thing about me. I had good reports dating back from the day I first joined the Job. 'Excuse me, sir,' I said, 'but who's written that report about me?' The Surgeon replied, 'Sorry, can't tell you that.' I was stunned. It seemed that my job was being torn away from me and I couldn't do anything about it. 'Look at it this way, officer,' he continued. 'Seventeen years' service plus seven tagged on for pension, you'd probably get £30,000 plus £700 a month.'

I stood up and insisted on having the Welfare Officer present, plus the Federation representative. I stormed out of his office and phoned them on the secretary's phone. I could hardly speak I was so upset. About ten minutes later all three of us were sitting in the Divisional Surgeon's office. Again, he repeated that I was stressed up and suggested that I be relieved of my duties on medical grounds. My two representatives also questioned the validity of the report and queried its author, but despite our attempts the report was kept face down on his desk. Eventually when threatened by the Federation representative with legal action if he didn't reveal the author of the report which alleged I'd gone mad, the doctor turned over the page, but didn't say anything. The author, it seemed, was my Detective Superintendent, whose report, based entirely upon rumour, stated that I was a queer who wasn't to be allowed to remain in the Job, and that the reason I had turned queer was because I was stressed up. He suggested I be let go on medical grounds.

I couldn't believe what I was reading. The sheer bloody cheek of it! Never a hint or anything. I'd never been to see the Detective Superintendent for anything, let alone this. I hardly knew the man. It felt as though my world was suddenly falling apart at the seams. I couldn't take it all in — I was totally devastated. Eventually we all left the Surgeon's office, leaving him in no doubt that I wasn't mentally ill.

I wanted to take it further. I needed to see the Chief Constable. My whole career depended upon what he thought about the matter. I went to see the Chief the next day again in the presence of the Welfare Officer and the Federation representative. I decided to come clean: I decided to explain to him that I was gay and that I wasn't mentally ill, as had been suggested. I also told him that I'd joined the support group for gay police officers [LAGPA]. To be honest, I expected to be blown out of the office with the wrath of Cain but my fears turned out to be unfounded. He sat in his chair and listened to everything put before him. He then stated he accepted everything I had said without reservation. He also surprised me by knowing quite a lot about the new gay police group. He said that he would investigate the false allegation of stress and speak with the Surgeon regarding the matter, about which he seemed genuinely concerned. We acknowledged, however, that neither of us would be able to stop the 'Serious Rumour Squad' from operating, and so we arranged that my sexual orientation would be announced in Police Orders, the force bulletin, which is very unusual but at least then everyone would know and that would be that. I also came off the Vice Squad to prevent any possible embarrassment to the Job.

Overall, I believe the whole experience was probably less traumatic than other colleagues in other forces have been subjected to. I'm pleased to be out and free of the double-life syndrome which followed me to and from work every day of my life. Those true friends I have in the Job, which probably number ten to fifteen, *haven't been affected at all by my admitting that I'm gay. If any-thing I think they quite like the idea of my being different. It doesn't stop them acting the same with me and on the odd occasion they've even tried to set me up with some chap, jokingly of course, but it helps them and me to come to terms with everything. Yes, I can definitely say I'm proud to be a cop. But more than that, I'm proud to be gay. It's a pity it couldn't have been this way seventeen years ago. Still a little progress is better than none.*

● *City of London WPC, age 42,*
seventeen years' service

I kept my sexuality a secret for a long time, but the whole force know about me now as a result of an incident at the London Lesbian and Gay Centre. I was there at a private party a couple of years ago when a guy there had a series of epileptic fits, which resulted in him kicking a table over and cutting himself to ribbons. He needed hospital treatment but there was an ambulance dispute going on at the time so I knew I wouldn't get anywhere on 999. The only way to bypass the system and get him to hospital was to call my force ambulance, and to do that I had to tell them who I was and where I was. I didn't really want to say that I was at the Gay Centre, so I just gave them the street and the number of the build-ing, but then some nosey idiot in the Met, who'd obviously seen the message come up, telephoned my station, told them what it was, and asked what the hell I was doing in a place like that. Unbe-known to me, my Inspector, who is a bit anti-female anyway, then put in a report about me which I saw some time later, saying that I 'frequented' the LLGC where 'certain marches' are arranged and depart from.

Anyway, after that my life became very difficult. Everyone had heard what had happened and working communication stopped in my office with the particular individual I was posted with, and he put a lot of bad word about me around the station. He also gave me an awful AQR, which was in total contradiction to all the others I'd had. After that, a lot of people who had been initially friendly to me became quite anti and I just couldn't do a thing right for a long time.

At the time of the incident I was a Divisional Training Officer. This was supposed to be a two-year attachment to our Force Training Centre, although you actually worked at a divisional level. It involved being responsible for the duties and training of probationers, especially within their first thirty-one weeks and also the update of legislation for everyone else on the division. I spent one year at one division then moved to another supposedly for another year. However, by now word had got around about my 'lesbianism' and the heads of the second division decided that they didn't need a lesbian in charge of their new impressionable probationers and so they started to try and trip me – which they couldn't. The FTC realized what was happening and tried to keep me out of their reach but my work life was made unbearable – especially when I was accused of trying to 'convert' the other WPCs on the division. In the end, I had to apply to be returned to division, and that's where I am now. Since then, I've had many reactions from very good to very bad. When it's averagely bad, it's normally just little things that get to you. If you are angry or upset about something for example, for whatever reason, it's not simply enough that you're angry or upset, it's all because you're a lesbian. Either that or it's your time of the month.

It wasn't until a couple of years ago that I understood racism. Now I feel as if I'm standing in the same place. When people all around you are making comments about you and people like you, it starts to get to you and unless you've been in that position yourself, and not just for eight hours a day, then you'll never know what it's like or be able to empathize properly.

My attitude has changed a lot in the last couple of years. Partly because I've accepted my sexuality now and partly because of what happened to me. I used to want to go up in the police but since I've accepted my sexuality, I see things in a different light and I'm not sure I want promotion any more. I think I might in a forward-thinking force but I don't really want to be associated with people who are collectively, to all intents and purposes, dinosaurs. In fact, if I'd known what I know now, I don't think I'd have bothered to join at all.

*   *   *

The third of the three pieces used to illustrate the concept of institutionalized homophobia was originally published in *Police Review* and is reprinted here with the kind permission of Lee Hunt, the first officer in Britain to come out publicly and brave the national media:[13]

In 1983 my partner and I, also a serving police officer, 'came out' by admitting to being homosexual and co-habitating. I believe we were the first police officers to do so. There was nothing abnormal about my progress in the service. I joined at 19, serving first in Norfolk and later in Hampshire, at Aldershot. I cannot say that, before I joined the service, I was aware of being homosexual; I never really had much time to think about it.

On leaving school, I joined the Hampshire Police Cadet Corps. Life was very busy and full right up to the time I joined the police service. There was never any reason for me to consider whether or not I should join because I was homosexual. The question simply never arose.

At Aldershot I met my partner, Richard. We were on the same relief and lived in the section house. Gradually our relationship became serious. We sought and gained permission to buy a house. Our relationship was taken for granted, and we attended all the usual parties and social events together. We did not thrust ourselves at anyone, but neither were we furtive or secretive. It did not affect our work and we remained popular among our colleagues.

In 1983 our relationship became known outside the police station and I was asked about it by a senior officer. I agreed with Richard to tell the officer the truth about our relationship. As a result, life changed dramatically. We were transferred to the county's vice squads, Richard to Southampton and me to Portsmouth. We were required to live at police hostels in Southampton and Fareham and not allowed to visit each other.

The emotional trauma was immense. We were put on monthly reports and required to attend a medical for no real reason. During the interview at which we learned our fate, the then deputy chief constable insisted that a record be taken by a shorthand writer. When I asked why the medical was needed, I received a shrug of the shoulders, leaving me to draw my own conclusions.

We were penalised financially, because our rent allowances were stopped. We had to rent out the house, and a chief superintendent demanded to know why I had not told the chief constable. He also asked if the two men in the house were homosexuals – they happened to be father and son. I was obliged to point out that, as I was not in receipt of a rent allowance, I did not have to inform the chief constable; the chief superintendent agreed.

Our lives became public knowledge, not through our blabbing but through other sources. At Easter that year our home was besieged by reporters and photographers. We were offered money for a story, but always referred callers to the press office at police headquarters. Our 'story' hit the headlines in the national press. The accounts were wild. Ironically, some 'gay' publications described us as 'pro-police – almost obsessively so'.

In the vice squads, we were not allowed to go anywhere near public toilets. During my attachment I had very little to do except tag on to the regular vice squad officers. The prosecuting authorities were very concerned that my presence on the vice squad would lead to accusations. There can be little doubt that these events, and others, were designed to bring about our resignations; they served no other purpose.

We sought the advice of the Federation straight away. It was not exactly a sympathetic hearing, but the advice was fair and concise. The upheaval in our lives was tremendous and we were seeking help. Having previously received glowing appraisals, I was shocked when my report said I was 'incompetent and unlikely to make an efficient police officer'. I found my personal and vehicle details on the collator's system – a result of fabricated information. It was expunged immediately by the sub-divisional commander after I complained. My medical history and conversations were being closely watched and reported directly to the Complaints and Discipline Department.

Having attended the medical as ordered by the DCC, I was detained at Southampton Central Police Station and interviewed about my movements that day. I was even required to prove that I had been ordered to attend the medical and had to produce the report given to me by my chief inspector. After a lengthy interview I was escorted out of the back door and told never to return.

This pressure continued for several years, but we stuck it out and largely prevailed. We showed ourselves to be effective police officers and gained the support of the vast majority of the people around us, for which we are grateful. Most of the pressure has now subsided.

As much as I would like to, it would be wrong of me to excuse the Federation's approach to my problems eight years ago. In July 1983, a Hampshire *Federation News* notice referred to the press revelations about us as a 'particularly unsavoury subject – gay policemen'. It recognised that such individuals existed but described them as 'unfortunate'. The police service, it said, had always made a priority of the protection of children from sick members of society. What, it asked, would parents think, now they knew we had homosexual officers?

That was followed by the circulation of an anti-gay motion which the Hampshire JBB was considering taking to the 1984 Federation Conference. The proposal proved unpopular and was dropped. None of this is meant to be a criticsm of any person. Indeed, my Federation rep came in for some stick over the stance he took with the then DCC on my behalf, as a point of principle for the good of the membership as a whole.

This brings me to the article on 'divided loyalties' by the chairman of the Met Federation, Mike Bennett ... His argument, a personal view, that the Federation should protect the rights of all police officers is sound, but some of his comments seemed clumsy and irrelevant. The general theme seemed to be that the lid should be kept on the whole subject in the best interests of gay officers themselves.

The world is moving forward, as Leslie Curtis, then the Federation chairman, recognised in 1983 when, in a letter referring to Richard and myself, he said: 'The police service has got to move with the times and our attitudes to the rights of the individual, albeit policemen or anybody else, must be honoured.'

It is clear that opinions on this subject will vary greatly, but this question of individual rights should cause concern. I suspect that the views of elected representatives have moved forward over the last seven years, but Mr Bennett's remarks had hints of the treatment I have described. To suggest that a police bondage or deviant sexual practices society might emerge trivialized the whole article.

The issue has to be treated sensibly. It may only affect a small number of individuals within the service, but how can any gay officer take the Federation seriously if its representatives make comments like that? If the debate were to continue in that tone, it would quickly become defensive and polarised.

If the arguments are not resolved and the Federation fails to fulfil its role by fighting all cases of prejudice, then it is only right that officers like myself should press for 'sexual orientation' to be included in all chief officers' statement of intent on discrimination. It would show that the service is serious in its attitude towards the community as a whole.

No one can dispute that there are a significant number of gay people in this country in all walks of life, so there should be no surprise that there are a sizeable number of gay policemen and women. If the service were more open about it, the opportunity to accuse the police of 'gay bashing' would be diminished.

For whatever reason, many gay people do not trust the police. Perhaps if they could speak to a gay police officer, they might be prepared to come forward with information, allowing otherwise difficult inquiries to be cleared up. These are practical advantages. All police officers are subject to regulations – what is there to fear?

Other issues which have arisen over the years have a bearing on this issue. The role of women in the service is one. At one time it was limited, but they are now an integral and essential part of the job. People from ethnic minority backgrounds once found entry into, and progress through, the service difficult. Now their role is regarded as invaluable.

Both groups have flourished since they gained the protection of anti-discrimination acts. But if you are, or suspected of being, homosexual, what then? It would be a shame if the aspirations and contributions of good police officers were hindered simply because their sexual orientation differed from that of the majority.

In the community, there are many self-help groups which campaign for various causes. So, if you are a police officer and happen to be gay, what could be more natural that to wish to talk to someone else in the same situation? Suggestions that such a group would bring the police service into disrepute smacks of stereotyping and a lack of understanding.

Against this background, should a police officer who is gay 'come out'? So long as you have completed probation, I say you should – although you have to be sure the Federation will support your rights. At a stroke you can remove all the pretence, and any chance of blackmail goes.

The Federation, if it really wants to fight for the rights of all officers, has to make up its mind on this issue. Otherwise pressure to form a separate association will increase – and I would not argue against that if it were to help those in a similar situation to me eight years ago.

My sexual orientation does not affect my work. Little regard is paid to it now, simply because I do not hide it and do not have to. My police and civilian colleagues can talk freely about the subject, but we also talk about many other issues. Richard and I socialise within the police service in the same way as we did eight years ago – only now everyone knows, and it doesn't seem to worry any of our colleagues or their families.

Some readers might feel that the past – and this subject – should be left alone, but that is burying your head in the sand. This is a live issue and it is not going to go away. I hope that no one will be annoyed or offended by my desire to chip in. After all, we each have an opinion and should respect the right to express it. This is my attempt to produce a balanced and sensible view of the matter.

The Acceptance of Lesbianism

The question of whether or not lesbians are more readily accepted than gay men in the police and suffer less prejudice and discrimination as a result is an interesting one, and one upon which policewomen are themselves divided. Robert Anthony has noted the existence of a double-edged sword which on the one hand demands the masculine virility which male officers often bring to the problems of policing, whilst at the same time trapping those female officers who display equal prowess 'safely in the pigeon hole of lesbianism'.[14] Some of the women I spoke to felt so strongly about the issue of lesbian visibility that they declined to assist with this study for fear of rocking the boat. The principal concern amongst these officers would appear to be the perceived threat that publicity would bring to the existence of a well-developed but informal lesbian network which has no male equivalent. This network is very protective of its affiliates, most of whom seem quite content with an effective yet largely invisible arrangement, and are concerned that the analysis of homosexual issues in the service, including the development of and publicity surrounding the new support group for gay and lesbian officers (although for many of these officers the 'lesbian' reference is seen as somewhat outmoded), would only draw attention to their existence. Many women, however, dislike this unassertive and slightly separatist tendency, preferring a more independent stance where they can mix comfortably with male gay colleagues when they find them.

Hence, it is the differing perceptions of the status of female homosexuality in the police which has caused the differing stances of women on this issue and of the following pieces. The first account deals with the network referred to above, whilst the two others contain some of the ideas around which the differences of opinion are based and highlight some of the opportunities for discrimination.

● *West Midlands WPC, age 28,*
eight years' service

I am a serving officer in the West Midlands police with eight and a half years' service. When I first made contact with a representative of LAGPA I was surprised to discover that it was mainly male officers who had expressed an interest. I personally know of only one gay male officer on my division, whereas I know of seven lesbians (out of a division of approximately 320 officers) but of course those are only the people who I definitely know are gay.

I believe that lesbian police officers feel less of a need to form or belong to such an association because informal networks already exist for them in a safe environment, that is, through sporting activities. As far as force sport is concerned, to the best of my knowledge, the main sport is hockey and I know of lesbian officers who have formed relationships with each other or civilians through meeting in this way. I have also known of civilians who have been connected with hockey and have subsequently joined the police because they have met and become aware of the number of lesbians that there are in the force. I believe that the fact that lesbian officers are associated with force hockey is an open secret and indeed when I was quite young in service I was asked if I played hockey, but I was unaware of the implications of the question at the time.

Another sport which has always been popular with lesbians from all walks of life is soccer, and although I am not aware of any force women's soccer teams, I know of lesbian officers who play for civilian teams and obviously use this safe environment for support. From speaking to officers involved in these sports it appears that the lesbians eventually suss each other out, although their sexuality is never discussed with the heterosexual members of the team and a straight front is put on in public. This sort of behaviour does not appeal to me, but I feel that many lesbian officers are happy with the situation and could find the LAGPA threatening.

I am not openly lesbian in that I discuss my private life, but I don't try to hide it and people presume that I am gay so I never get asked difficult questions. Because I haven't associated with other lesbian officers I have therefore not run the risk of exposing others who would prefer to remain closeted and who would be worried about being guilty by association.

I also feel that there is a greater acceptance of lesbians in the Job than gay men because traditionally, as have all uniform services, the police has attracted lesbians. The image of policewomen has changed and become more glamorous over the past few years through TV and films, and I would imagine that the number of lesbians joining the Job now as a percentage of women recruited is probably declining, whereas a few years ago the Job was seen as a job unsuitable for 'real' women and the percentage of lesbians was therefore higher. Even so, I would guess that proportionally, there are far more lesbians than gay men in the police.

● *Metropolitan WPC, age 24, one year's service*

When I joined the police service, I made a conscious decision to be open about my sexuality. At training school I got to know a few other lesbians and I mentioned to them that I was going to be open from the start. Their reaction was one of 'Don't!' I was made to believe that it wasn't important, that I had them to talk to about it and so why rock the boat. They made me doubt my decision and made me feel that it was better to just keep quiet. It all made me feel as if I should be ashamed of my life. Well, I'm not! I'm very proud of the woman I love and she deserves better than being tucked away like some dirty secret. So after ten weeks, I told some of the people in my class. Gossip being gossip, it didn't take long for it to spread, but I was happy that I was free from the heavy weight that had been with me. About a week later, however, I was cornered in a room by my lesbian friends and made to feel as if I'd committed a major crime. Friends of mine. I felt hurt and angry. How dare they make me feel guilty for being honest and open; for having had the courage to stand up and say, 'Yes, I'm gay, so what?' At this point I felt completely alone. I had hoped that they would respect my decision just as I respected theirs, but instead I was shoved out on my own to fend for myself. I don't regret coming out and I have had no problems on division. I still find it sad to think that those who made it most difficult for me were other gay people.

● *Metropolitan WPC, age 25, three years' service*

I think the men get it much harder than the women in the police if they're gay. Maybe it's different for women because the management don't really want women coming into the police for just a couple of years and then getting married and just using the Job for the training. Lesbians are more likely to make a career of it and be of long-term use, because we're not going to go off and get pregnant and leave. So maybe we're worth more to them in a way. Also, the stereotype of the male gay is effeminacy, which the police doesn't want, whereas the stereotype of the dyke is masculinity and the police need women who aren't afraid to get stuck in there and do the job. The other thing is that as lesbians we're not so threatening to the men as male gays are. Lots of them actually like the idea of lesbians. God knows why, but they seem to have far less of a problem with that than they do with the men.

● *Metropolitan woman Detective Inspector, age 34, eleven years' service*

A policewoman came to me because she knew that I was gay and a colleague of hers had come out to her and was suffering a lot of pain over it, so she wondered if I could talk to her about it. Another one wants to come and talk to me about career prospects. That can be a big worry for lesbians because the main thing about gay women is that they are petrified about coming out because they feel that they won't get promotion. I've spoken to a number of women who are paranoid about it. It's difficult enough for a

woman to prove her worth as a police officer, without the ad-
ditional stigma of homosexuality to cope with. That's why women
are more reluctant to come out than men if you ask me. I know I
felt that way for years. You're second best as it is in the police if
you're a woman, without all those additional problems to cope
with. And if you're lucky enough to be respected for being a good
police officer then the knowledge of your homosexuality could
neutralize or detract from that. Women feel that they will be looked
upon unfavourably if their orientation is known about, and since
they are more likely to do the full thirty years and make a career of
it, it is particularly important to them that there are no impedi-
ments to promotion. The police complain that they don't get to
keep their women long enough – so why don't they take advantage
of those who won't be leaving? It's because the police service want
to portray women as being feminine, heterosexual, 'normal'. These
are the women that they want to push through the ranks to encour-
age other women to join.

It is clear that, for women, the issues are as much to do with the
status of women in the police service generally as they are to do
with female sexual orientation. 'There appears to be a strong but
covert resentment of the competence of a woman who can get to
the heart of a problem, shows creativity and innovation, and
manages to acquire a reputation for getting things done,' wrote
Alison Halford in 1987.[15] Consequently, there is a feeling that
whatever a woman does she can never win – 'If you don't have a
drink with them you're a lesbian, if you do you're an alcoholic';[16]
thus, it can be difficult to rise above the status of relief 'plonk'.
Despite the fact that there is some disagreement over the status of
lesbianism in the police, the above observations suggest that whatever the differences of opinion, the concerns which are seen to
govern women's sentiments are distinct from those in the male
arena where there is no parallel conflict, and it seems likely that
there may be a significant experiential difference which separates
gay men and lesbians within the police structure.[17] A more detailed
analysis of the situation of the lesbian police officer must, however,
await further research.

Notes

1. But see, for example, J. B. Swerling, ' A study of police officers' values and their attitudes towards homosexual officers', Dissertation, California School of Professional Psychology, Los Angeles, 1978.
2. D. Bayley and H. Mendelsohn, *Minorities and the Police*, 1968, p. 144.
3. Policy Studies Institute, *Police and People in London*, Vols. 1–4, 1983.
4. Surveys by A. Niederhoffer, *Behind the Shield*, 1967, and P. Jacobs, *Prelude to Riot*, 1966.
5. In a recent study by the author, 61 per cent of respondents ($N = 36$) reported their conviction that the police were either 'slightly more' or 'much more' homophobic than the rest of society (see M. Burke, 'Homosexuality in the British police', Ph.D. thesis, University of Essex, 1993).
6. I. Westwood, 'Those well-known Christian virtues', *Police Review*, 18 January 1991, p. 149 (Letter).
7. R. Webb, 'Why all the hang-ups about sex?', *Police Review*, 18 January 1991, p. 149 (Letter).
8. See, for example, M. Banton, 'Categorial and Statistical Discrimination', *Ethnic and Racial Studies*, 6 (1983), whole issue. The police are not the only professional group to exercise stereotyping techniques and similar discourses have arisen in relation to store detectives and private security firms. N. South, *Policing for Profit*, 1988, refers to the tendency to 'typologise and stereotype' as 'security mentality' – a close relative of 'police mentality' – and in D. May, *Juvenile Shoplifters and the Organisation of Store Security*, 1978 (p. 151), one store detective demonstrates the tendency as follows:

   > It's difficult to explain ... You get to know them somehow or other. After a while you can tell the shoplifters the moment they walk into the store, and nine times out of ten you are right.

9. J. Skolnick, *Justice Without Trial*, 1966.
10. 'An examination of the non-verbal cues by which police officers perceive potential criminality', by Inspector D. R. Smith, Lancashire Constabulary (extracts from a paper presented whilst at the University of Liverpool).
11. J. R. Robinson, *Catching Criminals: Some More Basic Skills*, 1983, pp. 33–4.

12. A. C. Kinsey *et al.*, *Sexual Behaviour in the Human Male*, 1948, p. 615.
13. L. Hunt, 'When I "came out"', *Police Review*, 19 April 1991, pp. 804–5. Following the publication of Lee Hunt's article, the Editor of *Police Review* was contacted by the *Sun* for the officer's private telephone number. This was refused. The southern edition of the *Sun* (12 June 1991) then reprinted the original article, almost word for word, including the photograph. *Police Review* sued for breach of copyright and in an out-of-court settlement, the *Sun* agreed to pay £1,350 in damages.
14. R. Anthony, 'Homosexuality in the police', MA dissertation, University of Exeter, 1992, p. 4.
15. Reported by S. Boggan, 'Retirement ends two year nightmare', *Independent*, 22 July 1992, p. 4.
16. Reported by D. Campbell, '"Unwitting rebel" laid bare police fraternity', *Guardian*, 22 July 1992, p. 3.
17. Such findings appear to be paralleled by those of C. S. Chan, 'Issues of identity development among Asian–American lesbians and gay men' (*Journal of Counselling and Development*, 68 (1989), pp. 16–20), who found that Asian lesbians experience more discrimination connected with their ethnicity, while Asian gay men experienced more discrimination on the grounds of their homosexuality.

Chapter ten

Casualties

IF there is any truth in the adage that 'the policeman's lot is not a happy one' then the plight of the gay policeman or woman is far worse. In this chapter, the themes of prejudice and discrimination are further developed and the experiences of officers who, as a direct result of their sexuality, found themselves unable to continue serving in the police are explored. Three principal means of exit for gay officers are identified here: (a) voluntary resignation as a result of a rational, analytic decision to quit, (b) psychological deterioration resulting in voluntary retirement from the service or mandatory discharge, and (c) harassment or persecution following the discovery of an officer's sexual orientation, resulting in resignation under duress.

The officers in the first group are victims of institutionalized police heterosexism, and personnel in this category simply exercise their prerogative of opting out. Those in the second group are more likely to be casualties of the societal homosexual taboo, its homophobia, and of a consequent inability to accept their 'deviance'. Alternatively, breakdown may be a response to failure in the consolidation of sexual orientation and career. The double lives often led by officers who decide not to come out (examined in Chapter 7) mean that stability in life may be difficult to achieve, and there are numerous instances of officers suffering breakdowns and having to leave the service as a result of the pressures they face. The last and perhaps the most disturbing group houses those officers who are direct casualties of the system, 'the system' being that leviathan that ensures the waste of those officers who evade the menace of the preceding two snares. In this chapter, illustrations from each of these groups are offered.

● *Humberside PC, age 29, resigned with seven years' service*

I left the police because of my sexuality; because I got the impression that the blokes would automatically brand anyone who wasn't married by the time they were thirty as queer. I only had two or three years to go before I reached that age, and since I would never, ever, come out, and since I didn't want to be in the position of having to deny that I was gay for the rest of my service, I left. I just didn't want to be in that situation. In addition, after several years of looking around I finally had a relationship that I wanted to give everything to and I wasn't prepared to have another one ruined because of my job. Gay relationships are hard enough to maintain and I just wasn't prepared to risk this one by staying on. I wasn't out at work and I wasn't going to be because I knew that would be suicide. My dad's a Chief Superintendent in another force and he once told me that if they ever found out that someone was homosexual then they would make their life difficult in the hope that they would go, because the police just wasn't the right environment for them. I guess I expected that much from him but at the same time it made me quite angry. I wondered what he would have thought if he'd known that his son was gay. I like to think that it would have made him reconsider because he obviously had no idea about me. He was the one who encouraged me to join.

● *Metropolitan PC, age 33, resigned with fifteen years' service*

I used to hang out with this older women at the station and the others all thought I was bonking her. Everyone wanted to get into her knickers and they were all sick that I always had her with me. The person I really loved of course was another PC. I fell desperately in love with him and was besotted by him for two years such that, in the end, I had to leave the section house for my own sanity. *I told him what I felt for him once and I think he was actually quite flattered by the attention. It never affected our friendship either; in fact it made it stronger in many ways.*

But I never had a sex life. I was basically celibate. In fact I had no social life at all. I used my work to fill the aching gap I had in me. I became conscientious, smart, efficient, always on time. I had nothing else to do. I wasted so much time like that. Years. My supervisors wanted me to take rapid promotion but I couldn't because even though the system had expressed confidence in me I had no confidence in myself – no self-esteem. I felt inadequate both as a person and as a police officer. So I always felt I had to be the best of the best. And it gave me a drink problem. I used to get really upset if I got sent out on a job just before the pubs opened. I needed a drink before I could relax enough to work. Not that it made me a bad police officer. Being gay made me more scrupulous about being fair.

Looking back now, I think it was all that bottling it up that caused me to have the nervous breakdown and leave the police in the end. One felt completely suppressed through fear of judgement. I just could no longer combine the two variables of police and gay; I could no longer live as that schizoid entity. I also think that because I never allowed my sexual nature to mature properly I never grew up in a sense – as a whole, rounded person. An entire essential side of my nature was being denied all the time. And under those conditions something has got to go. In my case it was my mental health. I suffered some kind of a breakdown and got retired on the grounds of ill health. It was a refusal to be a gay policeman which got me. I could be one or the other but not both. I suppose it was a poor career move really. I should either never have joined, or been far more open from the beginning.

Things are much better now. I've found it easier to come to terms with being gay since I've left the Job. I'm more accepting of myself – less worried. I can't be blackmailed now and I don't care who finds out any more. It's existing in an environment where my sexuality doesn't matter that makes the difference. I'm not frightened of myself any more and I can really just be me and nobody cares. It's great. I could say that the police don't care either because there is a sense in which that's true. In general, the police don't

*mind what you do, so long as you're not found out, and so long as
you don't rock the boat. It's when you try to force the system to
change or see reality that the problems begin because then the
management structure, which is so moribund, has to start thinking,
and it's so big it just can't move quickly enough. So it attacks you
instead. That's why they hate being made to think or change the
status quo. It all costs too much effort.*

Coming to terms with one's homosexuality can be a difficult process regardless of occupation. It is almost inevitable that the stigmatized will sometimes feel ambivalent about the validity of their
difference due to the fact that they are in constant violation of the
codes that they unconsciously accept. As the sociologist I. Goffman
notes:

> ... a stigmatised person is first of all like anyone else, trained
> first of all in others' views of persons like himself...
>
> ... the standards he [sic] has incorporated from the wider
> society equip him to be intimately alive to what others see as
> his failing, inevitably causing him, if only for moments to
> agree that he does indeed fall short of what he really ought
> to be. Shame becomes a central possibility.[1]

Berzon makes the same point with specific reference to
homosexuality:

> In our formative years we were all exposed to the same
> antigay jokes as our nongay counterparts, the same stereo-
> types of lesbians and gay men, the same misinformation
> from our peers. For we gay people who have swallowed all
> this toxic material, it works against us from the inside while
> society's homophobes ... work against us from the outside.[2]

Self-esteem is lowered and anxiety is raised when disparity
exists between a person's 'ideal self' – what they would like to be –
and their 'real self' – what they know themselves to be (self-
concept).[3] Hence, the awareness of inferiority in the eyes of others

means that unless a robust counter-identity is in place to reply, disorder may result.

The extent to which a person is ultimately accepting of his or her sexual orientation varies considerably. The factors which affect patterns of acceptance or denial are numerous and include parental values and manner of upbringing, religious or political background, education, class, peer values and degree of residential urbanization. Occupation is also important. Indeed, if, as McDonald notes, the social context of identity formation is crucial,[4] we should not be surprised if gay police officers – who typically find themselves attempting to come to terms with an atypical sexual orientation in an environment devoid of social support systems – experience particular difficulty in coming to terms with their difference and are sometimes retarded in the development of their orientational identity.[5] As one constable put it:

> I just don't think the police is the right place to try and get to grips with something like homosexuality. It's no wonder some of them never manage to come to terms with it. You have to be either extraordinarily strong or extraordinarily thick-skinned.
>
> Metropolitan PC, age 29, four years' service

Several of the factors noted thus far are clearly evident in the following rather disturbing extracts from Stephen's diaries in which many of the classic problems of coming to terms with being gay are illustrated. For Stephen, a twenty-year-old constable stationed in south London, being a police officer is simply one of several obstacles that he is facing, and in this case, it is not simply the police service but society that must accept responsibility for the misery that this officer describes.

March 1989
Today I collected my letter of referral to a psychiatrist from my doctor. And some kind of prescription for depression. He wanted to know what was the matter with me. I just told him it was just the stress of being a policeman, which he seemed to believe OK. Perhaps this shrink will be able to help – I've tried everything else

*now. But I'm not sure if I'll be able to trust him – I don't trust
anyone any more – and this feeling of isolation is gradually destroy-
ing me. I'm beginning to think I'm paranoid, but I know inside that
it's justified. I can't rely on anyone any more. It's been proved to me
too many times. Nobody's interested in anyone but themselves.*

April 1989

*So much for the shrink. Fucking waste of time. Am I going
mad, or have I just got too many problems at the moment. I think I
must enjoy it subconsciously because I don't think it's ever going to
go away. But what can I do, who can I tell. Nobody. I can't afford
to lose what friends I've got and I can't destroy my family, so I have
to keep it inside. Perhaps it's just my environment. I seem to be
living many lives, but I don't fit fully into any of them. I am
becoming consumed with hatred and find something to despise in
everyone. My dreams are sometimes disturbingly violent, although
I can't remember the last time I had a nightmare.*

June 1989

*There must surely be others like me, but where are they?
Why me? What have I done wrong? Being gay is just not acceptable. But a gay policeman? I can neither be accepted by the gay
community as a 'pig' or by the police as a 'fucking queer'. I can only
hide within myself. But beneath the apathy, the hatred builds up,
because it's not my fault, is it? I can't help the way I feel. Why are
people so stupid?*

September 1989

*My interests in everything are beginning to dwindle. I
haven't got time for anyone any more. I am becoming a loner. I
wish I could tell someone – my best friend – but I can't. I could
never tell my mum. I can't afford to risk my job either. I believe in
God too. So I can't accept being gay to myself. I thought I was
getting used to it but now it keeps nagging at me. I know it says in
the Bible that homosexuality is wrong and will be punished, so
what can I do. I think I might eventually be able to accept myself
but if God won't accept me I don't think I'll ever be happy. I've
prayed to God to change but nothing happens – even though a
friend told me I'd be changed if I prayed. But who believes in God*

these days anyway. Being a Christian is a minority in itself, but a gay Christian is a living contradiction. A gay Christian copper can only be doomed to failure.

February 1990

I think I've almost given up hope; I can't help but feel that it's my destiny to be unhappy. My feelings of despondency and depression are with me daily now. I've got used to them, it's been a few years now, in fact I'm beginning to think that I need them ... Nobody knows what's going on in my head, but they never do, do they, which just makes me hate them even more.

April 1990

I don't know how much longer I can keep this up. Something's got to happen soon; it's been building up for too long. One of my friends on my shift has just flipped, poor bastard. Don't know what it is yet. He's in the local loony-bin at the moment doped up on drugs. Went to see him yesterday. Guess I'll be joining him soon.

Stephen made it clear to me that, for him, suicide would seem to be the only way out of his mess. He soon realized that the visits to the psychiatrist were not going to change him, nor did he feel that they would accomplish anything that he could not accomplish by himself. He felt that he had exhausted all available avenues and that there was no alternative means of ending his pain. Fortunately, after timely conversation with London Lesbian and Gay Switchboard, he decided to try one last possibility and his next step was to visit a gay youth group in north London. Although the experience proved demanding and somewhat traumatic at first, he managed to make a couple of friends whom he saw regularly, and through them he slowly began to relax in the fight against his orientation. However, he soon realized that he would never be able to develop fully as a person or be comfortable with his sexuality whilst in the police, since he was always worrying about being spotted in the gay pubs or clubs he was now visiting. Eventually, a year after rejecting suicide as the definitive answer to his problems, Stephen took the decision to quit the force having just completed his probation at the age of twenty.

Leaving the service would seem to have given Stephen the opportunity to properly explore and deal with his homosexual feelings free from tension and fear. His spiritual stumbling block remained, however, and this still bothered him greatly. He got involved with the Lesbian and Gay Christian Movement for a short while but this only led him to examine his beliefs more closely. He not only remained unconvinced that the two were mutually compatible but also decided that many of the things he had previously taken for granted were in fact untenable. Eventually, after several months of soul-searching, Stephen decided to discontinue his commitment to Christianity.

After years of desperation and having ditched the police, Christianity and the last of his hang-ups, it would seem that Stephen is finally happy with himself. He has told his parents who have stood by him and he has a new career in Manchester where he has been enjoying a steady relationship with his boyfriend Robert for the past year.

The officer relating the following set of incidents has requested that no personal details be disclosed.

My sole crime was a copy of Gay Times. *I was off sick at the time on crutches with a torn Achilles' tendon, when my Sergeant rang me at home to inform me with great glee that it might be better if I didn't bother returning to work. I asked him what he meant and he skirted around it for ages but wouldn't say anything concrete until I got pissed off with his antics and pinned him down. In the end he said that some gay magazines had been found with my name on them at work and that the boys at the station were all talking about it and wanted to know what was going on.*

After the call, the first thing to hit me was the fact that I'd never be able to go into work again. I had a house and car and suddenly it was all in jeopardy. I didn't know what was going to happen now. I felt so sick, I went to the bathroom and threw up. I know that sounds a bit dramatic but I knew exactly what them finding out meant for me.

A friend of mine who was also on sick leave was due to come and visit me that evening, and I didn't know what to do. I knew I should tell him before he heard from somebody else. So when he

arrived, we had a few stiff drinks and I told him that I had something to tell him that he might not find particularly pleasant. But
before I could start he told me that he already knew and had done
for two weeks. Apparently two weeks previous, while I was still off
sick, people had broken into my room at the station, which was
locked, and then broken into a locked wardrobe in the room, and
then into a locked chest in the wardrobe, and found a single copy of
Gay Times. Everyone already knew about this except for me
because I was off sick and the only reason I'd had the call was
because they knew that this guy was coming to see me and they
wanted to tell me before I heard it all from him. They'd even called
him up before he came over to see me and given him a bunch of shit
about 'Are you going to see your bum chum this evening?' After
that I tried to find out more about what had happened by ringing
the station but I couldn't speak to anyone. None of the senior
officers would speak to me – they were all suddenly and mysteri-
ously off on business and/or leave. I can't describe the feeling of
knowing what's going to happen but at the same time not knowing
how. I was totally devastated. I never cry but I was so scared and so
angry about the whole thing, it was one of the few occasions that I
did. God knows what my mate thought. Anyways, after that most
of them called me up. In fact out of my unit, which was one
[inspector], four [sergeants] and twenty-four [PCs], all but three
either called me, wrote to me or came to my house and said, 'Don't
you dare resign.' One said, 'You may be what you are but you're a
fucking good policeman and don't you dare give in.' That was nice.
I hadn't expected that. I'd thought they would all be against me.

A while after that the other phone calls started. The bad
ones. Mostly to my parents' house which scared my mum and the
whole family stiff. I know who was doing it. It was another officer
at my station, maybe with one other. And that went on for weeks
and weeks but I couldn't prove anything.

I was still off sick this whole time with little else to think
about except the loss of my career. I could never go back to work.
And even if I were to, I would just get sent to man a barrier or
something – it had already been intimated that that would be the
case and I wasn't going to do that.

I stopped going out almost immediately and things just

gradually began to go downhill. I guess thinking about it now what I actually had was a nervous breakdown, although I didn't recognize it as that at the time. But I don't see how it could be classed as anything else. I took the phone off the hook and I didn't leave the house for months. I didn't respond to anything. I wouldn't answer the door and I burned all correspondence which came through the door without even bothering to read it, including bills. I'd told my family and neighbours that I was going away for two months so they would leave me alone and the only time I left the house after that was at two in the morning to go to the all-night garage for a pint of milk or something. I have to say I contemplated suicide more than once. I just used to sit there like a moron staring into space. I used to just sit in my armchair. At first I'd get drunk but after a while I just used to sit and stare into space. And no one knew I was there. It was months before I saw anyone.

The only other time I left, was to go back to the station and resign. Nothing had happened to me, they had nothing on me, the only offences that had been committed were by them – namely burglary – but I was under so much pressure that I couldn't stand it, which was the whole idea of course. So about two months after the first call I got out of my chair and went in to resign. I was quite cool about it. I just got up, went in and did it.

Nobody could look me in the eye the whole time because they knew why I'd come in and I guess they felt embarrassed about the whole thing. I gave in all my gear: my warrant card, my gun, stick, all my uniform – everything. When you think of all the crap you have to go through to get into the Job and all the years of training, and the whole resignation thing took just ten minutes. Sign here, sign there and that was it. And I'm standing there looking at my gear all piled up on the floor – ten years of my life – just sitting there in a big heap, all packaged up and waiting to go off and be burned. It's totally humiliating. And I hadn't even done anything wrong. But I wasn't going to tolerate any more shit from them. So I said to this guy who was dealing with it, 'I don't give a fuck what happens to me now, I don't care about any of it any more but if there's one more phone call to my family, then you make it clear around here that I'm going public on the whole fucking thing, and I don't give a shite who I bring down with me.' I said, 'I know a lot of shit about everyone who works here and I'll squeal like a fucking pig if it happens again. So you make sure they get the message.' Then I just went back home again and sat in my chair.

I remember thinking that the only good thing about it all at that stage was that I couldn't be blackmailed any more. I had nothing left to lose. So I told the bastard to fuck off. That had started when I was contacted by a reserve constable that I worked with – that was before this Gay Times *incident. He called me at home and said that I ought to meet him if I wanted to do myself a favour. So I did. We met at a local bar. I had no idea what he wanted. Once we'd sat down he said, 'OK, this is the score' and he told me that he knew I was gay, which I realize now he couldn't have done at that stage, but he bluffed, and I panicked and swallowed the lot. He said, 'I'm the only one who knows. You could lose your job, you could lose everything you have. I don't mind either way, but I'm in financial debt and I need some cash.' And that's how it started. I guess I ended up paying him about eight and a half grand altogether. First a lump sum of £3,000 and then £200 a month after that for about two years. Always cash. I can't believe it. I could kick myself for paying a penny to the wee bastard now. But like I said, I was eventually able to tell him to fuck off, except that by then I'd already lost virtually everything I had anyway.*

In the end, it was a friend who got me out of the state I was in. She came around one day – God knows how she knew I was in there. She just started banging on the door and wouldn't go away. She knocked and knocked until it was driving me nuts. She must have stood there for about two hours. Eventually it was sending me out of my head and so I let her in. When she came in she just stared at me and I realized then that I hadn't shaved for weeks, or washed, and the whole place looked like a shit hole and she just spooked. She said, 'Right, I'm coming back here in three hours and I want you showered, I want that shite shaved off your face and we're going out.' She wanted to take me to a Simply Red concert. I just said, 'No, no, no.' But she said, 'You can do whatever you want but I'm back here in three hours, and if you don't let me in then I'm going to break the door down and we're going. You can kick and shout and scream as much as you like, and I'm not that strong but we're going if I have to drag you out of here. We are going.' I was quite shocked. I always thought she was so quiet and demure and unassuming. God knows where she got the strength from to be so aggressive. But I did, I actually moved. After she'd gone, I went and got washed and shaved and we went. And I remember actually starting to enjoy it, even though I was determined not to.

Altogether, I lost my house, my car, my credit status and I also lost £12,000 in debts that I owed by the time I resigned. It seems strange to think that I let it all happen now that I'm together about my sexuality, but I was only just coming out at the time. I was totally confused. Even I didn't know for sure what my real orientation was at that stage. But I just can't describe the pressure you're under once they find out. You know that being gay is just the worst thing that could happen to you in that situation.

Anyway, I hate to think of others going through the same thing which is why I'm doing this here. If it stops just one person going through what I did, then as far as I'm concerned it's worth telling others about it.

An analogous catalogue of events characterizes the following experiences of an RUC constable who refused to resign, and these nearly led to the serious injury of that officer and his partner in an incident in which the officer's motor vehicle had been tampered with.

● RUC Constable, age 29, resigned with nine years' service

At twenty years of age I joined the Royal Ulster Constabulary. It was a decision totally against my family's wishes and those of my peers, and everything was kept an almost total secret in case word got back to any terrorist group. In hindsight I must have been a very naive lad because I don't really think I knew what I was letting myself in for. But it was what I wanted to do. I suppose I had a feeling that I could help people – help a torn society to mend itself. I felt no hatred against anyone. People were people in my book. But if they broke the law then they paid for it with their liberty and/or a fine.

*I entered the training college in 1979 knowing I was gay. I
always had known but had never told anyone. I felt that it would,
or should, never interfere with my new career. Training went well. I
sailed through and enjoyed the crack as they say.*

*The one gay incident I did see at the training college is one
that I have never forgotten. I was asked by the Sergeant to deliver a
memo to one of the outlying huts. This was around eight thirty in
the evening. I was crossing a small field when I heard a low groan,
so I crept over to the side of a hut feeling that what I heard was not
from pain. Looking around the side of the hut, I saw the outlines of
two guys kissing and fondling each other. As I stood there, scared
of discovery and my heart pumping nineteen to the dozen, I could
not believe what I was seeing. As my eyes became more accustomed
to the light, I saw that they were two of the cadets that had joined
our squad. This had not been a chance meeting and both, I'm sure,
had been having a sexual relationship well before coming to the
college. I've never forgotten that incident. I was just lucky enough
to be in the right place at the right time to discover something I
needed to see. Knowing I was not the only one in the world helped
me get through the rough patches, although as for myself, even if I
had been approached by anyone to have sex I doubt I'd have
responded. I wasn't ready for anything physical then. I wasn't even
shaving.*

*After my passing-out parade I was stationed at Tennent
Street in the heart of Belfast. I was given a room there as recruits
were not allowed to live at home. Again, I enjoyed the comradeship
and felt at ease. But the job was not as easy as I had thought it
would be. I was given training for anti-terrorist attacks; I was given
a gun and trained specifically to kill and not wound.*

*Alcohol plays a big part in a policeman's life. It allows
escape into a sluggish world of forgetfulness until the morning. I
became one of the heavy drinkers at my station, being afraid to
refuse and be left out on a limb. That's the way it was then. I must
have kept the family of the licensee on two good holidays a year
with my contribution alone.*

*As the years passed, I was transferred to a few other
stations. The hunger strikes of 1981 were on everyone's minds and
I have never in my life encountered a more warlike situation than*

that year. Friends fell under bombs and bullets. Rocket attacks were frequent and a lot of good guys were lost by tiny pieces of shrapnel piercing their armoured vests. And I was injured by a hand-grenade bouncing off my head, and exploding on the ground beside me. I was a very lucky lad. The fuse was obviously that little bit longer than usual, otherwise by now I would be lying in some graveyard rotting with the others. But I got out of that one, only to be shot three times a few months later. They were not serious injuries as I was only hit in the legs. An armoured door protected my upper half. I can laugh about that now, thinking I was alright behind the door whilst my legs below the protective shield were getting splattered with armalite rounds.

I am afraid that after that I felt enough was enough and demanded a transfer. It was given to me and I was posted into a secret indoor unit that worked with the army. I learnt a hell of a lot there and my eyes were opened even wider when I realized just what was really going on. The intentions of the hierarchy just could not be believed by anyone not involved, so that I shall not bother to go into them here.

As the years passed I became more and more disillusioned with my lot. The war in Ulster was not for me. I got a transfer to a country station and bought a small semi-detached house. After adjusting to the quiet life, I became quite settled. It was also at this time that I met my partner. He was the first man that I ever had sex with. I was twenty-four and still a virgin. He was younger than me and more experienced in the ways of personal life. I fell in love immediately. He was so giving of himself and I returned that love. After a year, he moved in with me and I felt that no one could be happier. That is until the neighbours discovered that we were gay. A pure guess on their part – the usual gossip of two men living together, etc. This didn't bother me in the least. As long as they left us alone we would survive their ignorance and prejudice. My parents knew I was gay. I told my mother and she accepted it with a 'Be careful, Brian. People can hurt you if they know.' How right she was. Everything of hatred came from strangers. My family never lifted an eyebrow when they learnt of my orientation. I was the same son and brother they had always known and nothing would change simply because I was gay. Telling them was a very hard and stressful thing to do though. I didn't want them to reject me but also I did not want to live a lie, so I was glad when it was all over. And I was even happier knowing my family's support for me. My partner's parents knew when he was sixteen and after a short difficulty with his father they became closer. So life felt good and I felt that everything I ever wanted was within my reach. The love I had always sought was found and life could not put us down.

But of course in our happiness I hadn't reckoned on the police side of things and in 1987 the roof came in on our lives. It was a Monday morning and I was detailed overtime to oversee a local football match. I arrived at the station ready to change and head out when an Inspector passed my row of lockers and quickly said, 'Brian, the Chief wants a word.'

'Fuck the Chief,' I said jokingly. 'I want a word with a cup of tea first.'

'Up now!' he said angrily. I felt the joke hadn't really hit home but shrugged my shoulders and put my sports jacket back on and headed up to the Chief's office thinking that he was going to inform me that my transfer to first-aid training had been turned down. I knocked on the door and immediately it was opened. I was motioned by a finger to enter. I smiled and walked past the finger wondering why the atmosphere felt thick with negative vibes. In front of me sat two well-groomed men in civvies. I bid them good morning and smiled. They kind of growled at me and one of them stood up, and called my name. 'Yes' I answered, now wondering what the hell was wrong. It did not take three people to tell me I had been turned down. The Chief excused himself and left. The two men introduced themselves as a Chief Inspector and an Inspector from the Serious Crime Squad. My mind began to race as to why they wanted to see me. An involuntary nervousness ran through me. I thought that my previous station had received a court order for my shooting of a terrorist two years previously.

'We've received complaints from your neighbours, Constable. Very serious ones at that.'

'Yes?' I answered, waiting for more information. I knew by then it was because I was gay and was cohabiting with another man. My heart thumped. 'This is it,' I thought, 'they've come for me.' I was asked whether I was homosexual. Well, given their *knowledge from my good neighbours I could not deny them their answer. I told them I was. They moved uneasily in their seats. They spoke of sexual offences that I was supposed to have committed. This did indeed take the rug from under my feet.*

'What?' I said in confusion.

'YES!' A shout landed in my ear.

I do not know if there is anyone else who has faced the same ordeal, but I can tell you that all my nerve ends were numb. My head spun and my mouth went as flaky and as brittle as an old bone. The questioning went on and on for about two hours before switching to my gay friends. 'Who are they? Where do they live? What do they do?' No way was I divulging that information to them. I insisted on a solicitor. I was refused. I asked for a pen and paper. I was refused. In fact I was harassed short of physical violence but only because they knew that I would retaliate and bounce both of them off the back wall. During that interrogation the offences I was supposed to have committed were not mentioned again. They wanted information on the gay scene. Where the places were. Who frequented them. I became angry and shouted something about what the hell was I there for. They laughed. It was then that I noticed that one of them was wearing a Christian Police Association badge in his lapel. I hated these people enough already without knowing one of them was actually a Christian. Jesus, when I think about that badge.

Eight hours I spent in that office. Eight hours of questions and shouting. Finally, I told them that if they were not finished I would either have a solicitor or leave. Then a very strange thing happened. I felt the closeness of my partner. He felt so close I could have turned to see him there. 'You've got Patrick here, haven't you?' I asked. He looked at me blankly. The phone rang. After a moment he looked at me. 'Yes,' he said, 'he's just been brought in.'

'What the hell for?' I shouted. 'He's done nothing wrong.'

'Fuck you, arse bandit,' he smirked.

On the ground floor my partner was going through hell. They did not tell him what was wrong. They also knew he was diabetic and refused him insulin. Of course I didn't know at the time but they were throwing everything at him, scaring him witless. I was told to go to the canteen and get a bite to eat. I gladly left and smoked twenty cigarettes in a series of clouds. Then they sent up one of the local detectives who I thought was a friend to question me quietly. I told him to fuck off or I would pull his guts out from the brain cell in his arse.

After another few hours of unrelenting questions on everything but the alleged offences they decided they had had enough and let me go. My partner was waiting outside the station having been finally thrown out with no insulin or money to obtain the vital sugar he needed to bring his blood-sugar level to a normal pitch. He could have dropped into a coma and they would have spat on him where he lay. We helped each other home and I fed him. We both sat and cried all evening wondering what on earth was going to happen to us now. I felt an awful guilt that he had had to suffer so much for nothing.

Those first few days seemed as if the world had slowed down and every car that passed was 'them' coming for us again. We knew we had done nothing wrong, yet we also knew what they were capable of. It really seemed as if the roof of the world had collapsed on us and we were slowly suffocating. If it were not for other gay friends and of course our respective families giving us their support I do not know how we would have coped. Police cars kept passing the house at regular intervals but not by chance. We lived in a cul-de-sac.

A few days later I was informed by a Chief Inspector that I could return to work after they had sorted the situation out. I have always had a suspicious mind and told Patrick that we may have to do something other than wait for them to act again. I went on sick leave. It sounds a simple thing to do and a short-term solution to a more serious problem, but I can assure you that it saved a lot of wrangling in the end. In fact that was the wisest decision I took. The next day the Chief Inspector called at the house. Patrick and I thought that it was to give me permission to return to work. I had no intention of returning. My mind was still racing to keep one step ahead of them. He informed me that I was to be suspended from duty (on full pay) and a report sent to the Director of Public Prosecutions for court action. I should have known. I should never have pinned my hopes on a quick settlement.

Depression fell upon Patrick and I for a while and com-

munication between us was strained. Later we just held each other
tightly and cried. Patrick was very strong-willed and sat me down
and told me that no matter what came of the situation we would
deal with it, and deal with it together. We did just that, but it
seemed bloody hard to face each day with any enthusiasm.

The most surprising thing happened around a week later. I
was sitting with a cup of tea, sipping away, when the telephone
rang. My heart leapt. Any sudden noise had me on edge. I picked up
the receiver and waited for abuse. A woman's voice asked if Brian
was there. 'Yes, this is Brian,' I said. To cut a long story short she
was one of the girls I worked with and she just wanted to send us
her support as she found it unfair what was happening to me. I
thanked her and felt pleased that she had taken the trouble to
phone. This call was followed by around twenty similar ones, all
supporting. Even the cleaners! I was told that stories were going
around at the station and as usual they were exaggerated at every
turn, but in the main, most knew me well enough to ignore them
until they had had a chance to speak to me personally. It seemed all
but the born-again Christians were behind us. One Christian even
went to the trouble of watching our house for days on end to see
what evil emanated from 'that house'. How bloody silly can you
get? And this was supposed to be an impartial police person. Then I
got a visit from the RUC welfare branch. A lady spoke solemnly to
me and asked if I needed anything. I told her politely that I needed
nothing from them. She then asked me if I had God in my life. I
couldn't believe it! Another bloody Bible-thumper at my door.
'Pray, Brian, and you shall be forgiven,' she said. I almost had to
throw her out. The last thing we needed was her telling me to pray.
Thankfully she left without further trouble and I sat wondering
when these people would just go away. I don't mean to run Christianity down but when you see it head on you'll discover yourself
how closed-minded most of these people are. A quick talk with
them and you're forgiven.

Over the next few weeks we had to endure a kind of ritual-
istic fear and silence from all and sundry. If we left the house, we
didn't know what we would to return to. We expected bricks and
firebombs to be delivered via the front window at every moment.
People in the street turned their backs as we passed. That we could

put up with. One woman actually crossed the street and stopped right in front of me. I was about to excuse myself and pass around her when she spat in my face.

A few days later, a representative of the police called and advised me to resign. I had to play a very shrewd game here to secure any financial future for myself and Patrick. I readily agreed to resign. He left happily and I left for the doctor's office to play the best part of a paranoid human you have ever seen. I got a four-weeks' sick line from him and got it photocopied. I then sent this into RUC headquarters and awaited another visit. They called within four days and again asked me to resign. I said I would and this went on for a while. After some weeks of bluffing and more 'Are you going to resign?' 'Yes, of course I am', I think they caught on to my ploy. I woke up one morning, a Monday I think it was, and the phone rang. A gay friend warned me that he had some bad news for me and that I should sit down. I panicked as I had thought someone had died. 'Listen, Brian,' he said softly, 'they've put everything in the papers.' He read out to me what the paper said – what I was supposed to have done and when, and then the angry outcry for blood. None of it was true. I honestly could not believe what was said. Could this be me they're talking about? Obviously those 'within' had decided to be more positive to get rid of me and released a pack of lies to the papers. My name was not mentioned but it may as well have been. Everything bar my house number was there in print. Unfortunately I could not sue as no names were mentioned, or any addresses, so in fact everyone knew who it was that they were talking about but I could only sit there and take it. I must say since then I have never bought a newspaper. I would not give them a penny for their anti-gay propaganda.

For days on end I shook nervously. I could not eat or sleep. Patrick and I were coming to the end of our tether. On the Sunday following the paper incident we visited my mum's. We had been invited to dinner and offered a chance to escape our tormentors. We got no further than the kitchen when my mum handed me a paper. The Sunday version of the weekly. There it was again. On page eleven in a long column. 'GAY COP TO BE THROWN OUT OF RUC.' My head went light and I fell into a dead faint. For the first time in my life I fainted. Patrick helped me to a chair and I was given a cup of tea. I started to cry again and so did Patrick. We held each other for a while and my mum left us to it. She cried in the other room, as once again they too had hit a low spot.

It was pointed out to me later that we were fortunate to be out to our parents and luckily we had already informed them of what was happening. What the police had hoped for in going to the papers was that the whole thing would come as a terrible shock to our families, who they wrongly assumed didn't know, and that would put further pressure on me to resign. They never guessed our parents already knew we were gay. I was grateful for the support given by our respective parents and the love they showed us. But of course if they hadn't already known about us then I doubt that I could have explained anything in such a way that they would have believed it.

After the paper incidents, I had a call from the RUC Federation representative whom I had also known as a friend. He conveyed to me his support and also offered me a helping hand in any way he could. I thanked him and asked about a solicitor for court. He told me that I would have to wait and see what the DPP said first and to get one thing out of the way before diving into another. He gave me confidence to carry on and fight for my mental freedom and the right to live as we chose. We were hurting no one but the ignorant scum who thrived on gossip and scandal. This whole thing was happening to me simply because I had the courage to live with another man and continue my career as a police officer.

Three weeks later the papers were filled with gay witch-hunts within the RUC. One man, a heterosexual Inspector, was videoed in his back lounge wearing his wife's clothes while she was shopping. He resigned immediately. Another was set up as I was. Again, an immediate resignation. Fifteen to twenty others went the same way and I stood fighting them. I was not going to give in to their pressures, although I cannot blame the others for resigning. They had different situations, and some also had wives and children to look after. The unfortunate thing for them was that most of the wives left their husbands with kids in tow to go some place else. Those poor guys were left totally in the cold with two committing suicide because of unnamed scum. It all seemed that there would be no let-up in the hunt for victims. Spies were sent forth to spot anyone in the services and to report back. There was a flurry of resources used to get anyone on suspicion of being gay. I wondered who was organizing all this and who was to be next. The Sunday World *newspaper latched on to the hunts and one brave reporter questioned the high profile inquisition of the RUC. He asked why there were now so many gay men (and now two lesbian) police officers being hounded out of the force. A special gay information centre was set up somewhere in the north of Ireland, but it seemed to die a death shortly after opening its lines. Maybe if it had been organized to help heterosexuals then it would be financed by local government.*

Anyway, things seemed to cool down over the weeks. The difficulties remained though. Should Patrick and I move home? Who would give us a place to live? Where would we be safe? All these questions ran through our heads daily, but in reality there was no big choice. If we moved they would simply follow. If we shared a house with friends then they would also be persecuted. Hard as it was, we decided to sit our ground until it was over.

I was still attending the doctor and on one appointment he sat me down and spoke quietly to me. He told me that a friend of his (a very high-ranking officer and also well known to myself) had told him of what was going on in the force and that he thought it was all wrong. I had served under this officer in the early 1980s and he knew I was not the stereotyped gay but a sturdy officer who did not run in the face of a gun battle or riot. Anyway, the doctor also found these happenings frightening and told me that he would support me where he could and handed me a sick line for six months. Six months! I could hardly believe it. Here was a man who would gain nothing from helping me; he was a just heterosexual male who found his own society sickening. I left his surgery 'a happy homosexual', feeling for that moment unafraid to face the authorities and their lies. When I got into the car, Patrick saw the smile on my face. Telling him what had happened he just grabbed me, and then for the first time in what seemed like years we laughed together.

Everything seemed to be turning in our favour as far as the false charges were concerned. We ignored people's disgusted looks as each of us gained strength. We even bought a bottle of Moët et

Chandon in the event of something really worthwhile celebrating.
OK, we were not in any way out of the woods, but it would not go
to waste in any event. We would either celebrate or commiserate
our end in this affair.

At around the same time as all the goings on in the papers,
we decided to take the car and go for a long drive, away from home
and people. We needed the time away to get some piece of mind for
a short time. With everything packed in a makeshift hamper, we
made our way to our destination. The sun was out and once we had
reached a safe distance we gave a sigh of relief, feeling free of our
burdens. After ten or so miles I told Patrick that I would do nothing
but lie in a soft patch of grass and take in the silence of the country-
side. He nodded, and as he did, the engine roared, the accelerator
pedal dropped forward and the car began to gain speed. Taken
totally by surprise I applied the brakes only to find the engine
pulling hard. Within a short time we were nearing ninety miles per
hour. I manoeuvred the car as best I could around bends, parked
cars and hills. Nothing would slow us down. I was sure that we
were not going to get out of that situation alive. I looked at Patrick.
He sat rigid in his seat willing me to do something. I looked ahead.
I saw a field with newly turned soil in it and decided to run the car
into that. Maybe we could still get out alive if I drove in at the right
angle and we both held on for dear life. Then I thought of just
turning off the engine and braking fast, keeping the steering wheel
as straight as possible. Taking a chance, for everything here was
chance, I turned the ignition key off so that the engine died, then on
again and set the gears into neutral so as not to start the engine or
have the wheels lock into position. I held my foot firmly on the
brakes, but just enough to stop the car skidding. It worked. The car
slowed down and we came to a halt. The silence was overwhelm-
ing. I slumped over the steering wheel and could not help hearing
the thumping of my heart. Sweat began to pour from me. Then we
both jumped out of the car. After a few moments of just looking at
the car, I opened the bonnet and looked inside. After some search-
ing we found the accelerator cable. Using a screwdriver I un-
fastened the catches and examined the wire. In horror I asked
Patrick to look at the neatly cut wires. All had been cut but one or
two flimsy strands which were slightly frayed. If we had crashed

nothing untoward would have been noticed. But having been lucky we had the evidence in front of us. Some unnamed people had tried to kill us both. But even having the cable examined by an expert would not help us. We just had to be more careful than ever and check everything before moving the car anywhere. I had been close to death on many occasions but this one, having Patrick there with me, angered me deeply. After a little investigating of my own I found who exactly had carried out the deed. I would have damaged him physically had it not been for the fact that it would have only mounted more ammunition against us.

All this seems hard to believe I know, but I have tried to understate rather than overstate events. Sitting here now thinking back, I find it hard to comprehend what was happening to us. Why go to such lengths to rid yourself of a gay officer? They knew I would not speak out in public; they knew I was no longer a threat to them. So why go to all that trouble for one gay man? I wish I knew.

Six months after the initial questioning, the very same Chief Inspector called round to our home again. I expected nothing from him but contempt and his face showed every sign of it. He almost choked the words out when he said that there was to be no further action against us. I did not move a muscle. Instead I asked him if that was all. He said that disciplinary action would also be taken out against me for my unsociable lifestyle. I again asked him if that was all. He nodded. I stood up and told him to leave my home immediately. I did not want him there any longer. Inside myself I felt an almost fatal urge to attack him for having put us through sheer hell, but then Patrick looked at me and seeing my face, quickly led him down the hall and out the front door, slamming it behind him. When Patrick returned he found me with my head in my hands crying from sheer relief. He joined me and we must have held each other for the longest time. The champagne we had bought was finally opened and we granted each other good health. It was the best news we could have had. The disciplinary hearing would be nothing compared to this.

After taking advice from my Federation representative and consultations with Patrick, I found that my only safe route out of the RUC was to be medically discharged. After all, I had been shot *and had been in grenade attacks on a few occasions, so why not use this to my advantage. I needed no more persuading. On the Monday morning following the visit from the Chief Inspector, I made an appointment with a psychologist. I informed him (without telling him the whole story) that I found that I could no longer be part of the service as I was unstable. A quick fifteen-minute diagnosis was made and I was given a certificate of almost total insanity. That done I returned to my own doctor who agreed with the psychologist's findings, but wondered how I had bluffed him. I smiled and said nothing. He returned the smile, gave me a letter for the medical board and wished me all the luck in the world.*

In the interim, Patrick was on the lookout for a place for us to live temporarily. A hideaway if you like. We had no idea what would happen should I be given an honourable discharge. We had to cover my disappearance for a long time so that memories would fade and vendettas be forgotten or at least pushed away into a file.

Our lives in the gay world became better. We made many more friends on the scene. There was one club we used to go to in Belfast called the Carpenter Club. It was a wonderful place. I felt at last that I could go wherever I pleased, and did. I had been to gay pubs before but always with a careful eye out for you know who. It didn't matter now that they came into the pubs, I felt free. I had a feeling of almost total contempt for them, and when the test was placed before me, I sat upright as they passed. I said nothing, just simply looked them in the eye and dared them to question me.

Towards the end of 1988, I was summoned to headquarters for a meeting with the force psychologist. Passing known faces and ignoring jibes, I waltzed down the long corridors to a door marked 'Force Doctor'. On entering and giving my name, etc. I was asked to wait. Fifteen minutes later I was greeted by a thin man who seemed to need help. His face had a painful expression as if to say, 'All this crap for a few pounds.' He showed me to a very low chair. I ignored it and sat in the higher one. His chair. He looked stunned. Well, I thought, if he thinks I'm loony then this should satisfy him. He did not sit in the other chair though. He chose a desktop which rose above my head by two inches. After all this supremacy crap, the meeting itself lasted no more than three minutes. He began to talk and then I stopped him abruptly. 'Look,' I said staring him straight in the eye, 'if we are going to discuss my sexuality, then I must tell you that I am quite comfortable with it and find no reason for you to waste your time trying to convince me otherwise.' A moment's silence followed, then he slowly nodded, twice at first, then faster. 'Right,' he said standing up, 'I do not think there is any more to be said. You can go now.' And that was it. I went home feeling a kind of contentment that he actually went into this meeting with all kinds of propositions for aversion therapy and such, and I had just sidestepped it. It seemed that they were all falling over trying to get me on something. If I'd told them I couldn't handle my sexuality, they would have found a way of giving me dishonourable discharge. That would not have worried me in the ordinary sense, but I did not fight them this far to give up on my right to a deserving service record, thereby allowing them to taint any other gay officers they might hunt out. Someone had to make a stand. We live in an age now where, if we can find the courage, we must face these kind of people and say, 'You have no right to hunt me like a dog and tear me apart for my sexuality. I am prepared to face you and fight for my right to sexual freedom.'

On 18 October 1988, I received a letter informing me that I was now officially 'honourably' discharged from the RUC. There was no ceremony. No handshakes for a good service record. What I got just arrived in the post. I received a cheque for £15,000 and a pension of £300 a month (index-linked) for the rest of my life. We had actually won! All the terrible experiences of the past were fogged for that moment. It is still hard to describe the joy Patrick and I felt at finally being free from such a totally oppressive system. Two weeks and many celebrations later, we moved house to a flat in Newtownabbey, County Antrim. Our good neighbours fled the street for the sanctuary of their houses as we departed. I saw no need to gloat and simply smiled as we passed their beady eyes peering through the flittering blinds of supposed normal living. I wished them no goodness whatsoever and hoped that they would one day get something of a taste of our experiences. Before reaching the end of the road, I decided to leave my own mark on the street. Asking Patrick to slow the car, I opened the window and spat my contempt on the road, cleaning my mouth of their hatred. Then we drove on into a new life and an ever closer bond.

As I write, it is almost three years since I was discharged from the RUC. We have moved again and now live in a beautiful home which we love dearly. The two years spent in the flat were a hiding exercise and a break before starting out again. Something akin to holding your breath whilst a bad smell passes. We are happier now than ever before. Faces that I have known in the past (in the force) have looked at my smiling face and wondered why I am not what they expect from a homosexual. That stereotypical pervert that loves men but is gloomy and sad in life. I hope they pinched themselves and thought again. But they probably didn't. At least they will know that they have not and will not break us. We are still in love and stronger now than we have ever been. I am totally open without pushing my sexuality down anyone's throat. If they don't like me they can go elsewhere, I am staying where I am now, with Patrick by my side being the strong-willed lad he had always been. There were those that said I should have resigned when the whole thing fell open on us and there were numerous times when I wished that I had. I'm glad now that we did not give in. I would also say to other gay men and women that everyone is entitled to a career. In hindsight I made a mistake in ever joining the police, but I have also learnt by it and will use my experiences to help others should they need it.

Notes

1. I. Goffman, *Stigma: Notes on the Management of Spoiled Identity*, 1963, pp. 160 and 18.
2. B. Berzon, *Positively Gay*, 1979, p. 3.
3. R. C. Atchley, 'The ageing self', *Psychotherapy: Theory, Research, and Practice*, 19 (1982), pp. 388–96.
4. G. J. McDonald, 'Individual differences in the coming out process for gay men: implications for theoretical models', *Journal of Homosexuality*, 8 (1982), pp. 47–60.
5. Research suggests that the accomplishment of a homosexual identity may take a number of years, anything from six (B. M. Dank, 'Coming out in the gay world', *Psychiatry*, 34 (1971), pp. 180–97) to ten (R. R. Troiden, 'Becoming homosexual: a model of homosexual identity acquisition', *Psychiatry*, 42 (1979), pp. 362–73).

The author's research did not provide data by which a comparison of identity formation might be made; thus the view that police officers endure an extended period of identity organization remains conjecture at this time (see M. Burke, 'Homosexuality in the British police', Ph.D. thesis, University of Essex, 1993).

Chapter eleven

A Unique Contribution?

THE difficulties associated with what sociologists call *simultaneous position occupancy* and the resultant marginality of the gay or lesbian police officer were examined in Chapter 3. The reverse face of this coin, however, suggests that the subjective approach of an insider combined with the objectivity of an outsider means that marginal individuals are often adept and capable critics of the dominant society, able to recognize the inconsistencies and hypocrisy of the unconscious majority. As Stonequist has said, 'The gap between its moral pretensions and its actual achievements jumps to his eye.'[1] The sociologist Georg Simmel similarly describes his notion of the 'stranger', of one who lives in intimate association with the world but who never identifies with it so completely that they are unable to view it with a certain critical detachment. 'Inevitably he becomes, relatively to his cultural milieu, the individual with the wider horizon, the keener intelligence, the more detached and rational viewpoint.'[2]

Most lesbian and gay officers believe that their eventual acceptance within the police will not only help to improve their own situation but will also result in dividends for the police as employers. Firstly, they possess the detailed knowledge and experience necessary to communicate and work with minority communities more effectively, but more importantly, many such officers believe that having to fight their way through a hostile and inhospitable world has led to the development of many police-serviceable qualities.

● *Thames Valley Drugs Squad PC,*
age 26, resigned with five years' service

I think because of what we go through we become sensitized
to many of society's problems and are able to stand back and assess
things in a diversity of ways. We know what it's like to be innocent
and at the wrong end of the firing line. I certainly had a lot to offer
the police and I think that they lost a lot when I went. For a start, I
was more broad-minded, more compassionate, less aggressive and
less likely to run into violent confrontations through insensitivity
than most of my colleagues. So I always questioned things and they
didn't much appreciate that. I also think I appreciated people's
problems more. Not just those from my own group but from all
minority groups. I think we're more tolerant than most people and
are good at facing new situations more open-mindedly and more
maturely. From my experience once they're happy with themselves
and not screwed up about it, gay people don't have so much to
prove, so they don't get drawn into the canteen culture; they don't
need the police corporate identity because they're more independently minded. They've had to be. The police should draw on their
multicultural resources. But they don't because they don't know
what they're losing and even if they did, they'd be more worried
about their macho image than what people like me had to offer.

● *Devon and Cornwall PC, age 41,*
eighteen years' service

I'm potentially a much more useful asset to the police than
they realize, and a useful asset to the gay community as well. There
is definitely room for liaison here. I'm beneficial to both groups
because I'm influential. Most problems are caused through ignorance. I understand both sides – I understand the parts that neither
of the others does. I could get shot of all the nasty stereotypes and
explain to both parties what things look like from the other side of
the fence. Unfortunately, the Job just isn't that bothered with it at
the moment, but they will be eventually. Just like it took time to
take the ethnic issue seriously. They've already realized that ethnic

*minorities have a big police contribution to make in today's multi-
cultural society, and gay officers have got just as big contribution to
make. Of course you may not want such a multicultural society,
but that's a different question. Since we've got one now, the right
police service for it will be one that reflects its diversity. That
principle is basic to the concept of policing any society by consent.
It's only right that the police draw from all areas of society and be
representative. If the police are drawn only from one particular
group, then by excluding other groups they distance themselves
from all those who are not part of mainstream society, and that
kind of a police service could never work.*

● *Metropolitan PC, age 25, four years' service*

*We're already making use of our known gay officers at my
station. If we have a licensing problem for example at a gay pub or
club, then they get gay officers to deal with it to try and avoid a
confrontation. Also, there was an incident where this guy was killed
in a motorway pile-up a while back and someone had to inform
his other half, who was a guy. Anyway the CAD operator, who
obviously knew about me, called me back to the station on the
radio and asked if I could deal with a death message. So I and
another PC went round there to tell him what had happened, which
is about the most unpleasant task you can get in the police. I think
we dealt with it very well – or at least as well as it could be dealt
with under the circumstances. I felt it was lucky that I was on duty
really because if someone else had gone, they might have been too
embarrassed or too frightened to deal with it properly and they
might have left prematurely. Not that I came out to him or anything, but I was able to deal with it in a sympathetic way because I
understood what was going on. I was able to take it seriously
because I could empathize; I knew what having that happen to you
must have felt like, and so what came from me was genuine. I didn't
treat it as a farce. Others might have found the situation slightly
comical.*

● *Durham Detective Inspector, age 37, fifteen years' service*

At the very least, gay officers can help mitigate the organizational and cultural homophobia that exists in the police. The extent to which they can do this will be governed of course by their situation in terms of rank, station, department, and undoubtedly, by the extent to which they have accepted their own homosexuality. This mitigation will, in many cases, inevitably be covert and isolated. However, there are other situations where it can perhaps be more open and more structured. A good example of this occurred in the force in which I served several years ago. A homosexual man was murdered and it was thought that his sexuality was a significant factor in the offence. Enquiries were therefore concentrated on the gay community, not only within the force area but also within the region. A Detective Sergeant thought in some quarters to be gay was appointed as the liaison officer with the gay community.

I should emphasize that it is only supposition on my part that the officer's appointment and the opinion held by certain people were connected but even if they were not, the case is certainly a good example of the type of contribution that gay and lesbian officers can make to policing over and above that which they make in their day-to-day work.

A couple of years later, there was another murder in the same area. As it turned out, there was no homosexual connection but at one stage in the enquiry there was a possibility that there might have been one. I was given the job of researching the previous investigation to discover any connection between the deceased in the latter case and persons interviewed in the former. (But why me?!)

Reading the statements taken from the many gay men interviewed during the course of the first enquiry left me feeling very angry. Why on earth some detectives in this type of investigation feel the need to go into intimate and technical detail of people's sex lives defeats me. It's almost voyeuristic. They certainly wouldn't do it if the subject was straight. The enquiry had obviously taken on the nature, not exactly of a witch-hunt, but it certainly went beyond what I think was necessary. It seemed to have got wrapped up in trying to discover every single member of a 'homosexual network' in the area and in doing so, lost sight of its real goal. People were interviewed because they knew someone who knew someone who knew the deceased. That investigation was a good example of the ignorance prevalent in many police officers and of the continuing need for education. Perhaps an 'out' gay liaison officer would have been able to prevent a lot of unnecessary effort in that case as well as providing a little of that education.

In addition to whatever contribution lesbian and gay police officers have to offer the police service, it may also be worthwhile thinking about what such officers could offer to the gay community and to society at large.

It will be a long time before the gay community (and especially gay men) will be able to deal with the police in an atmosphere of complete trust. One way of building that trust might be to encourage the recruitment of gays and lesbians in much the same way that the recruitment of ethnic minorities is encouraged now. This would send positive signals to the gay community and also to the rest of the public. To have it officially accepted that being homosexual and a police officer is OK would do a lot to help break down prejudice and received opinion on the subject and to demolish taboos. This has perhaps already been started with the 'coming out' of the Lesbian and Gay Police Association and the many favourable comments made regarding its existence in certain influential quarters.

Of course officers can only provide these additional 'services' if they are relaxed about themselves and allowed to operate in an atmosphere of acceptance. Where this is not the case, officers will not only be unable to assist both the police and the gay communities but may be a positive hindrance and may even be unable to perform their regular duties properly. This was illustrated to me a few years ago when I was a uniformed constable. At the time I was just coming to realize that I was homosexual. By coincidence at the same time a couple of other probationers had been caught in a gay club in another part of the force area when it had been visited by the Plain Clothes Department. This was the talking-point of the moment and certainly the dominant opinion on my shift was very anti-gay. The town in which I was serving didn't have any gay pubs or, as far as I was aware at the time, very many gay people. However, one Friday night I was called to an incident in the town centre which turned out to be quite a nasty case of queerbashing. A gang of yobs had beaten up two gay men. When I arrived, the offenders had left but the victims' friends were all at the scene. I was surrounded by a group of very angry and quite effeminate gay men and a larger number of very angry and quite uneffeminate lesbians. I'm afraid I didn't handle the situation very well at all. I was absolutely petrified with fear. And I didn't want to be involved at any price.

I'm very ashamed of my actions now, even though I understand the reasons for them. I went through the motions of taking details and circulating descriptions over the air but I just wanted to get away before the Sergeant or anyone else arrived at the scene. The last thing I wanted was for someone else to arrive and realize the nature of the incident. This would have only given more cause for mirth and anti-gay jokes in the canteen. The other reason I didn't want that to happen was because it made me feel so uncomfortable. Whenever the subject of homosexuality was mentioned I used to blush very deeply and start to shake.

Anyway, my reluctance to get involved obviously communicated itself to the victims and their friends who were quite rightly disgusted, and said so. No doubt it confirmed all their prejudices about the police. It also allowed the offenders to get away with it.

● *Hertfordshire PC, age 32, ten years' service*

It's becoming more and more apparent these days that there are millions of people out there who are living alternative lives of varying kinds with corresponding alternative values. None of them and all of them are valid because the days of a single Christian ethic are over. Today there exists a multiplicity of lifestyles and you can't go about treating everyone the same. Even the law recognizes that in exempting Sikhs from wearing crash helmets on motor cycles. That's the way it is today and we have to be able to adapt as a police service if we are going to stay afloat.

Everyone has got something to contribute to this job. There is so much to understand out there. It's a very complicated society we live in – you don't need to be a sociologist to see that. There's black, white, blue, green – call them what you will. If we can learn to come to terms with just a few of the differences then we will all get along better, and homosexuality is one of the things which the Job has had a problem with for a long time.

That gay cops can be an asset in related incidents has been proven in New York's Greenwich Village. In May 1990, after a bomb wrecked a popular local club known as Uncle Charlie's, it was largely due to the action of gay cop Edgar Rodrigues, who was immediately on the scene and dealing with the community, that a major public-order incident was averted. However, not all officers see the liaison exercise working out quite so smoothly.

● *West Midlands PC, age 37,*
twelve years' service

    I'm not all that sure about gay/police liaison really. I think that anyone who tried to liaise between the two would just end up taking shit from both sides, and in the end their heads would blow up. That's what happened with the black issue. The best way to solve these things is just to have more of them in the Job.

● *Metropolitan WPC Home Beat officer,*
age 34, sixteen years' service

    I think that we're in a unique position to bridge the gap between the two communities and help inform and direct police policy in that area. But once that happens, you have to watch out because then you really do have two groups tugging at your loyalties. If you go to some kind of an incident at a gay establishment, or if you're there socially when the police arrive for something, people might expect you to get involved and liaise with the police to sort things out. That's OK but I think that the Job would really have a problem with it if it got political. I've been in that sort of situation before and I refused to get involved.

● *Metropolitan PC, age 34, five years' service*

I'm concerned about the possibility of the police using gay officers to go into gay pubs to find offences simply because they know that those officers will feel comfortable in those venues and not stand out so much. If that happens then those officers will find themselves involved in controversial legislation involving their own community and that will eventually destroy all the bridges that are being built to bring the two closer together. The officers might also have to give evidence in court and may well suffer personal threats as a result. That's not to say that homosexual officers will be totally biased and not deal with their own like everyone else in 99 per cent of cases, I'm just saying that where the legislation is clearly unfair or discriminatory, it could cause a problem. It would be the same as asking a black officer in South Africa to seek out blacks who were breaking the old apartheid laws. There is a line to be drawn.

Notes

1. E. V. Stonequist, *The Marginal Man*, 1961, p. 155.
2. R. Park, in his introduction to Stonequist, *The Marginal Man*, pp. xvii–xviii.

Chapter twelve

Equal Opportunities

THE testimonials of officers thus far demonstrate a widespread fear of discrimination and/or blackmail on the grounds of a differing sexual orientation and it is clear that such fears are exacerbated by the lack of an effective equal opportunities policy in most forces. The South Yorkshire Constabulary was the first of Britain's fifty-two police forces to underwrite an equal opportunities policy that included the words 'sexual orientation' and yet despite leading the way on this important issue, the Chief Constable of the force, Richard Wells, does not view the move as a particularly radical one and sees no reason why the decision should cause problems. 'There is a widespread and irrational fear – particularly amongst men – about homosexuality,' says Wells, who continues:

> Because of this and because of the feeling that their sexual preference is best kept secret, there must be severe pressure on gay police officers, of whatever sex. Police work is difficult enough already without extra pressures of that sort and I would welcome more openness, understanding and tolerance. In the current climate, secrecy in a police officer about sexual orientation can add, quite unhealthily, to opportunities for blackmail and will also stifle debate on an important social issue.[1]

The inclusion of a sexual orientation clause in a British police service's equal opportunities policy is a major step forward in the battle against heterosexism, although perhaps predictably, it is a move which has resulted in some discord as other forces are pressured to follow the South Yorkshire example.[2] But it is not the first time that the police have suffered this kind of difficulty. There was controversy during the mid-1960s when Britain's ethnic minorities were first invited to become a part of the 'Thin Blue Line' leading up to the recruitment of the Met's first black officer, Norrell Roberts, in 1967; and between 1972 and 1974, when women were first fully integrated into the service, there was a similar crisis.

Socio-psychological research into the nature of prejudice has suggested that frequent amenable, equal-status contact with members of 'outgroups' can significantly reduce levels of prejudice with respect to those minorities. One might predict in accordance with such findings that the attitudes of police officers towards people of colour, women, homosexuals and other minorities will be directly influenced by the proportion of those group members that exist within the service itself. There are two key questions. Firstly, have sexism and misogyny in the police decreased since the acceptance and large-scale recruitment of women? Secondly, have racism and xenophobia decreased since the active recruitment from ethnic minorities? Although there is little hard data with which one might begin to construct a comprehensive reply to such questions, I suspect that the answer to both questions would be yes.

The implicit inference, then, is that by having visible lesbians and gay men in the police service, levels of homosexual antipathy might be lowered. This hypothesis might be partially tested by investigating the effect of gay and lesbian recruitment and equal opportunities policy implementation in countries such as the Netherlands and on the east and west coasts of the USA.

Decreased levels of prejudice ought to result in a corresponding reduction in discrimination. Decriminalization or other legislative modification in favour of legal equality would also help to erode the problem. It would do so in several ways. Firstly, it would dispense practical aid to the problem by offering both a legal and, in the case of an equal opportunities statement, an internal means of redress. In addition, a change in the law would demonstrate a more open-minded establishment view which set an official and authoritative norm, helping to create an effective self-fulfilling prophecy over the long term. The 1976 Race Relations Act is believed to have generated a significant change in attitude towards blacks in this way simply by defining discrimination on the basis of colour as unacceptable. However, the process of wider attitude change may take many years to accomplish leaving 'expatriates' to cope with everyday grass-roots prejudice just as they had done before during the interim. It is no doubt for that reason that many officers feel that an equal opportunities policy covering sexual orientation would be of little functional value to them.

● *Metropolitan WDS, age 34, resigned with nine years' service*

Equal opps. means nothing to me because I don't care what's introduced – the Job can say it's OK, the Federation can say it's OK – but it's the blokes on the relief you have to work with. Attitudes might be changing at the top, but it will be a long time before PCs accept that they are working with gay officers. No way would it have tempted me to come out.

● *Sussex PC, age 25, six years' service*

Having such a policy is fine in an abstract sense – it might give people more confidence – but it's still got to be positively and effectively applied in all areas of the police service. Just because you have some form of protection against discrimination doesn't mean that an out police officer is going to survive very long in the police. There are already equal opportunities in other police forces and that hasn't stopped people's lives being made uncomfortable to the extent that they have had to leave. We've had equal opps. for blacks and women for some time now and it hasn't stopped them from having a hard time either. I think it's a question of educating society; it's society that has to change at the end of the day, not just the police.

● *Metropolitan PC, age 24, six months' service*

I doubt it would make much difference at the moment – I have to concentrate on getting through probation first – but I might need it at some stage in the future if I come up against somebody who's above me who's a complete bigot. It would be nice to have it there as backup. Also, whilst I'd like to see equal opportunities for everyone in the police, I don't want to see gay people getting into the police if they're not suitable just because they're gay. I don't agree with that.

An additional concern for many officers is that even if an effective policy were to be introduced for their benefit, it would probably not be effective across all departments and might only provide equal prospects for promotion up to a certain rank.

● *Metropolitan YACS PS, age 34, seven years' service*

Certain areas of work are particularly sensitive for the police. Take the Youth and Community Section for example. Even now equal opportunities are in down here, what do you think your chances of getting a transfer to that section would be if they knew you were gay? They're nil. Because if it ever got out that a gay or lesbian police officer had anything to do with teaching children then there would probably be a public outcry. That's because a lot of people out there still believe that if you're gay that means that you want to molest little kids, or convert them, which is such a load of crap. But the police would rather not have to deal with that kind of allegation, so although with a new equal opps. policy they wouldn't be able to refuse you on the grounds of your sexual orientation, they'd simply find another reason. If you were already in the section when they found out, then again, they'd find a reason to move you. It's not hard. If they knew about me I'd be out by the end of the week.

● *Metropolitan PS, age 29, ten years' service*

Equal opportunities is an interesting subject because it's not as simple as it sounds at first. It could be, but nothing's simple for the police. For example, will equal opps. cover every specialized department within a force? These are the kind of things that will worry them. What about SB? Can you be a shot? And what about Royalty Protection? I mean, I've already avoided applying for a job with the Royal Family because of the vetting. Chances are, any equal opportunities statement won't include some of those things because they're seen as 'super-sensitive'. But that will be an unofficial policy, you can be sure. In reality of course, there's no reason why all of them shouldn't be included. To suggest otherwise is to pander to the prejudice that has dominated the discussions on the subject for so long and it makes a mockery of any policy that may be in existence in that force by showing it to be nothing more than a device which serves to placate, but which is not truly believed by those who implement it.

But let's take the objections anyway. SB is a classic. If you want to work in such a department, so the argument says, you should be firstly totally stable and secondly not open to blackmail. And homosexuals are potentially neither. So the argument says. The second point is easily despatched by announcing an equal opps. policy and allowing officers to come out, thereby negating the possibility of blackmail. In the case of the first objection, to believe that homosexuals are inherently less stable than heterosexuals is unsubstantiated and there is no evidence to suggest that such is the case. Where homosexuals are found to be unstable, such instability is not inherent, but either a proportional embodiment of the instability in the heterosexual world, or as likely, the instability is caused by the stress of living a double life. Again, equal opportunities would go some way to relieve this. The same instability argument is applicable to shots. If they are unstable, then like heterosexuals they should be refused the opportunity, after testing, to obtain a certificate. Otherwise, ability is the only valid criterion for the job.

A standard Youth and Community argument might put forward two positions: (a) that homosexuals are more likely to take an interest in young children than heterosexuals, and (b) that if parents found out about homosexual officers teaching their 'babies' in schools, they might cause a stink and cause the police embarrassment. OK, firstly, statistics clearly show that the vast majority of child sexual abuse is heterosexual – most commonly perpetrated by *father or stepfather on daughter or stepdaughter. That argument is plainly spurious.*

The second argument against officers being allowed to enter the YACS is hardly better. Are the police to lead the way on social issues and set an example based on a greater experience and understanding of social issues, or do we simply let the public dictate an outdated morality to us? In other words, if we are convinced that we are doing the right thing in introducing equal opportunities for lesbians and gay men, having properly researched the issue, then we should have the guts to stick by that conviction and challenge the prejudice of the public whenever they throw it at us as a reason for maintaining a prejudicial stance on the issue. If we know better than they do, then we should tell them that they're wrong; that their notions are outdated and invalid. The police service is big enough to stand up for itself and oughtn't to allow itself to be beaten down by some ignorant mother who kicks up a fuss because the policeman or woman who gave a talk to her little Johnny simply happened to be gay.

● *Greater Manchester Chief Inspector, age 31, twelve years' service*

Going back to discrimination, the way I see it continuing is like this: even if sexual orientation were to be included in police services' equal opportunities policies, then it still would not follow that homosexual officers would be equally likely to get promotion. Imagine that one of the many important questions when considering someone for promotion, particularly above Inspector, is, 'Has this officer got the necessary credibility to carry the confidence of his or her junior officers if promoted to the rank?' If those on the board felt that, rightly or wrongly, because of that person's sexual orientation they would be unable to carry that confidence, then I think that a board could probably justify the position that the individual in question ought not to be promoted – unless they had a number of compensating qualities. If other – say, good leadership – qualities were there, however, then there's no reason why being gay per se should be sufficient to result in a significant loss of confi-

dence. In fact, if equal opportunities were to come in and a force wanted to show that they were taking the issue seriously, then it is conceivable that they might actually positively discriminate in your favour on that basis. You can never tell which way it will go.

One important area of discrimination certainly not coming within the scope of current police equal opportunities policies concerns pension rights. At present, police pensions pay out a half-pension to the surviving spouse of a married pensioner who dies. However, the pension ceases altogether for a 'single' police pensioner who dies, even one who has been living with a partner for several years.

The fact that some officers are pessimistic about the effectiveness of any police policy that purported to offer equal opportunities to lesbian and gay police officers is interesting but irrelevant when it comes to determining whether or not such a policy should exist. As paragraph 9 of the Home Office Circular 87/1989, 'Equal opportunities policies in the police service', states,

> It is not enough for a force to claim to be an equal opportunities employer. Chief officers of police must take the necessary steps to identify and eliminate discriminatory practices and to guard against the risk of discriminating unwittingly.[3]

Despite the cynicism of some officers, it seems that most would welcome such a policy, and many believe that it would also benefit the police as an organization.

● *Metropolitan Crime Support Group PC, age 36, ten years' service*

I believe that clear equal opportunities policy statements would lessen the risk of overt discrimination, allowing gay and lesbian officers to become more open about their sexuality should they wish to. Apart from greatly improving the quality of life for the officers themselves, there would be several possible advantages to the police service:

1. The service would be able to place lesbian and gay officers in positions where their sexuality could be of practical use, for example in the investigation of gay murders and queer-bashing, or in community liaison roles.

2. *The public and especially the gay community would have greater confidence that the police service was genuinely seeking to represent all sections of the community, rather than simply paying lip-service to that ideal. A continued refusal to include orientation can only add credence to the claims of pressure groups such as the Gay London Policing Group [GALOP] of the 'overwhelmingly prejudiced attitudes [of the police] towards homosexuals'.*

3. *Officers might be less likely to resort to 'socially unacceptable' sexual behaviour, thereby reducing the damage to the service resulting from criminal prosecutions and the ensuing adverse publicity.*

● *Metropolitan Mounted WPC, age 24, six years' service*

Including sexual orientation in our statement would show that the Job was taking the whole thing seriously. They'd be making an effort for those already serving and also showing that it wasn't a problem as far as recruitment is concerned. Additionally of course, I would then be able to invoke the force grievance procedure, which is very important. I used to be a bit sceptical about how much the whole thing would work but a couple of recent cases have shown that when something goes wrong, managers are, to an extent, individually liable as far as damages are concerned, and that might make a real difference, since the best way to hit a police officer is through his pocket.

For the most part, the observations of these officers are somewhat academic because the vast majority of forces do not yet have fully effective equal opportunities policies. Many are now researching the issue but in most cases the challenge of sexual orientation would appear to be overwhelming. The irony of the situation lies in the fact that the dilemma which now threatens police credibility with the lesbian and gay communities was ultimately of their own making, since the only truly comprehensive equal opportunities policy is the one which is effective *without referencing any specific group as receiving special protection under its various clauses.* However, once the step has been taken to allude to certain groups under the terms of a policy, then the next best policy is that one which mentions all possible minorities, since to embrace some groups is to reject others via the laws of exclusion. Thus, most police forces are now in the difficult position that, having elected to include 'sex or marital status, colour, race, nationality, and ethnic or national origins', they effectively exclude all other categories, including sexual orientation and disability. In order to justify this position, the police have employed various arguments, few of which would appear to have cut any ice with their gay officers.

● *Manchester WPS, age 27, eight years' service*

I love the arguments that the police are using to avoid put-ting sexual orientation in. One is that they aren't doing it because it would be wrong to discriminate in favour of a specific minority, as one Superintendent said in one of the police magazines.[4] I couldn't believe it. So what about the Met's Personnel and Training Depart-ment then? Everyone knows that they have been spending tens of thousands of pounds on a massive, high-quality recruitment campaign aimed at the ethnic communities. We've been bending over backwards for years now to get them in, and positive discrimi-nation is the name of the game when it comes to getting them through the system. The other argument is that they don't need to include anything special because they're not prejudiced against homosexuals. Does that mean then that they admit to being preju-diced against coloured minorities? It's hilarious.

In some forces, it seems that the situation caused by the lack of orientation-'friendly' equal opportunities policies has resulted in a peculiar ethical paradox, as explained by the following constable.

● *Metropolitan PC, age 27, six years' service*

Many public bodies have already issued policy statements of non-discrimination on the grounds of sexual orientation. These include some twenty government departments including: Customs and Excise, Ministry of Defence, Department of Social Security, Home Office, Department of Health, and Department of Education and Science.[5] It will be noticed that the Home Office figures in this list, a fact which created a somewhat contradictory situation within the Metropolitan Police until 1992 and probably still does so in other forces.

Police civil staff enjoy the same conditions of employment, etc. as Home Office civil servants; accordingly, the Metropolitan Police Office adopted for its civil staff a strongly worded equal opportunities policy which included sexual orientation. Any breach of this policy by civil staff was treated as a serious disciplinary matter. In stark contrast, the equal opportunities policy adopted by the force to cover its police officers was much weaker, and notably did not extend cover to sexual orientation.

The operation of two separate policies within the one organization can lead to situations where, for example, two gay men could be working from the same office, one a member of the civil staff, enjoying full protection from discrimination by civil staff management (but apparently with nothing to protect him from discrimination by police management), and the other, a police officer, with no protection against such discrimination whatsoever. This situation is clearly contrary to paragraph 24 of the Home Office guidelines. The HO circular to all forces [No. 87/1989, 'Equal opportunities policies in the police service'] states, 'Where police officers and police civilians are working together ... it is essential that there should be, so far as possible, consistency of treatment in the application of equal opportunities policies.'

Little comparative research would appear to have been done on police equal opportunities policies, but it seems likely that other forces are still in a situation where lesbian and gay civilian staff are being covered by comprehensive local authority policies whilst their police colleagues go unprotected. Finally, the issue of promotion has featured highly among the concerns of officers. Hence, the last word on the subject of equal opportunities goes to Richard Wells, the Chief Constable of the South Yorkshire Constabulary:

> Provided that an officer's sexual conduct, as with anyone else, is within the law I see no reason why they shouldn't be treated absolutely equally in terms of promotion or work opportunity.[6]

The South Yorkshire equal opportunities policy not only stands in testimony of that declaration, it also illustrates the general viability of such policies in Britain. Only reluctance and trepidation prevent their universal employment. (The full South Yorkshire policy is reprinted in Appendix B.)

Notes

1. *Police Review*, 18 January 1991, p. 105.
2. At the time of writing, South Yorkshire, West Yorkshire, Bedfordshire, Lancashire, Leicestershire, Avon and Somerset, Hertfordshire, Derbyshire and the Metropolitan Police have included the words 'sexual orientation' in their equal opportunities policies. Others forces are expected to follow in the near future.
3. See also Appendix C for further extracts from this circular.
4. *Police Review*, 8 June 1990. Reported comments of Superintendent Ian Buchan.
5. Now the Department for Education.
6. *Police Review*, 18 January 1991, p. 105.

Chapter thirteen

The Lesbian and Gay Police Association

The reported formation of a Lesbian and Gay Police
Association ... is a development never envisaged by
contributors to the first *Police Journal* and one which
will have caused ex-police officers to shake their heads
in utter disbelief ... There is, surely, nothing gay about
buggery, and society should be reluctant to accept it as
'normal'.[1]

THE passage from resistance to tolerance and eventual
acceptance trodden by some of the most influential British police
forces in respect of the Lesbian and Gay Police Association
(LAGPA) will be of interest to any general scholar of the police,
whilst its impact on police politics and culture at all levels – from
the initial training of recruits, to matters of welfare and equal
opportunities policies, to discipline and grievance procedures – is
potentially immense. But the founding of a gay police group in
Britain at this time also raises questions in the arena of sociology
and sexual politics. Why Britain? Why 1990? The development of a
specific organization for homosexual and bisexual police officers is
significant because it represents an important historical milestone in
the evolution of sexual politics in Britain, and perhaps globally.
I say globally, not because Britain is unique but because the formation of such a group appears to represent an international trend. A

number of similar groups have been discovered by the author during the course of this research; with two notable exceptions, they appear to have developed almost in parallel (but independently) and in some cases are synchronous with their British counterpart. Those exceptions are embodied in the San Francisco and New York associations (Golden State Peace Officers Association (GSPOA), founded 1979, and Gay Officers Action League (GOAL), founded 1983), whose cities' non-heterosexual populations might have been expected to anticipate such events elsewhere in the world by the interval which in fact occurred. That countries like the Netherlands, famed for their acceptance of sexual diversity, were not the first to organize in this realm is perhaps more surprising. Yet the situations of these countries are not analogous. Indeed, it may be the very tolerance of nations like Holland which is responsible for their comparative impassivity in this regard; the urgency of the situation is, perhaps, less acute. Nevertheless, it is still more urgent than in those countries which do not simply tolerate sexual diversity but appear to embrace it. In such countries, it seems that the need for support networks like LAGPA is all but negligible. A case in point is Denmark. It had been suggested to the author that there was a lesbian and gay police group in existence in Denmark. It transpired after protracted enquiries, however, that although the country has no shortage of gay police officers, there was, for good reason, no support group. Jens Boesen, a Danish officer with sixteen years' service, explained in a letter to the author:

> I have always been openly gay and I've never had any problems being a gay officer. Homosexuality is no big deal here; the attitude to sexual behaviours is very relaxed. My partner and I walk hand in hand on the street and nobody really cares. As you probably know, gay people can marry in Denmark and so I did last year to an American. We've even appeared at police parties as the married couple we are and there have been no problems. I don't know of any gay police officers who have had problems in or outside the force because of their sexuality. A gay police group just isn't needed in Denmark.

There appear, then, to be grounds for identifying several broad categories of (Western) nation with regard to the development of 'gay police' support groups. This might go some way towards explaining the existence (or non-existence) of such groups, as well as discrepancies in the timing of their evolution. Firstly, there are those countries whose sexual ethic would seem to leave them without demand for such an organization – as is ostensibly the case in Denmark. Then, there are those whose sexual ethic is less permissive, and these may be further subdivided. Within the less permissive countries there may be certain states or cities, with large, stable homosexual populations and 'citizen-friendly' constitutions (viz. New York and San Francisco) where gay rights were further advanced, years before the swell empowered other nations.

An in-depth analysis of gay police officers internationally and of their sociological significance in relation to their societies would undoubtedly be a profitable exercise. It might transpire, for example, that the development of the homosexual police group could be used as a crude yardstick for evaluating the impact of lesbian and gay politics within different cultures. Such an analysis must, however, await future research. Nevertheless, I have attempted, using the information available, to provide a brief outline of the various gay police groups known of at this time, both in order to give some sense of perspective to the circumstances leading to the formation of the Lesbian and Gay Police Association in Britain, and in order that some comparison between groups may be made.

GOAL

In 1979, a New York City police officer named Charles Cochrane, a Sergeant with fourteen years' service in the police department, took legal advice prior to testifying before the city council in support of a controversial new gay rights bill. In doing so, Cochrane became the first New York cop publicly to declare himself gay. It was hoped that the bill in question would outlaw discrimination against homosexuals with regard to employment, thus safeguarding those already working in, and facilitating those seeking positions in, 'sensitive' occupations such as teaching, social work and the police.

In giving evidence, Cochrane came out, in one huge leap, to his friends, his colleagues, the police department, his parents and the city. Whilst the bill failed at the committee stage (though it would eventually be passed in March 1986), Charles Cochrane became an overnight inspiration within the gay communities. However, the legal advice that he had taken before testifying advised him that the state law would not afford him protection from subsequent discrimination by the police department should they choose to take exception to either his political endeavour or his sexual orientation. Yet despite this, Cochrane found himself with a good deal of unexpected respect from within the department, and to his surprise he was left largely unmolested.

Autumn four years on: Cochrane and a New Jersey police officer, Sam Ciccone, meet in St Joseph's Catholic Church in Greenwich Village and wait in response to the 400 outreach posters they have distributed around the city's police department precincts. They knew that there must be others like them in the department, it was simply a question of finding them. They also knew that everyone had seen their posters, but plucking up the courage to appear on the night would be quite a different matter. Despite the risks and the inclement weather, a total of eleven police officers surfaced for that first meeting, and in what could hardly be described as a secular inauguration, the Gay Officers Action League (GOAL) was born.

It was clear from the beginning, however, that an initiative like GOAL would not escape controversy; the organization was not without its vocal critics – most vociferously from within the department itself – and the group received scores of vicious phone calls over the following months, including several death-threats. In addition, when in February 1983 the League (which was by now 55 strong) applied for membership of the NYPD branch of the Brotherhood in Action, a national fraternal group formed to promote 'tolerance and understanding', GOAL was denied admission on moral grounds. When Cochrane appealed to the highest authority in the department, Police Commissioner Ward, the Brotherhood was instructed that federal law prohibited discrimination in public agencies. Ward ordered that the group should grant GOAL admission or disband. It disbanded.

Despite such difficulties the early members of GOAL refused to concede defeat and now, a decade later, the Gay Officers Action League is still addressing issues affecting lesbian and gay communities. Both of the original co-founders, Cochrane and Ciccone, are now retired from the force with Ciccone the executive director of a group that now has in excess of 300 current members and has seen hundreds more pass through its hands. 'Without GOAL, you feel you're alone,' says Edgar Rodrigues, a Sergeant on Greenwich Village's Sixth Precinct, 'but, when you go to a meeting, you learn you're one of many.'[2] Because of GOAL's existence, Rodrigues never entertained the idea that he was 'the only one', unlike so many of those who went before him. As part of a weighty fraternity, he could talk to others who he knew would relate to his own experience – not simply of being gay – but of being a gay police officer. Thus, GOAL has made a major impact on the lives of a sizeable minority of the city's 27,000 police officers. 'It's the only time some of our guys can relax,' says Ciccone.[3]

Today, GOAL is an extremely active and politically influential force in New York City, with its members spending a considerable amount of their free time involved in the organization's activities. Much of the day-to-day work involves reaching out to various social, professional and community-based groups in order to challenge prejudice and promote tolerance and understanding within both the police and the gay communities. GOAL has steered the NYPD forward in equal opportunities work for nearly a decade now and holds a number of impressive pioneering records: the Gay Officers Action League was the first gay group in the United States to be both recognized and have its services called upon by US police agencies, its resources are now regularly employed by the myriad of criminal justice agencies across New England, and members' photographs on police recruitment posters are nothing unusual. Its members were also the first to march openly under the GOAL banner in the annual Lesbian and Gay Pride festivals in New York, Philadelphia, Boston and Dallas. A GOAL member sits on the mayor's Police Council, and a number of the company are trained as instructors for the department's multicultural education programme. In addition, the organization is committed to an impressive itinerary of internal activities each year, including regular encounters with all sections of the media: between June 1990 and May 1991, GOAL and its members appeared in ninety-six magazine and newspaper articles, were interviewed in sixteen radio broadcasts, and made twenty-eight television appearances. Members appeared at sixty-eight general speaking engagements and were involved in over 100 police and community-based meetings. A staggering 5,000 pieces of correspondence arrived for the group's attention during this period and nearly 3,500 GOAL newsletters were distributed. Not surprisingly, Ciccone reports in a letter to the author that 'GOAL has significantly altered the attitudes and beliefs that were once held by people within these agencies towards lesbian and gay people.'

The Gay Officers Action League is not the only gay police social group in the world, not even within the United States. In California there are three further organizations: Golden State Peace Officers Association (GSPOA), Pride Behind the Badge (PBB), and the Society of Law Officers (SOLO).

GSPOA

In 1979, an informal group of San Francisco deputy sheriffs and police officers began meeting at a yearly retreat near the Russian River. The outing began as a small party and by 1981 had grown into a larger group affectionately known as Pigs in Paradise. As the group grew in numbers, the need for a more structured, state-wide, professional peace officers association became apparent. This need was answered in August of 1985, when the Golden State Peace Officers Association (GSPOA) was developed from the group of friends that was originally Pigs in Paradise. Since then, over 100 men and women from law enforcement agencies throughout the United States have joined the Association and worked to make its professional, social and charitable events a success. There are currently 107 members, from California, Nevada, Michigan, British Columbia and Oregon.

The group uses the term 'peace officers' because it is not only police officers from regular city police departments who are permitted to join. GSPOA currently has representatives from twenty-eight different law enforcement agencies including the California Highway Patrol, California State Park Rangers and the US Park Police. Members also include the County Deputy Sheriff, prison guards, District Attorneys and private investigators.

The goals of the group are as follows:

1. To promote fellowship among its members and to provide resources for exchange of information within the Association and other associations.

2. To foster educational opportunities for the Association through a variety of means, including conferences, workshops and seminars.

3. To engage in charitable activities which benefit the gay and lesbian community.

4. To network with other organizations that have similar interests and objectives.

5. To provide a forum for planning and implementation of activities and programmes for the benefit of the Association and its members.

6. To publish a regular newsletter (*The Hog Caller*).

PBB

Pride Behind the Badge (PBB) is the name of the group based in Los Angeles. It was officially formed in April 1991, although members had been meeting unofficially since 1988. The group has approximately seventy paid-up members, plus an additional seventy-five who participate in some way but have declined full-paid membership. PBB's associate membership programme also permits fire fighters, reserve police officers, district and city attorneys, and officers outside of southern California to join. Approximately 35 per cent of the total involved are women and the group also represents a large variety of federal, state and municipal police agencies. The group exists primarily as a social and support organization but it tries to address political issues where they affect either the organization or the individuals that are a part of it. The group hosts regular monthly meetings but social and speaking engagements are weekly. The group also publishes a monthly newsletter, *PBB News.*

SOLO

The Society of Law Officers (SOLO) was formed on 31 October 1990 in San Diego. The group was founded by six law enforcement officers: two San Diego police officers, the San Diego County Deputy Marshal, the Deputy District Attorney and a former FBI special agent. The aim of SOLO is to provide a discreet professional network, along with social activities for its members. The group has also established a biweekly 'rap' group where members are able to discuss issues of importance, and has a 'speaker's bureau' which addresses groups about SOLO and issues related to law enforcement. The Society currently has over seventy members representing a cross-section of the state, local and federal law enforcement agencies of San Diego and Imperial counties, with roughly equal numbers of men and women taking part. In June 1991, San Diego police chief Bob Burgreen attended a SOLO meeting where he expressed his support for both the group and for lesbians and gay men as part of the law enforcement community.

Gay-CUF

In 1990 in Toronto, Canada, Brian Aguiar set up the Gay Cops United Foundation (Gay-CUF). Their mandate includes: providing support and solidarity as well as a means of social interaction for its members; the promotion of equality within the police department; and liaison between the police and the gay community.

Aguiar knew that he was gay when he signed up in 1976 but he thought he could keep the two parts of his life separate. 'From what I've seen and experienced, it's still not acceptable for anyone in the police force to be homosexual. There's a very macho image. Being gay is a no-no.'[4] However, over the years he found himself unable to maintain this position: 'You do a lot of damage to yourself by hiding ... coming out is the best thing I've done in my life in a long time,' he says. Despite a distinct lack of encouragement from police counsellors, Aguiar set up his group and began advertising it around his division using posters that he'd made himself. Most of these were ripped down as fast as they were put up, or else defaced with anti-gay graffiti. The establishment hoped that Gay-CUF would not last: 'They thought we were going to go away,' Aguiar says, 'but we haven't.' What they can do, he maintains, is to use 'abnormal methods to make life miserable at work'.

In Canada, sexual orientation is not a factor in hiring-and-firing decisions, a situation that, according to the director of information for Metro police, predates the inclusion of gay rights protection in the Ontario human rights code of 1986. Nevertheless, Aguiar told me: 'Gay-CUF is not accepted by the Toronto police. In fact, if they had a choice they wouldn't hesitate to get rid of the group, and me with it.' Aguiar has filed a detailed complaint with the Ontario Human Rights Commission.

WPH

In Holland, the Werkgroep Politie en Homoseksualiteit (WPH) was set up in May 1985 by ten men and two women in order that officers throughout the country could come together for support and talk about their experiences within the Dutch police system. The struggle for equal rights was also on the agenda and to that end the group has achieved some interesting successes. Most notably, an officer's (same-sex) partner is now officially recognized as a spouse and as such, in cases of death, the surviving partner is entitled to financial benefits. The group has about fifty regular members of whom about 40 per cent are female. WPH is supported and receives small bursaries from the police structure.

Werkgroep Homo-emancipatie

The Werkgroep Homo-emancipatie is a newer, smaller group for gay and lesbian police (and police civil staff) in The

Hague. Its membership, which is mostly female, meets about once a month. It has produced a small booklet for the use of colleagues who want to know more about how to deal sympathetically with the gay community and the group is also hoping to create a short film for police use in the near future. Like WPH, this group is also supported and receives small bursaries from the police structure.

LAGPA

Whilst there have undoubtedly always been gay and lesbian police officers in Britain, most of them have remained hidden and unaware of the existence of others in their situation. One result of this is that there has been little support for these officers in times of difficulty, save the goodwill of the odd force chaplain, since the admission of emotional or psychological difficulties in the police via the police welfare system is perceived as occupational suicide, a consequence of which is that there is little confidence in the police welfare system. Until recently, for lesbian or gay officers with difficulties, the only practical alternative to police welfare was to seek assistance outside the service – perhaps by means of a specialist referral via the officer's GP. Unfortunately, for most non-heterosexual men and women serving in Britain's police forces, high levels of anxiety and distrust ensure that having one's sexual orientation as a matter of record, even with a GP, is not a viable option. Accordingly, there has been a strong tendency for homosexual officers to remain isolated, lonely and fearful. At the time when I began work on this book in 1990, only a negligible percentage had come out at work, and despite that openness with their colleagues, none had ever been prepared to come out publicly and brave the Cochrane syndrome – the flood of national media publicity that would surely engulf them.

These facts are reported in the past tense because during the summer of 1990, at about the same time as the Canadian group Gay-CUF was forming, a British equivalent began to evolve – quite independently and without any knowledge of its Canadian counterpart – after a handful of gay men, who had somehow managed to find each other, realized that there was a real need for the kind of support that was being offered in other countries. In addition, on 19 April 1991, as a result of publicity surrounding the development of LAGPA, Hampshire PC Lee Hunt came out publicly in *Police Review*, a national police magazine on sale to the general public.[5]

The Association's beginnings can be traced to an impromptu barbecue hosted by a game PC one August evening in 1990 in a small north London garden. When about a dozen officers arrived, several of them with their lovers, the euphoria was almost tangible. It was difficult for the officers to believe that all of those who surrounded them – most of whom they had never met before – were gay police officers. Such an event had been unthinkable only six months earlier. New friendships were formed that night and the foundations of what was soon to become the Lesbian and Gay Police Association (LAGPA) were laid.

From its beginnings the cluster grew silently, mostly by word of mouth, and it developed further through discreet advertising in the gay press. Initially the group was casual, unstructured and lacked direction or purpose, but as it matured it became more sophisticated. A committee was eventually formed and within a few months its members took a decision to reveal the new Association's existence to the Metropolitan Police, the force from which most of its members were derived. Before doing this, it was decided to approach the National Police Federation of England and Wales, the police 'union', to seek their support in pursuit of the following aims:

1. To work towards equal opportunities for lesbians and gay police officers.
2. To offer support and advice for lesbian and gay officers.
3. To work towards better relations between the police and the gay community.

In the meantime, the Association attempted to acquire discreet links with sympathetic ears both in the police and in the lesbian and gay communities, whilst at the same time taking care to keep a low profile to avoid the scrutiny of tabloid reporters. Although a voluntary news blackout had been running in the gay press since the Association's unfolding whilst it gained strength, the same courtesy could not be expected of the national press. And on

18 January 1991, after a 'confidential' meeting between Association committee members and the Editor of *Police Review*, Brian Hilliard, LAGPA was exposed despite protests from committee members that the neophyte organization was not yet ready for its existence to be disclosed to the general public. *Police Review* had decided in publishing the news of the group's existence that 'it was better that its formation and objectives were brought to notice in a responsible fashion rather than through the sensationalist headlines in the tabloid press.'[6] In keeping with that philosophy, news of the article was then duly leaked to a number of newspapers the result of which was a wave of national publicity dispersing the information rapidly to both the police and the public alike. Reports appeared in the following publications in 1991: *Police* (February); the *Daily Star* (22 February); the *Sport* (22 February); the *Daily Mail* (25 January); the *Independent* (18 and 19 January); the *Guardian* (18 and 19 January); the *Daily Telegraph* (25 January); the *Pink Paper* (3 and 25 January, 4 May); *Capital Gay* (25 January, 1 February); and the *Sun* (no date, February).[7] In addition, the programmes 'After Dark', 'The London Programme', 'Dispatches', 'Public Eye', 'Sky News',[8] BBC Radio 2[9] and 'Gloria Live' were also interested in covering the story.

On receipt of the news, the natural reaction of many senior officers was to panic. Most knew nothing about the new Association, and LAGPA was a tumour in the police structure that they had neither anticipated nor wished for at a time when the image of the service was being so carefully nurtured. However, the most perturbing reaction came from a corner of the organization where the London members of LAGPA had hoped to receive support.

On 25 January 1991, the Chair of the Metropolitan Police Federation, Sergeant Michael Bennett, lashed out in a reply to Hilliard's original but sympathetic exposé. Entitled 'Divided loyalties' the article put together a *mélange* of disjointed arguments, first attempting to establish the poor character of a former police officer (the present author) and then linking that individual's research work with the Association in order to suggest that the involvement of former police officers 'would only bring discredit to such an association'.[10] The piece concluded with a plea for someone in authority to ban the Association before the police were forced to tolerate the emergence of a 'Police Bondage Association' or a 'Deviant Sexual Practices Society'.[11] A charitable view of such a passionate attack might identify the hallmarks of a man who had little understanding of the phenomenon which seemed overnight to have besieged his already beleaguered service. A less charitable interpretation might identify an article designed to ensure the early demise of the Association, the scuttling of any research, and with these, any prospect for embarrassment.

According to the Editor of *Police Review*, Bennett's piece on 'Divided loyalties' resulted in a deluge of letters. One of the first to take Bennett up on his arguments was Mark Thompson, a heterosexual officer from his own force. In a letter to *Police Review* (26 April 1991) he wrote:

> I am not black, I am not gay, I am not a woman. I cannot know what officers from these groups, who are suffering discrimination, are going through but I can empathise. I should not have to, but as long as discrimination continues (and it does, though good signs for the future are all around us) then I shall. I am a police officer and so are people from many groups in society. That they are police officers is enough for me. The only assumptions I shall make about them is that they are honest and loyal.
>
> I agree with PC Hunt's view of Mike Bennett's article, which I felt was appalling. I want the person who represents me at the Federation to be someone who understands policing and social issues. If he's misread the gay issue what else has he misread?

Despite the level of hostility generated by Bennett's sentiments, it would be unfair to exploit his misunderstanding of the situation in order to provide a scapegoat for any intolerance that there may be in the police. He does not stand alone in his views, to be sure; his infamous outcry regarding police bondage and deviant sexual practices associations was little more than a variation of a letter published in the same magazine two weeks earlier (see pages 125–6).

Despite its potential appeal to the rank and file, it would appear that Bennett's article lacked credibility with senior officers, and the publicity which followed his piece served only to embarrass the organization he was trying to defend at a time when the Met were clearly trying to rid themselves of their reputation for intolerance of minority groups. In the wake of Bennett's outburst, force reactions to the LAGPA were mixed but all appeared to treat the group with a notable degree of caution, and none were prepared to risk an attempt at further attacking the organization. To date, no witch-hunt has been instigated, something that would have undoubtedly been witnessed ten years ago, and this has bewildered a number of older officers who were confident of the Association's downfall.

There are probably several reasons for the lack of the expected offensive, one of which was surely the group's intangible and necessarily secretive membership. Although the police were aware of the Association's existence, information regarding the group was sporadic and the lack of effective equal opportunities policies ensured that those involved in running the organization remained elusive. Pseudonyms or first names only were used when contacting members of the police structure; hence, the Association's membership remained frustratingly incorporeal to those who desperately needed to know the nature of their antagonist, making both its fortitude and the extent of its influence extremely difficult to judge. There was a good deal of speculation over exactly how influential the group might be, and conjecture continued for some time regarding: (a) how many members the group had acquired, (b) how many forces were involved, and (c) how many senior officers were represented within its membership. Reports quoted anything from 60 to (in the case of the *Sunday Mirror*) 500 officers, from thirteen to twenty-five forces and ranking from police constable to Chief Superintendent. An impressive and potentially influential body!

The Association, I believe, was seen as being one which meant business; an assembly which was seriously political, highly unpredictable and potentially dangerous. It arrived seemingly overnight, unannounced, and caught the establishment off guard. The police were fearful of the Association's intangibility and few could be certain of how far its members might be prepared to go in order to assert their rights against a bigoted employer. The structure was, therefore, reluctant to risk provoking the organization into a mode of high-profile, politicized behaviour that would undoubtedly lead to unwarranted publicity and provide tabloid newspapers with endless weeks of titillation. Yet I think that there was also the feeling that an old-style witch-hunt, still popular in some forces, would, if it were to be instigated at least in the Met (the chief catchment force for the group), be ill-conceived and ineffective. With the increased emphasis on human rights and equal opportunities characteristic of the 1990s, such a hunt might not only fail but could backfire with further risk of 'gay police' publicity.

Thus, the strategic mistake of the police (assuming that it was their ambition to quash the Association) was that they believed that they were no longer dealing with ordinary police officers whose behaviour they could predict and explain, but something else, something foreign and precarious. It was the police's own prejudice and misunderstanding of what it meant to be homosexual that turned LAGPA into a giant that was to be feared and not goaded, hence, in a strange twist of irony, the very prejudice which was expected to result in the Association's obliteration actually frustrated its would-be exterminators.

The need for a group like LAGPA has been questioned by its opponents. I hope that the testimonies of the officers throughout this book have responded adequately to their objections. In our present society, to be called 'homosexual' is to carry a stigma. It is to be degraded, denounced, devalued and treated as different. It can lead to ostracism, discrimination and physical attack. For many men and women in this situation, isolation is a serious problem, and this can be lessened by the refuge offered by the company of sympathetic others who have shared their experiences and with whom they can find a non-prejudicial ear. The most convincing answer to the question for me arrived in the form of an emotional letter from a West Yorkshire PC, who, after hearing about this research, wrote asking for the Association's contact address and assurance that the group was not bogus: 'I just can't believe that there are other coppers in the same boat as me – who understand what it's like ... my stomach turns over every time I think about it.' Despite sporadic attacks on their integrity, the Lesbian and Gay Police Association have managed to maintain a relatively dignified silence in the debate surrounding their existence. In the remainder of this chapter, many of their members speak out for the first time in giving their reactions to the furore.

● *Lancashire Chief Inspector, age 39, twenty years' service*

The request from an individual, who purports to represent the welfare of police officers, for such a group to be banned is misguided and unfortunate. With every police claim that there is no need for such a group, the need for that support grows stronger. Frankly, Britain's police services can ill-afford either to ban this group, or to be so complacent on this issue when they have failed for so long on minority issues, and when most do not include the words 'sexual orientation' in their equal opportunities policies. As one editorial in the Independent *said, if the police service wish to prove that they regard unfair treatment of minorities as unacceptable, only by 'ostentatious measures' can they convince the world that this is really so.[12]*

If, as Mike Bennett admits, he is 'old-fashioned and not tolerant enough for today's generation', then perhaps he ought not to be in a position where he may be called upon to represent people whose lifestyles he clearly finds distasteful. How much confidence can an officer with any kind of personal problem now have in approaching the Federation for assistance? His claim that the Federation has never had an instance of discrimination on the grounds of sexual orientation brought to its attention is hardly surprising. And yet in just six months, the Lesbian and Gay Police Association is reported to have over eighty members. I believe that the facts speak for themselves.

He says that he is speaking from a personal point of view. The public reaction following James Anderton's outburst on Aids suggests that such comment is unacceptable from a person in his position and is likely to be interpreted as official policy. Such remarks not only serve to increase suspicion and fear on the part of those officers who require assistance from the Federation, but help to reinforce the belief in the gay community that they are indeed treated in a prejudicial manner.

● *Metropolitan Traffic Division WPC, age 32, eight years' service*

I've heard rumours that some people in the Job think LAGPA is some kind of dating agency. I just can't believe it when I hear stuff like that. Where do they get these people from? It's simply a support group set up for us, by us. Nothing more. And it's bloody brilliant. Can't they see that if society didn't exclude us to such a great extent in the first place then there wouldn't be a need for it? There's nothing that I would like more than to be fully integrated into society. It's not our fault that we're not now, is it?

● *Metropolitan PC, age 34, nine years' service*

If I split up with a partner or something, I can't just go and talk to anyone and get support or sympathy from them like most people do. People tend not to take it seriously if it's a gay relationship. They can't understand why you're upset. It's so good to know there are other people like you in the Job, having to put up with the same crap. The new gay police group is unbelievable. I was so pleased when I found out that I wasn't the only one. It really made my day. You can't imagine what that means to me. God, I wish it existed a long time ago. For the past nine years in fact. For the first time in my career I've been able to speak to someone like myself. It's a big morale booster to meet others in the same job with similar problems and concerns. It isn't often that one can open up with colleagues at work, but if they are gay too, then there's an awful lot to talk about, swapping stories about incidents at work, or even who's good-looking on the relief! Same as any straight PC would do. That's really important because if most gay PCs are like me, we tend to keep the majority of our social life to ourselves and talk in

*vague generalities at work: 'I went out last night with some friends
...' 'Some people came round for dinner ...'*

● *Metropolitan PC, age 25, one year's service*

I spend most of my time with gay cops. I have done for the
past year – even before I joined. I've known about the gay police
group since it started – I went out with one of the guys in it – so at
least I've always known that there are others like me. In fact it gave
me extra confidence to join. I think it's a great thing and I have
strong feelings about it. I've made a lot of good friends.

● *Metropolitan Home Beat PC, age 37,*
resigned with sixteen years' service

All I want is a little more tolerance and understanding. I'm
not dangerous to the community, but the community is dangerous
to me – I know that because I've experienced it firsthand. And it's
all to do with fear. I'm waiting for the day when this world is
mature enough to deal with its fears instead of burning them at the
stake. As for myself, if this group had been around when I was in
the Job then I would probably still be in it now. I think it's a great
idea. Especially for the young ones. Who else can a gay copper talk
to?

● *West Mercia PC, age 22, three years' service*

The Job needs to make it easier for the people who are gay to
feel more acceptable and one of the ways they can do that is not to
make a big fuss about the group. It's not doing any harm. And
having us in the force helps to break down prejudice because when
other officers meet gays on the streets it helps them to see that
they're OK too. As far as I'm concerned, LAGPA is well needed.
I'm really pleased to have joined at the time when it's got going. I
consider myself very lucky in that respect. I'd like to see more
senior officers in the group, although I understand why it's difficult
for them.

● *Metropolitan WDC, age 34,*
fourteen years' service

What the police welfare system is clearly incapable of doing is looking after the needs of their gay and lesbian officers. Most of them have no real understanding, that much has already been demonstrated, and without that they are totally useless to us. But it's not just a question of understanding or tolerance. There need to be officers in welfare who are trained in issues surrounding HIV and Aids. Police officers are not immune to it – several have already died – not that that's common knowledge of course. It's all hushed up and I've heard some pretty horrendous stories about how lovers have been treated by the police during funeral arrangements, etc. I doubt that most of the people in police welfare know the first thing about HIV – it's out of their league. So how are they going to care for their officers who are HIV positive? A support group on the other hand contains a lot of collective experience and knowledge. Nobody in the group is going to have ignorant ideas about it and nobody is going to say anything insensitive. I wouldn't trust the Job with the knowledge of my HIV status on my deathbed.

● *Royal Parks Police PC, age 29,*
four years' service

I'm not a member of this group yet, but if people ask why a group like LAGPA is needed, I would say it's because on the whole the police display a lack of sensitivity and respect. The misdemeanours they deal with are not simply treated as offences, police officers tend to make these grand moral judgements on people as well, and I've both witnessed it and been subjected to it. And if they know you're gay, then you can expect the same treatment as the public get.

At school I used to get bullied and got called 'poof'. I don't need that any more and a group provides a sanctuary where you know you won't get shat on. Nobody says anything about ethnic officers having their group, but that's probably because officially they don't have one, but they do, and so do women, and two lots of

Christians, not forgetting our wonderful Masons. So why can't we? Bennett says, 'Why the police service? We do not have a homosexual milkmen's association, or one for bank clerks.' Well, I don't know about milkmen or bank clerks but I do know of a British Telecom Lesbian and Gay Workers Group, a Lesbian and Gay Medical Association, a London Underground Lesbian and Gay Workers Group (and another one for British Rail), and another for the BBC. Then there's Rank Outsiders for the armed forces, and so it goes on ad nauseam. If you look in Gay Times, *the listings of groups cover several pages. If he contacted the Transport and General Workers Lesbian and Gay Group I suspect he would even find his milkmen. Why do cops so often mix with cops in their spare time rather than with civilians, and why nine times out of ten do they marry them? It's because nobody else understands them or the way they think; because nobody else is capable of seeing the world in quite the same way as they do. It's natural to want to hang out with people like yourself – everybody does it. It means you have something in common. So that's why. It's quite simple really. There's nothing subversive in the idea.*

At the time of writing, the Association's membership stands at between sixty and eighty and seems unlikely to rise above a couple of hundred, even once properly established.[13] Thus, whilst it is clear that the controversy surrounding the group's inception has prevented many potential members from joining, only a minority of potential associates are likely to become members.

● *Thames Valley PC, age 38, sixteen years' service*

I suppose I've slept with about ten coppers in my entire service, but none of them have come forward to join the group. In fact, lots of them are married now. So from my own experience alone, I would say that for every one officer that joins the group, there are probably at least ten others out there who don't, but who have definite tendencies.

This is an interesting comment from the point of view of crude statistical analyses of homosexual frequencies. Research data suggest that around 10 per cent of the population may be significantly homosexual. If this officer's hypothesis were applied to a mature police group membership like GOAL, which is around 300, a multiplication of ten would bring it to around 3,000, which is, in fact, just over 10 per cent of the NYPD's manpower of about 27,000 (London's Metropolitan Police equals 28,500); the suggestion being that *only 10 per cent of the 10 per cent* of lesbian, gay or bisexual officers will choose to join such associations. It would seem that those who do join are more politically orientated, confident, 'out' or, in police terms, 'radical' than those who have not yet come forward. This has resulted in an in-built tendency to undersample those with deep anxieties regarding their dilemma in this research, and it is the author's belief that most gay officers harbour a mixture of perplexity and trepidation which is so concentrated that the idea of coming out in either life sphere, that is, as 'poof' or 'police' – let alone approaching an out organization such as LAGPA – is inconceivable.

In conclusion, I would make one further observation on the subject of a British police lesbian and gay social group and of non-heterosexuality in the police in general with specific regard to police discipline. A number of the Association's opponents have suggested that membership of LAGPA could render officers liable to a charge of 'bringing the force into disrepute', and this has caused some concern – indeed, some officers fear that simply being homosexual may be sufficient cause for their dismissal (see page 107). It is manifest that this infamous catch-all is entirely contingent upon a police service choosing to define homosexuality as 'disreputable' in the first place. Accordingly, any force using such an article against an officer as a means of discipline would *ipso facto* be guilty of both harbouring and exhibiting homophobia. Such an inference is analytical. There is no logical retreat.

Notes

1. R. W. Stone, Editor, *Police Journal*, April 1990, p. 93.
2. M. Santangelo, 'Badge: marching with New York's gay cops', *Daily News Magazine* (US), 24 June 1990, pp. 8–11.

3. Ibid., p. 10.
4. Interview with Glenn Wheeler, *Now* (Canada), p. 17.
5. Hunt's article, 'When I "Came Out"', is reproduced in Chapter 9.
6. Editorial, *Police Review*, 25 January 1991, p. 164.
7. Most of the reporting at this time was reasonably positive with the exception of the obvious. The *Daily Star* (22 February 1991) ran an article with the leader, 'Limp Arm of the Law'. The text began: 'There's a touch of pink in the thin blue line as pansy policemen come out of the closet.' It continued with lines like 'Ooh! It's a fairy cop, mate' and finished with a further piece, accompanied by a photograph of reporter Mark Christy taking to the streets in a police uniform (with handbag, lipstick, earrings and wig) in an attempt to discern the reaction of the public toward the notion of gay policemen.
8. Sky 'Newsline' eventually transmitted a half-hour piece on homosexuality in the police on 15 May 1991, using an anonymous member of LAGPA. Michael Bennett, Chair of the Metropolitan Police Federation, also appeared, asking for the Association to be banned.
9. BBC Radio 2 transmitted a one-and-a-half-hour programme on homosexuality, hosted by Claire Rayner on 13 May 1991, which included a ten-minute interview with a member of LAGPA.
10. M. Bennett, 'Divided loyalties', *Police Review*, 25 January 1991, p. 164.
11. Ibid., p. 165.
12. *Independent*, 19 December 1991, p. 18.
13. Estimated using membership criteria from established gay police organizations, e.g. GOAL, which has a force size similar to that of London's Metropolitan Police, the main catchment force for LAGPA.

Epilogue

IT was my ambition at the beginning of this project to assemble a balanced and constructive overview of the circumstances of lesbian and gay police officers serving in Britain's police services today. To that end, in addition to the police officers themselves, prominent members of both the police and gay communities were also invited to submit their observations and opinions on the issue, in what were to become two supplementary sections of the book. Both were offered an extensive platform with editorial control over their contributions.

From the gay community, the following organizations were approached: the Gay Business Association (GBA); the Gay London Policing Group (GALOP); journalists from the London and national gay press; and a number of other high-profile community-based organizations. None of those approached rejected the petition; indeed, all were enthusiastic to contribute to the research effort.

From the Metropolitan Police, Britain's largest force (and the chief catchment territory for the purposes of this book), the following departments were contacted: the Equal Opportunities Unit (PT1) and the Community Liaison Branch (TO31) at New Scotland Yard; the Metropolitan Police Federation; and the Commissioner, Sir Peter Imbert. The following *national* police organizations, which, between them, comprehensively represent the totality of officers of England, Wales, and in the case of ACPO, Northern Ireland, were also approached: the Association of Chief Police Officers (ACPO); the Police Superintendents Association and the National Police Federation.

Only three replies were received from the police. All declined the invitation to contribute. Of those that failed to reply, reactions were varied.

The National Police Federation failed to respond to both the original approach and a follow-up letter. A number of subsequent attempts were made to verify receipt of the correspondence by telephone; however, on each occasion, both the Chairman, Alan Eastwood, and the Secretary were either 'not in', or 'too busy' to answer the telephone.

Sergeant Michael Bennett of the Metropolitan Police Federation also declined the invitation to contribute his point of view to this book. He later expressed the view that 'because contributors can remain anonymous, I suspect some stories would distress Hans Christian Andersen.'[1] I doubt that such is true, although I do concede that some of the accounts are distressing. The supposition that (had he still been alive) a learned man from a country noted for its tolerance of sexual diversity would feel offended requires some degree of presumptuousness. It seems more probable that Andersen would query why the officers felt the need to remain anonymous; after all, as a gay man himself,[2] he would undoubtedly find himself in sympathy with many of the officers' testimonies, and would have been well versed in the rhetoric of the ignorant and the reckless.

My letter to the Commissioner, who suffered a heart attack shortly afterwards, was redirected to another department from whom I heard not a peep. However, the advice of a reliable source at New Scotland Yard is that it was catapulted from department to department, ricocheting its way across several desktops, unable to find a taker, and is apparently still mobile somewhere on the fifth floor. The last of the letters was apparently mislaid upon arrival and never found.

The net result of the police initiative, which required six months of letter writing, letter chasing and phone calls, was that not a single department in the Met, nor any of the national representative bodies contacted, would accept the offer of a free platform on the issue. Whilst this state of affairs was not wholly unanticipated, it nevertheless left me with a difficult decision with regard to the corresponding section of the book that was to be given over to lesbian and gay communities; it was only after some deliberation that the decision was made, in the name of symmetry and equilibrium, to abandon that section and bequeath the entire forum solely to those officers who were the authentic domain of the study.

Apart from the book becoming somewhat thinner, I discovered that without the palliation of the police contribution, the nature and feel of the end-product was somewhat less encouraging than I had originally hoped for. Perhaps that much was to be expected; the overall thrust of the book remained, after all, illustrative of the need for change. Nonetheless, I believe that there is room for some optimism with regard to the future, and I would like to offer a few points of mitigation on behalf of those police personnel who either declined to contribute their observations or were not granted the opportunity.

Over the past ten years or so, the educational standard of police officers has been steadily rising.[3] The number of graduates in the police has increased dramatically in recent years and today's police officer is more academically qualified than at any other time. A number of these graduates have now risen to senior ranks and have taken with them their more progressive thinking. In this way, they are beginning to have a direct effect on police policy, gradually filling the shoes of those increasingly outmoded officers from what is now known as the 'old school' of policing, where cautioning a juvenile recidivist meant giving him 'a clip around the ear'. Additionally, most (urban) police services have suffered substantial change since the ethnic unrest of the early 1980s and subsequent reformation imposed by the Scarman Report of 1981. That document has acted as a catalyst for broad change, its reverberations still being felt in many forces – although most of the transformation has gone largely unnoticed by a critical public.

Further, whilst the leopard is unlikely to change its spots, the animal's environment may eventually lead to its significant mutation. Much effort has gone into reshaping the image of the police (in particular the Met), and successive police Commissioners have attempted to increase public confidence by remoulding the organization from a 'force' into a 'service', with an increased emphasis on professionalism. 'Professionalism' was the buzz-word of the late 1980s after 1985 saw the then Commissioner of the Met, now Sir Kenneth Newman, produce a handbook for all 27,000 members of his force entitled *The Principles of Policing and Guidance for Professional Behaviour*. His successor, Sir Peter Imbert, produced during his own office the Plus Programme innovation, with the aim of creating a better quality of public service through listening more closely to the needs of the community. Such efforts have resulted in the evolution of a more socially and politically aware police service, particularly within the ethnic centres of Britain. It is no longer possible to remain ignorant of the consequences of insensitive policing (or of the current, less police-protective, police complaints system).

In addition, a consensus of opinion has been developing which suggests that some of the recent lessons learnt by the police in their dealings with the black and Asian communities might effectively be applied to other minorities, including lesbian and gay communities. In London, one of the Plus Programme's heirs is the London Lesbian and Gay Policing Initiative (LLGPI) in which both the police and members of lesbian and gay communities meet regularly at Scotland Yard to discuss gay-related policing issues. These encounters represent a significant landmark in communication history between these two traditionally antagonistic groups.[4] The decision of several forces to include the words 'sexual orientation' in their equal opportunities policies suggests that other forces also intend to exercise increased sensitivity in this regard.

Perhaps the single largest catalyst for such changes was provided internally by the unexpected emergence of the Lesbian and Gay Police Association. It will be several years before the response to that challenge can be properly analysed; attempts at force reorganization take many years of implementation before their influence is detectable and inevitably have little effect on officers who are too long in the tooth to change their ways or even notice the difference. But new recruits, one hopes, will be joining a radically different service to that of their predecessors, and one would like to think that in the case of negative experience most of the officers in this book are recounting events which could not – at least in those forces that have instigated change – be repeated.[5] The status of the non-heterosexual police officer is only just evolving. The early signs suggest room for cautious optimism; certainly the response to Brian Morgan's letter on the Christian ethic (see pages 125–6) and the similar response to both Folkes' and Bennett's comments suggest that intolerance is on the decrease. Such changes have not gone unnoticed by lesbian and gay police officers.

● *Cumbria Detective Inspector, age 35, fifteen years' service*

I was quite surprised some months ago when I overheard a Detective Sergeant talking to a couple of DCs about a third DC whom I used to work with, and who I thought might be gay. The Sergeant in question obviously thought the same, but evidently it was of no consequence to him. He said that this DC was a first-class detective and a nice guy and all that mattered was whether or not he could do his job. Whether he was gay, or whatever, was immaterial. If the Sergeant had voiced that kind of opinion a few years ago people would have undoubtedly talked about him as well. The fact that he felt able to voice his opinion, and the fact that those he was talking to obviously agreed with him shows how far we have progressed.

There are also other officers whom I used to work with and who have known about me for several years. It obviously makes no difference to them (that I know of) and they apparently have not told very many people about me – at least if they have it hasn't made any difference, or it hasn't yet reached certain influential quarters – because I've been promoted twice.

A further area of police mitigation with respect to the problems faced by non-heterosexual officers, and one which has been touched on in this book, is that in many cases the difficulties faced by the individual at work may rest more with their own lack of self-acceptance than with their police employer (see, for example, pages 160–3) although it has to be said that lack of self-acceptance is normally the result of societal disapproval. Furthermore, not all of the genuine obstacles faced by homosexual officers in the police service are police specific; many other occupations provide similar barriers to promotion and opportunities for nervous breakdowns, as noted on pages 108–9 in the narrative provided by the Detective Sergeant.

It has been suggested that for the police, like the rest of society, there is an inherent tendency to accept the common homosexual stereotypes because they see little in either their home or their work lives which questions them. Perhaps the arrival of the openly gay or lesbian police officer will change that. I would hope that the experiences of the officers who have given so much of themselves in these pages will help to stimulate that change; that they will make a difference to those officers who thought that there was no problem, who thought that there were only a few 'queers' in the police or that this was a non-issue for the service. Perhaps they will encourage those officers to reassess their faith. Such is not unheard of, and in the final narratives, the combination of open-mindedness plus, in the first illustration, an encounter with a 'real, live' lesbian provides the stimulus for change and illustrates how affirmative experience can serve to alter opinion.

● *Lancashire woman Chief Inspector, age 34, nine years' service*

Not all that long ago, I was on a course at the police college, and one of the courses that I took there was a class on counselling skills. It was towards the end of my time – I'd been there a couple of weeks – and during that particular counselling session I told everyone present that I was gay, because it was relevant. Well, I saw this Superintendent's face who was sitting there visibly change, which was a bit worrying. Afterwards, he asked if he could have a word with me and so I said, 'Sure.' He told me that he absolutely detested homosexuals. Then he said, 'But I like you. I've known you for a number of weeks now and I hadn't got the faintest idea that you were gay. This is my dilemma. What do I now do about you? Will you talk to me about it?' Despite what he'd said, I thought it was quite brave of him to come out and admit a thing like that to me; he was obviously open to listening to me at least, so we had a bit of a discussion and he was much happier about it all afterwards.

● *Metropolitan PC, age 35, nine years' service*

Being gay, people automatically think that you can't do the job properly. There were a few people at my station who had a problem with my sexuality, saying that a poof couldn't possibly do the job properly, but attitudes towards me changed almost over-night after a nasty drugs incident where I got shot at in the street. Fortunately, the gun jammed when this bloke tried to shoot me and I chased and arrested him as he ran off. Then I went back to work as if nothing had happened. The people at work respected that and they decided that I wasn't such a bad bloke after all, and that I wasn't a wimp just because I'm gay.

I think I've had to work twice as hard to prove myself over the years. It's a bit like being a woman in the Job in that respect. You have to constantly prove your worth. But I'm sure it's made me a better policeman because it's made me work that much harder.

At a more general level, it is hoped that by shedding light on some of the concerns of gay and lesbian police officers, this book might help to inform future policy around issues of sexual orientation, stimulate good practice, and allow those forces that have not already done so to develop acceptable equal opportunities policies within this domain as they have done in relation to the ethnic minorities. The problems faced by a large minority of their work-force are real. Increased sensitivity will help to increase their com-mitment and loyalty, and arrest the tendency for officers to see their jobs as precarious 'meal-tickets'.

In conclusion, it might seem that the police and the gay communities represent two distinct groups separated by a chasm through which members of neither group may pass; that 'police officers' and 'homosexuals' come from, and live in, separate worlds; that their essential selves are fundamentally different and that there is no overlap of thought or ideology. Yet the complexity of the world we live in stretches far beyond the tolerance of theoretical parameters. In practice, there is no exclusivity in terms of thought or behaviour on either side and the complete picture affirms not only a natural tendency for the overall polarization of ideologies, but also an area of considerable overlap. Those persons who are members of both the homosexual and the police communities (i.e. gay, lesbian or bisexual police officers) would seem to be the best candidates to exploit that overlap for the benefit of both groups in order to promote a greater tolerance and understanding between them. With the recognition and acceptance by Britain's largest and most influential force of a support group for lesbian and gay police officers and the equal opportunities advancements in very recent years, it is clear that the future holds some promise of improvement for the lot of the gay police officer. As Ernie Gash, Secretary of the Police Federation Equal Opportunities Committee, has stated:

> We have to admire and respect the integrity and personal courage of those of our colleagues who have 'come out' about their sexuality ... Gay police officers oblige us to face the truth about equality ... To put it bluntly, that means our culture has got to change. Just as it is no longer acceptable to make crude jibes or derogatory comments about women officers and black people, so it is time to cut out the offensive and wounding 'jokes' about gay people. The world has changed ...[6]

British views surrounding all aspects of sexuality have been steeped in fear and superstition for centuries. As a member of a new and increasingly progressive European empire, Britain must learn to deliver itself from the primitive hobgoblin that has compromised for so long our ability to approach matters of sex and sexuality in an intelligent fashion. We *must* learn to come to terms with simple sexual diversity in all its harmlessness. It is not enough to concede passively that we live in a pluralistic society. In order to make progress, we must seek both to believe and to understand the workings of alternative potential through our experience of others' lives. The case of the newly baptized Superintendent (see page 229) demonstrates admirably that such understandings *can* and *are* being achieved by those who wish to better their understanding of the world we live in.

It is perhaps fitting that the final contribution in this book be left to the eminent British philosopher Bertrand Russell, a man whose accomplishments were ruthlessly decried earlier this century due to his 'permissive' ideology concerning matters of sex. His observations remain pertinent today:

> A habit of basing convictions upon evidence, and of giving them only that degree of certainty which the evidence warrants, would, if it became general, cure most of the ills from which the world is suffering ... The world that I should wish to see would be one freed from the virulence of group hostilities and capable of realizing that happiness for all is to be derived rather from co-operation than from strife. I should wish to see a world in which education aimed at mental freedom rather than at imprisoning the minds of the young in a rigid armour of dogma calculated to protect them through life against the shafts of impartial evidence. The world needs open hearts and minds, and it is not through rigid systems, whether old or new, that these can be derived ...[7]

Notes

1. M. Bennett, 'Divided loyalties', *Police Review*, 25 January 1991, pp. 164–5.
2. H. C. Andersen, *The True Story of My Life*, 1921.
3. 'There are now more graduates in the police than in the army, navy and air force put together. Nearly 6 per cent of the intake are graduates.' Home Secretary Kenneth Baker to Preston ACPO conference. (Reported in the *Job*, 18 October 1991.) The relationship between prejudice and education was delineated by G. Allport in his celebrated work, *The Nature of Prejudice*, 1958.
4. It remains to be seen whether Paul Condon, appointed Commissioner of the Metropolitan Police in January 1993, will lend effective support to such negotiations.
5. Nonetheless, it has to be said that many of the officers I interviewed were young in service. Their reports indicate that whilst there are

pockets of change throughout the service, there still exists a core of 'bad attitude' towards homosexuality.

6. E. Gash, 'We are all equal', *Police*, May 1992, p. 16.
7. B. Russell, *Why I Am Not a Christian*, 1957 (reprinted 1988, Preface, p. 10).

Appendix A

Police Rank Structure

Metropolitan Police	*County Forces*
Commissioner	Chief Constable
Deputy Commissioner (DC)	Deputy Chief Constable (DCC)
Assistant Commissioner (AC)	Assistant Chief Constable (ACC)
Deputy Assistant Commissioner (DAC)	
Commander	
Chief Superintendent	Chief Superintendent
Superintendent	Superintendent
Chief Inspector	Chief Inspector
Inspector	Inspector
Sergeant (PS)	Sergeant
Constable (PC)	Constable

Appendix B

A Comparison of Equal Opportunities Statements

THE following are good examples of positive policies intended to extend equal opportunities protection to all officers regardless of sexual orientation. The first is from the New York Police Department (Police Commissioner: Benjamin Ward) and is dated July 1989. The second is from South Yorkshire Police (Chief Constable: Richard Wells) and was published February 1991; South Yorkshire was Britain's first force to include the words 'sexual orientation'.

I. Equal Employment Opportunity Policy Statement

The New York City Police Department, which has long been committed to the fundamental principles of fair and equal employment opportunities for men and women of every racial, religious and ethnic background of the city's population, is pleased to renew herewith its traditional pledge to achieve and maintain these policies and practices for the benefit of all citizens who seek or are presently employed within the Department.

As Commissioner of the New York City Police Department,

it is my privilege to reaffirm this Department's commitment to these principles. As in the past, Deputy Commissioner George L. Sanchez is charged with the responsibility of implementing and coordinating the Department's Equal Employment Opportunity Program, to review and monitor all employment practices which affect recruitment, hiring, promotions, transfers and disciplinary procedures.

Deputy Commissioner Sanchez is further empowered to investigate all complaints and allegations of employment discrimination or harassment based on race, color, religion, sex, national origin, handicap, age, sexual orientation or Vietnam Era and Special Disabled Veterans status consistent with City, State, and Federal guidelines.

Inquiries or allegations concerned with any aspect of employment discrimination may be directed to the Office of Equal Employment Opportunity, New York City Police Department, One Police Plaza, Room 1204, New York, N.Y. 10038-1497, (212) 374-5330.

The Police Department's entire written EEO Program is available for inspection and study during hours at the Public Inquiry Section, Police Headquarters, One Police Plaza, Room 152A.

(signed)
Benjamin Ward
Police Commissioner

II. *Equal Opportunities in the South Yorkshire Police*

1. The South Yorkshire Police declares that it is opposed to any form of treatment which is less, or more, favourable, whether through direct or indirect discrimination, in respect of all members and employees, together with all applicants seeking employment, on grounds of sex or sexual orientation, marital/parental status, colour, race, nationality, ethnic or national origins, religious beliefs, creed; or are disadvantaged by conditions or requirements

which cannot be shown to be justified. The South Yorkshire Police also seeks to ensure that employees are not victimised or subjected to sexual or racial harassment.

2. The South Yorkshire Police similarly declares opposition to any form of less, or more, favourable treatment accorded to all members and employees, together with all applicants seeking employment, on the grounds of non-job related handicaps. This policy applies to disabled people within the medically advised limits of their disability.

3. The South Yorkshire Police recognises its obligations under both the Sex Discrimination Act 1975 and the Race Relations Act 1976 and fully supports the spirit and intent of the related Codes of Practice in respect of both pieces of legislation leading towards the goals of elimination of discrimination on grounds of sex, marriage and race, in respect of such legislation, and the promotion of equal opportunity in employment.

● Scope of Policy

4. The policy relates to all employment matters affecting individuals and groups whether they are actual or potential members or employees. It extends to all currently serving members and employees of the South Yorkshire Police, irrespective of the body which determines their pay and conditions of employment. It therefore includes all serving police officers of all ranks, all civilian employees, including traffic wardens and all full-time and part-time employees. It also includes all members of the special constabulary in respect of the office which they hold.

5. The policy is designed to be effective principally in terms of ethnic minority and sex discrimination, but the policy also applies generally to any aspect of employment where unfair discrimination may exist.

● Employment Practices

6. The Chief Constable states, in agreement with the staff associations, his wholehearted support for the principles and practice of equal opportunity. It is the duty of all employees to accept

their personal responsibility for fostering a fully integrated community at work by adhering to the principles of equal opportunity and maintaining racial harmony. The South Yorkshire Police will, therefore, actively promote equal opportunity through the application of employment policies which will ensure that individuals receive treatment which is fair, equitable and consistent with their relevant aptitudes, potential, skills and abilities.

7. It will ensure that individuals are recruited and selected, promoted and treated on objective criteria having regard to relevant aptitudes, potential, skills and abilities. In particular, no applicant, member or employee will be placed at a disadvantage by requirements or conditions which are not necessary to the performance of the job or which could constitute indirect unfair discrimination.

8. The South Yorkshire Police recognises the problems that sexual harassment could cause in the workplace and is committed to ensuring that such unacceptable behaviour does not take place. Sexual harassment is gross misconduct and as unfair discriminatory conduct, will be dealt with accordingly.

9. The South Yorkshire Police Working Party on equal opportunities will monitor employment practices. The successful implementation of this policy document is dependent on regular examination of progress towards equal opportunity and the development of local initiatives and, in consultation with the Staff Associations, the Equal Opportunities Working Party will be responsible to the Chief Constable for ensuring primarily that the spirit and intent of this document is maintained in respect of employment practices.

● *Monitoring and Review Arrangements*

10. The South Yorkshire Police recognises that the regular monitoring of ethnic origin and sex of all members and employees is essential to ensure thorough reviews of the effectiveness of its equal opportunities policy and to this end, will maintain and improve, as necessary, equal opportunity monitoring arrangements.

11. The practical application of this policy document will be subject to review from time to time to ensure that it continues to

remain fully effective and this will primarily be the responsibility of Staff Services Department together with the ongoing monitoring of the Equal Opportunities Working Party.

Responsibilities

12. All members and employees of the South Yorkshire Police share the responsibility of ensuring that the equal opportunities policies outlined in this document operate fairly and effectively. The major responsibilities in this direction, however, devolve as follows:

1. Senior officers, managers and supervisors, are responsible for the operation of the equal opportunities policy in their own division/departments/area of responsibility. The Chief Superintendent (Staff Services) is responsible for ensuring consistent application of the policy.

2. The day-to-day monitoring of equal opportunities will be the responsibility of the Chief Superintendent (Staff Services), who will act as a central reference point for all.

Grievance and Disciplinary Procedures

13. The South Yorkshire Police is anxious to ensure that individual members, employees or groups of employees, who believe they have experienced direct or indirect discrimination are properly represented. Any such persons who feel that they have been treated unfairly in connection with their employment, should raise such a grievance through the appropriate Force grievance procedure, when every effort will be made to secure a satisfactory resolution. The procedure is shown at Appendix 'A' [not reproduced here].

14. The South Yorkshire Police will ensure that any member or employee making a complaint of unfair discrimination will be protected from victimisation. The South Yorkshire Police will not tolerate contraventions of its equal opportunities policy by any of its members or employees.

● *Implementation of Policy*

15. The South Yorkshire Police will actively promote personnel practices which help to eradicate the assumptions and stereotypes which can often be at the root of unfair discrimination. The action taken will include the following areas:

1. *Recruitment and Selection*
The South Yorkshire Police will conduct ongoing reviews of procedures relating to recruitment, job descriptions, and selection methods to eliminate the possibility of unfair discrimination (direct or indirect) and to ensure that decisions are taken on job-related criteria. When vacancies are advertised, such advertising, both in placement and content, will be compatible with the terms of this policy document.

2. *Training*
The South Yorkshire Police will provide suitable and relevant equal opportunities training, as necessary. It will take into account all the recommendations made by both the equal opportunities working party and the training department together with any future legal requirements, operating within the financial constraints of the South Yorkshire Police.

3. *Conditions of Employment*
The South Yorkshire Police will ensure ongoing reviews of all relevant policies on matters relating to grading schemes, leave of absence and working time to ensure fair application to all employees, together with similar reviews for career development and promotion prospects of all regular police officers.

● *Communication*

16. The Chief Constable will seek to ensure that the policy is brought to the attention of all the members and employees. Such action will include the following measures:

1. All future recruitment advertising will include the phrase:

> '*The South Yorkshire Police is committed to being an equal opportunity employer*'.

2. All application forms for persons seeking any form of employment with the South Yorkshire Police will incorporate an equal opportunities statement.

Appendix C

Extracts from Home Office Circular 87/1989, 'Equal opportunities policies in the police service'

● *Paragraphs 1–4*

The government is firmly committed to the concept of equal opportunities, to the framework of law in which it is embodied and to the aim of introducing equal opportunities policies and working towards their full implementation throughout central government and the public services for which it has responsibility.

The *object* of equal opportunities policies in employment is to ensure that fair and non-discriminatory treatment is given by management to all applicants for employment with the organisation, to all the employees of the organisation, and by those employees to each other. The *effects* of equal opportunities policies will be to secure for the organisation the best recruits from the widest available range of candidates; to ensure that the best use is made of the skills and abilities of all employees; and, less directly, to reinforce the professionalism and image of the organisation itself.

The implementation of equal opportunities policies is particularly important in the police service. There is a clear link between a commitment to equal opportunities principles in police recruitment and employment, with which this circular is concerned, and the expression of those principles in the high professional standards of conduct on which the reputation of the service depends. Unfair or unlawful discriminatory practices not only lead to resentment on the part of those who suffer from them: they also affect adversely public perceptions of the police as a service and as a career. The creation within the police service of a genuine belief in equal opportunities, coupled with the knowledge that unfair or unlawful discriminatory practices will not be tolerated, should yield benefits not only within the service itself but in a more positive public belief in its fairness and professionalism and improved relationships with the wider community.

Equal opportunities policies need not be concerned solely with the elimination of discrimination based on race, sex or marital status. No-one is immune from the fear of the effects of unfair discrimination, and the implementation of policies designed to eliminate such discrimination should be of benefit to all...

● *Paragraphs 9–10*

It is not enough for a force to claim to be an equal opportunities employer. Chief officers of police must take the necessary steps to identify and eliminate discriminatory practices and to guard against the risk of discriminating unwittingly.

Chief officers of police who have not already done so should therefore prepare, in consultation with the police authority and the local representatives of the police staff associations, a written statement of their equal opportunities policies...

● *Paragraph 18*

... While posts must always be filled, and promotions awarded, solely on grounds of merit, there is scope, in order to ensure equal opportunities to members of the groups which have in the past had less access to particular employment and are under-represented in it, to take action to attract more applicants from those groups or otherwise improve their opportunities.

● *Paragraph 24*

... Where police officers and police civilians are working together, however, it is essential that there should be, so far as possible, consistency of treatment in the application of equal opportunities policies.

Appendix D

Age of Consent Laws in Council of Europe Countries in 1993

THE following is reproduced from a Stonewall (London) document. Stonewall is a lesbian and gay lobbying organization for legal and social equality.

Where two ages are shown, this is either because a higher age applies where the older person is in a position of authority or influence over the younger *or* because sexual activity is legal at the lower age unless the younger person subsequently complains.

| Country | Age of consent | | |
	Heterosexual	Lesbian sex	Gay sex
Austria	14	14	18
Belgium	16	16	16
Bulgaria	14	14	14
Cyprus	16	16	n.a.[1]
Czech Republic	15	15	15
Denmark	15/18	15/18	15/18
Finland	16	18	18
France	15/18	15/18	15/18
Germany	14	14	18
Greece	15	15	15
Hungary	14	18	18

Country	Age of consent		
	Heterosexual	*Lesbian sex*	*Gay sex*
Iceland	14	14	14
Ireland	17	17	n.a.[2]
Italy	14/16	14/16	14/16
Liechtenstein	14	14	18
Luxembourg	16	16	16
Malta	12/18	12/18	12/18
Netherlands	12/16	12/16	12/16
Norway	16	16	16
Poland	15	15	15
Portugal	16	16	16
San Marino	14/16	14/16	14/16
Slovak Republic	15	15	15
Spain	12/18	12/18	12/18
Sweden	15	15	15
Switzerland	16	16	16
Turkey	18	18	18
United Kingdom	16	16	21

There is now an equal or common age of consent in 20 out of 28 Council of
Europe Countries.

 ● *Notes*

1.   Gay male sex is still illegal in Cyprus. The European Court is
expected to rule against Cyprus in *Modinos* v. *Cyprus*.
2.   Gay male sex is still illegal in Ireland, but the new coalition government has given an undertaking that it will bring in legislation to
reform the law later this year.

Gay Police International

Britain

Lesbian and Gay Police Association (LAGPA), BM LAGPA,
London WC1N 3XX.

Canada

Gay Cops United Foundation (Gay-CUF), PO Box 234,
Station P, Toronto, Ontario M5S 2S7.

Netherlands

Werkgroep Politie en Homoseksualiteit (WPH), Postbus 27,
6950 AA Dieren.
Werkgroep Homo-emancipatie, Postbus 553, 2501 CG Den Haag.

USA

Gay Officers Action League (GOAL), PO Box 2038,
Canal Street Station, New York, New York 10013.
Golden State Peace Officers Association (GSPOA), PO Box 14006,
San Francisco, California 94114-0006.
Pride Behind the Badge (PBB), PO Box 88517, Los Angeles,
California 90009.
Society of Law Officers (SOLO), PO Box 34205, San Diego,
California 92163-4205.

Glossary

THIS glossary contains a selection of both the police and the gay vernacular used in the main text.

Job Speak

ACPO Acronym for the Association of Chief Police Officers (England, Wales and Northern Ireland).

AQR Acronym for Annual Qualification Report. Met term for the annual written appraisal of junior officers by supervisory officers. Now called Annual Performance Appraisal (APA).

Area car *See* RT car.

Body A person (body) who has been arrested or may potentially be arrested.

CAD Acronym for Computer Aided Dispatch, the police message dispatch system.

Cadet The minimum recruitment age for the police in Britain is eighteen and a half. Candidates who are below the recruitment age may, however, in certain forces apply to join the police cadets until they have reached the required age.

Canteen culture Term used to describe the popular police mentality, which has its roots in the police canteen.

Carrier Umbrella term for the large, emergency minibus-style vehicle, normally carrying a number of officers. Generally used for public order events. In the Met such officers are now 'shield-trained' equipped with riot gear, and part of a group referred to as the TSG. Such units have been unpopular with the public since their association with the death of Blair Peach during the Southall riot of 1979. Since then the concept has been regularly reshaped and renamed. Known as the SPG (Special Patrol Group) in the 1970s, it has since been known as the IRU (Instant Response Unit), DSU (Divisional Support Unit) and is now called the TSG (Territorial Support Group).

CID Acronym for Criminal Investigation Department. Responsible for the investigation of all crime.

CPS Acronym for Crown Prosecution Service. The responsibility for the prosecution of offences was removed from the police and handed over to the CPS in late 1986.

DC Acronym for Detective Constable.

Demo Verbal shorthand for public order DEMOnstration.

Federation The National Police Federation of England and Wales was set up in 1919 by an Act of Parliament. Crudely speaking, it performs for police officers the same duties that a trade union does for its members, i.e. matters affecting welfare, including the police annual pay rise. All officers are obliged to become members and fees are normally automatically subtracted from pay. No other body is legally permitted to perform its functions. Each force in England and Wales is served by a branch of the Federation and most major stations within that force are served by a rep responsible for dealing with the concerns of individual officers.

GBH Acronym for Grievous Bodily Harm.

Ground That area covered by a particular police station.

Group *See* Relief.

Guv'nor Any officer of inspector rank and above. (*See* Appendix A.)

Home Beat Constable responsible for a particular beat within a division. Officers normally patrol alone during the day getting to know the residents of their beat, and are separate and supplementary to the relief system. (Met term.)

Landline Telephone.

Met Shorthand for the Metropolitan Police, London.

NFA Acronym for No Further Action.

NSY Acronym for New Scotland Yard.

Operator The officer occupying the front passenger seat in the area/ RT car. Responsible for the operation of the emergency lights, 'two tones', Force radio, and map reading on the way to emergency calls. In the Met postings are usually on a monthly basis. The operator is normally junior in service to the driver.

Parade At the beginning of each shift, all relief officers 'parade' in the parade room to receive their postings for that tour of duty.

PC Acronym for Police Constable.

Plonk A common derogatory police expression for woman police constable (WPC).

Plus Shorthand for 'The Plus Programme', the Metropolitan Police initiative for providing a better service to London's public.

POLAC Term referring to road traffic accident involving a police vehicle (POLice ACcident).

PR Acronym for personal radio, as distinct from those found in police vehicles.

PS Acronym for Police Sergeant.

R & DPG Acronym for Royal and Diplomatic Protection Group.

Relief (Met) police term for a 'shift' (soon to become 'team'). Known as a 'section' or 'group' in other forces.

RT car The main marked police vehicle responsible for responding to 999 emergencies on a given area. Also known as the 'area' car. (Met terms.)

RTA Acronym for Road Traffic Accident.

Rumour Control Gossip and rumour concerning other officers are rife in most police forces, much of it having its origins in the canteen. The police grapevine is particularly effective and when there is important gossip to be had it is not unknown for a rumour to circulate around the Met's 800 square miles in less than twenty-four hours.

SB Acronym for Special Branch.

Section *See* Relief.

Section house Police residence housing large numbers of (usually single and relatively young in service) police officers.

Shot Officer trained and authorized to carry a firearm on police duty.

Skipper Slang for Police Sergeant (PS).

Spade Derogatory term for a black person. (Origin: 'Black as the ace of spades'.)

Special Constabulary Supplementary force of unpaid, part-time, uniform police volunteers. Broadly equivalent to the Territorial Army.

Stitch up Verb: to fabricate evidence against. Noun: a case in which evidence has been fabricated, leaving the quarry no way out.

The Job Popular and universal expression amongst officers meaning 'the police organization'.

TSG Acronym for Territorial Support Group. (*See* Carrier.)

WDC Acronym for Woman Detective Constable.

WDS Acronym for Woman Detective Sergeant.

WPC Acronym for Woman Police Constable.

WPS Acronym for Woman Police Sergeant.

YACS Acronym for Youth and Community Section. Formerly Juvenile Bureau. (Met terms.)

Gay Speak

Camp From theatrical sixteenth-century England; camping = the wearing of women's costume in plays. The term became linguistically popular in the late 1960s and is now amongst the most widely used of gay slang. A term with multiple definitions today, especially in the USA; most commonly, it describes the outrageously theatrical and often effeminate behaviour of some gay men.

Coming out The term 'coming out' was originally used in the élite circles of the 1920s, referring to the entry of a débutante onto the social scene. It was borrowed by the contemporary homosexual subculture to mean 'coming out of the closet', the imaginary cupboard in which their sexuality was hidden. The term has come to embody a number of meanings today, including the similar entry of the neophyte homosexual onto the gay scene and the disclosure of one's sexual orientation to others.

Cottaging Expression for the picking up of sexual partners in public conveniences.

Cruising The search for a partner, normally in an open space such as a park.

Out The state of having come out. (*See* Coming out.)

Outing The exposure of someone as homosexual against their will.

Pride Short term for the festive Lesbian and Gay Pride marches through the streets of Britain each summer.

Queen From the British 'Quean': a woman of low morals. Used most commonly today by gay men to refer to other gay men. It is usually employed in a less pejorative manner than when used by heterosexuals to describe homosexuals.

Selected Reading

Aandewiel, J. *et al. Politie en Homoseksualiteit*, Interfacultaire Werkgroep Homostudies, Rijksuniversiteit te Utrecht, 1985.

Anthony, R. 'Homosexuality in the police', MA thesis, Faculty of Social (Police) Studies, University of Exeter, 1991.

Averill, B. and Giteck, L. 'On the beat with gay cops: caution and closets in New York', *Advocate* (US), 14 May 1981, pp. 15–16.

Bennett, M. 'Divided loyalties', *Police Review*, 25 January 1991, pp. 164–5.

Bernstein, H. 'When a cop comes out', *Mandate* (US), July 1981, pp. 48–52.

Burke, M. 'Cop culture and homosexuality', *Police Journal*, 45 (1992), 30–9.

Burke, M. 'Homosexuality in the British police', Ph.D. thesis, University of Essex, 1993.

Clark, J. 'Cops: out of the closet', *Toronto Star*, 4 May 1991, pp. G1 and 3.

Daley, H. and Furbank, P. N. *This Small Cloud: A Personal Memoir*, London: Weidenfeld & Nicolson, 1986.

Derbyshire, P. 'Gays and the police', *Police Review*, 8 June 1990, pp. 1144–5.

Dyer, K. (ed.) *Gays in Uniform*, Boston: Alyson, 1990.

Folkes, A. 'They do not belong', *Police*, December 1992, p. 26.

Gash, E. 'We are all equal', *Police*, May 1992, p. 16.

Giteck, L. 'May the force be with us: recruiting gay rookies', *Advocate* (US), 20 September 1979, pp. 20–3.

Giteck, L. 'On the beat with gay cops: fighting harassment in San Francisco', *Advocate* (US), 14 May 1981, pp. 15 and 17.

Hilliard, B. 'Coming out', *Police Review*, 18 January 1991, p. 119.

Massa, R. 'One of New York's finest', *Village Voice* (US), 25 November 1981, pp. 15 and 106.

Mitteager, J. 'NYPD's gay cops', *National Centurion* (US), 2 (1) (1984), pp. 33–6 and 71.

Morgan, B. 'Sexual morals are important', *Police Review*, 11 January 1991, p. 97 (Letter).

Police, 'Gay police: we're not all that different', January 1980, pp. 32–3.

Police Review, Editorial, 21 December 1990, p. 2492.

Police Review, Editorial, 18 January 1991, p. 104.

Police Review, 'Gay officers' association set up to fight discrimination', 18 January 1991, pp. 104–5.

Police Review, 'What it means to be gay', 1 February 1991, p. 253 (Letter).

Popert, K. 'Gay cops unite', *Xtra!* (Toronto), 24 August 1990, p. 1.

Richardson, C. 'They've only just begun', *Gay Times*, June 1991, pp. 14–15.

Santangelo, M. 'Badge: marching with New York's gay cops', *Daily News Magazine* (US), 24 June 1990, pp. 8–11.

Seabrook, M. *Conduct Unbecoming*, London: GMP, 1991.

Seabrook, M. 'Homosexuality and the police', *New Law Journal*, 6 March 1992, pp. 325–6.

Signorile, M. 'True blue', *Outweek* (US), 10 December 1989, pp. 38–41.

Stonewall Group (London), *Memoranda Submitted to the Select Committee on the Armed Forces Bill*, April 1991.

Swerling, J. B. 'A study of police officers' values and their attitudes towards homosexual officers', Dissertation, California School of Professional Psychology, Los Angeles, 1978.

Wheeler, G. 'Officers form group to reach out to gay police', *Now* (Canada), 10 (14), 6–12 December 1990, p. 17.

Windibank, M. 'Straight talking: a training manual for police officers working with lesbians and gay men', unpublished, 1990.

Index